FROMMER'S

WASHINGTON, D.C.

by RENA BULKIN AND FAYE HAMMEL

D0684522

□

1989–1990

Copyright © 1977, 1979, 1981, 1983, 1985, 1987, 1989
by Simon & Schuster, Inc.

All rights reserved
including the right of reproduction
in whole or in part in any form

Published by Prentice Hall Trade Division
A Division of Simon & Schuster, Inc.
Gulf + Western Building
One Gulf + Western Plaza
New York, NY 10023

ISBN 0-13-048612-4
ISSN 0899-3246

Manufactured in the United States of America

Text Design: Levavi & Levavi, Inc.

*Although every effort was made to ensure the accuracy
of price information appearing in this book,
it should be kept in mind that prices
can and do fluctuate in the course of time.*

CONTENTS

MAPS

Inflation Alert

It is hardly a secret that inflation continues to batter the United States as it does everywhere else. The author of this book has spent laborious hours attempting to ensure the accuracy of prices appearing in this guide. As we go to press, we believe we have obtained the most reliable data possible. Nonetheless, in the lifetime of this edition—particularly its second year (1990)—the wise traveler will add 15% to 20% to the prices quoted throughout these pages.

CHAPTER I

AN INTRODUCTION TO WASHINGTON, D.C.

□ □ □

As home to one of the world's major powers, Washington, D.C., offers its own special brand of excitement. Here, a visitor can linger in the halls and chambers where great statesmen formulated the democratic process; listen to Senate debates; hear the Supreme Court in session; visit the National Archives, where our most cherished documents—the Declaration of Independence, the Constitution, and the Bill of Rights—are enshrined; find inspiration in magnificent monuments to our greatest presidents and check out the palatial digs of our current leader; learn how the FBI works to thwart crime; watch dollar bills churn out at the Bureau of Engraving and Printing; tour the Pentagon, America's military headquarters. In short, experience firsthand just how our government works.

Edifices of gleaming marble are the background to Washington sightseeing. And surrounding the city's grand beaux arts buildings are spacious boulevards and tranquil tree-lined streets, grassy malls and parks, and circular plazas with splashing fountains and statuary at the focal points. This is a lushly verdant city, as millions of flowers create a dazzling riot of color in spring and summer, and every April the famous Japanese cherry trees burst into bloom along the Tidal Basin like a pink snowstorm. In almost every respect, our capital is a showplace, one of the most beautiful cities in the country. But that hasn't always been the case. . . .

WASHINGTON—THEN AND NOW

Probably not an American alive thinks of Washington as a capital in the wilderness. But back in 1800, when the Congress moved from its temporary home in Philadelphia to its new permanent seat of government on the Potomac, that's precisely what it was.

The Continental Congress had decided as early as 1783 that a federal city should be established as a permanent locale for their meetings. But even then, the question of slavery created a gap between the North and the South. The northern states insisted that the new capital be in the North, while southerners championed a national seat of government in their precincts.

Wrangling about a location for the capital continued until 1790, when New Yorker Alexander Hamilton and Virginian Thomas Jefferson resolved the dispute (over dinner in a Manhattan restaurant) with a compromise. In exchange for the South's agreement to pay our national Revolutionary War debts, the capital would be located in the South. Furthermore, it would be named Washington after our first president and (probably more important) a resident of the Commonwealth of Virginia.

By Act of Congress, George Washington was given full authority to choose a site "not exceeding ten miles square on the River Potomac at some space between the mouths of the eastern branch [of the Potomac] and the Conogocheague for the permanent seat of the Government of the United States."

ENTER PIERRE L'ENFANT: Virginia and Maryland, by agreement, ceded land for the new capital. It was to be known as the Federal District, and to include Georgetown in Maryland and Alexandria in Virginia. In 1791 Pierre Charles L'Enfant was employed by George Washington to survey the land and plan the city. L'Enfant, a Frenchman, had distinguished himself as an engineer in the Revolutionary Army. He had also remodeled New York's City Hall to serve as the first seat for our federal government.

L'Enfant's masterplan (which you can see in the Library of Congress) proposed "a presidential palace" linked to the "home of Congress" by a vast green mall. In describing how he happened to choose the hill at the west end of Jenkins Heights as the site for the capitol, he poetized that "it stands as a pedestal waiting for a monument."

Assisting L'Enfant in laying out the design was Benjamin Banneker, a black surveyor, inventor, and mathematician. He was specifically responsible for drawing up the District boundary that affected the state of Maryland.

L'Enfant, though a genius, was also a temperamental artist. He had no patience for practical politics and refused to cooperate with building commissioners or Washington's appointed surveyor, Andrew Ellicott. And he ignored Washington's repeated requests to produce a preliminary blueprint so that fundraising could begin. His situation became increasingly difficult, and in 1792 he was fired. For the next few decades L'Enfant was often seen "haunting the lobbies of the Capitol . . . pacing the newly marked avenues"—keeping a jaundiced eye on the developing city.

When L'Enfant died in 1825, the fact that he had designed Washington had been practically forgotten. His superb plans were gathering dust, the city that had begun with such grandiose vision muddled along as a nondescript small town. L'Enfant was buried without fanfare, and it wasn't until 1909 that his grave was moved to Arlington Cemetery (near the Kennedy gravesites), to rest on a hill looking out over the city that owes him so much.

But let's return to 1792. A nationwide competition was held for the design of the Capitol Building to be erected on the hill L'Enfant had designated. The winner was a young physician, an amateur architect named William Thornton, who later founded the Patent Office. (Architects in those days had little professional standing.) In the words of Thomas Jefferson, another amateur architect, the Capitol plan "captivated the eye and judgment of all." George Washington noted that "grandeur, simplicity, and convenience appear to be so well combined in this plan."

And so the cornerstone for the Capitol Building was laid September 18, 1793, beside the banks of what the Indians called "The River of Swans," the Potomac.

The competition to design the "presidential palace" was won by an Irishman, James Hoban, who received $500 for his plan. Other entrants included Thomas Jefferson, who had submitted his design anonymously. Hoban hailed from North Carolina, where he had designed that state's capitol building. Because the White House's cornerstone was laid in 1792, it holds the distinction of being the oldest public building in Washington. George Washington, however, never occupied the mansion, and is, in fact, the only American president never to have resided there. John Adams, our second president, became the first tenant on November 1, 1800—before the house was fully completed.

A CITY RISES: In the considerable period before the public buildings were completed, it was suggested that the Congress meet alternately in Trenton, New Jersey, and Annapolis, Maryland—that is, part of the time in the North, part of the time in the South. This idea of shifting meetings was rejected when Francis Hopkinson suggested, sardonically, that a Federal Town be built on a platform on wheels and rolled back and forth between two places of residence. Other responses were bawdier.

By 1800 one wing of the Capitol Building was ready for the legislators. They moved down from Philadelphia, the last temporary capital, in the fall of that year.

"A single packet sloop brought all the office furniture of the departments, besides seven large boxes and five small ones, containing the archives of government." Very small potatoes, compared to the 86 packing cases Thomas Jefferson brought back to the States with him from Paris in 1790 after serving as minister to France.

As the first tenants in the White House, President and Mrs. Adams headed from Baltimore cross country, and they got so hopelessly lost that they "wandered for two hours without finding a guide or path." When they finally arrived, however, Abigail Adams pronounced that "it is a beautiful spot, capable of any improvement."

Mrs. Adams, a Yankee of grit and gumption, finding "not the least fence, yard, or other convenience," hung the laundry out to dry in the East Room.

Pennsylvania Avenue, on paper the principal boulevard between the Capitol and the presidential palace, was then a muddy morass of a pathway covered with alder bushes. Where the path reached Georgetown, "houses had been erected, which bore the name of *The Six Buildings*," a putdown to those who harbored ideas that it was a blossoming megalopolis.

Never mind. The new Federal Capital was in business. And John Adams wasted no time in delivering his presidential address to the first joint session of Congress. To this day, only the president is privileged to address the House and the Senate in joint session. (Chief executives may extend the privilege, however, to foreign heads of state, to national heroes, and to other worthy individuals, at their discretion.)

Yet the grumbling continued. Secretary of the Treasury Oliver Wolcott wrote to his wife in Connecticut that he couldn't see "how the members of Congress can possibly secure lodgings, unless they consent to live like scholars in a college or monks in a monastery, crowded ten or twenty in a house, and otherwise secluded from society. . . ."

John Cotton, also from Connecticut, had other complaints: "A sidewalk was attempted in one instance by a covering formed of the chips hewed from the Capitol. It extended but a little way and was of little value, for in dry weather the sharp fragments cut our shoes, and in wet weather covered them with white mortar."

Newspapers all over the country quipped about "the palace in the wilderness" and referred to Pennsylvania Avenue as "the great Serbonian bog." Georgetown was called "a city of houses without streets" and Washington "a city of streets without houses."

Thomas Moore, Ireland's national lyricist, on a visit in 1804 cracked:

And what was Goose Greek once is Tiber now.
This fam'd metropolis, where fancy sees,
Squares in morasses, obelisks in trees;
Which second sighted seers e'en now adorn,
With shrines unbuilt and heroes yet unborn.

Speculation escalated land prices in the capital. Congress had agreed to purchase land at £26 to the acre for public building sites. Land surrounding these sites was to be sold, with half the proceeds from the sale of lots to go to the landowners, half to the government for the erection of government buildings.

But as land prices rose ferociously high around the Capitol Building, those who would have preferred to live in the area were forced to buy elsewhere. As a result, settlement shifted toward the northwest, and even today most fashionable town houses and embassies are found in the Northwest section. The area along Pennsylvania Avenue remained a soggy bog. And when the land speculation syndicate fell apart in 1796, financial support for constructing government buildings went down the drain too.

Jefferson, when he assumed the presidency in 1801, had to secure money from Congress for public buildings. He planted poplar trees along Pennsylvania Avenue, doing what he could to make that "Appian Way of the Republic" something better than a "slough of despond." The Library of Congress was established, too, at this time.

During the Jefferson Administration three municipal corporations also were established on May 3, 1802, which would split the District of Columbia into the City of Washington, the City of Georgetown, and the County of Washington. The twin cities were to endure until 1871 when their charters were abolished, and the entire area again became the District of Columbia.

Building went on slowly, but no sooner had the youthful Congress seen James and Dolley Madison installed in the White House than it became necessary to declare war. England had been impressing American seamen, and disputes over western land worsened the situation. The War of 1812 had started.

A CITY BURNS: On August 24, 1814, the British fleet sailed into Chesapeake Bay and marched on the capital. Admiral George Cockburn (pronounced Co-burn by the British) was in charge of the attack.

Fortunately, everybody knew that they were coming. Dolley Madison stubbornly stayed on in the White House, determined to save all she could. She hustled important documents off to Lewisburg, 35 miles northwest of Washington, for protection. Then when friends insisted that she leave for her own safety, at the last minute she cut Gilbert Stuart's portrait of George Washington out of its frame, rolled it up, and hied off to a nearby army camp where she spent the night in a tent, a soldier guarding the entrance. This famous portrait, probably the oldest original possession in the White House, hangs today on the East Room's east wall, where you may see it. Dolley Madison knew George Washington well—her younger sister, Lucy, was married to Washington's nephew—and she considered the portrait a remarkable likeness. Dolley saved another painting too—a portrait of herself—which also hangs in the White House.

Luckily for our budding nation, the rains came on that fateful night. A torrential storm halted the flames that might have destroyed the city completely.

Then, the British gone, the Madisons moved back into town. They set up housekeeping at Octagon House, on the corner of 18th Street and New York Avenue, and the gala parties Dolley threw helped relieve the pall over Washington left by the war.

The Madisons remained at Octagon House until 1815, when they moved to the northwest corner of Pennsylvania Avenue and 19th Street, to a place known simply as "The Seven Buildings," early housing for the Department of State. There they stayed until the executive mansion was rebuilt, its charred walls painted white in March 1817. Ever since, the president's palace has been called the White House.

A CITY REBUILDS: After the British withdrew, Congress first met in the Blodgett Hotel, then moved into a brick building across from the burned-out Capitol. It was here that James Monroe's inauguration (1817) settled a dispute over whether that ceremony should use the Senate's "fine red chairs" or "the plain democratic ones of the House." He took the oath on the porch of what became known as the "Brick Capitol," which stood where the Supreme Court now stands, beginning the tradition of taking the presidential oath in open air, sometimes a chilly event in January.

Monroe also refurnished the burned-out White House with $15,567.43 in French-designed furniture, very Napoleonic. (Jefferson, Madison, and Monroe all had a taste for things French, and it's still reflected throughout the White House. More recently, First Lady Jacqueline Kennedy, also French oriented, was responsible for refurnishing and redecorating the White House to reveal its original French character.)

Repair work on the Capitol Building was directed by Benjamin Latrobe, an Englishman who had taken over responsibility for its construction in 1803. Slowly he replaced the gutted wood with marble, brick, and metal. It was reoccupied by the Congress in 1819.

By 1822, only 22 years after its founding and eight years after being burned, the capital city boasted a population of nearly 15,000 people.

In 1829 the Smithsonian Institution was created when an Englishman, James Smithson, left half a million dollars "to found at Washington, under the name of the Smithsonian Institution, an establishment for the increase and diffusion of knowledge among men." Smithson never visited the United States, but the cornerstone for his great legacy, the now-sprawling Smithsonian, was laid in 1847. The first building in the complex is a red-brick castle of Norman inspiration. The original building is located on the Mall, and it was reopened to the public after undergoing considerable restoration in 1972.

Government building continued booming: by 1842 the present Treasury Building—blocking the vista from the White House to the Capitol and spoiling L'Enfant's original plan—was completed. Andrew Jackson had tired of waiting for the appointed commission to choose a Treasury site, so he marched out of the White House one day, pointed to a spot, and said that the Treasury cornerstone would be laid there. His will was done . . . plunk in the middle of Pennsylvania Avenue!

MID-19TH-CENTURY WASHINGTON: From all this, you might assume that Washington was well on its way from villagehood to cityhood. Gas lights were lit on the Capitol grounds in 1847. But by 1860 no more than Pennsylvania Avenue had been lit. "Pigs roamed the principal thoroughfares, pavements but for a few patches were lacking, and open sewers carried off refuse." A visiting Anthony Trollope declared Washington "as melancholy and miserable a town as the mind of man could conceive." Soon things would get even worse.

The Civil War turned the capital into an armed camp. It was the principal supply depot of the North and an important medical center. The rotunda of the Capitol Building—its nine-million-pound, cast-iron dome completed in 1865—was used as a barracks, referred to by the soldiers as "the big tent." Later it became a troop hospital, and here American poet Walt Whitman wandered among the wounded, helping where he could. Altogether, 3,000 troops were billeted in the Capitol. Basement committee rooms were converted into bakeries, and the "Old Brick Capitol" became a military prison.

The Civil War ended when Lee surrendered to Grant on April 8, 1865. The greatest parade in the capital's history took place when the Civil War ended. To the tune of fife and drums, troops marched down Pennsylvania Avenue for two full days and nights. Less than a week later, on April 14, President Abraham Lincoln was shot at Ford's Theater by John Wilkes Booth, and the city went into mourning.

The war's legacy was poverty, unemployment, and disease. Washington's population swelled with uneducated, agrarian ex-slaves who had come here seeking protection, and tenement slums arose within a stone's throw of the Capitol.

SUDDEN EXPANSION: In 1870 several factions attempted to transfer the national capital to another city. St. Louis bid several million dollars for the honor, and Horace Greeley suggested that the capital go west. But the move never got under way seriously and Congress went ahead and voted $500,000 to build the Departments of State and War and the Navy Building.

Enter "Boss Shepherd" and another era. Governor Alexander R. Shepherd was chosen to head a territorial government established in the District of Columbia from 1871 to 1874. Under his guidance, the L'Enfant plan was finally executed in earnest. Three hundred miles of half-laid streets were improved. Nearly every thickly populated thoroughfare was paved either with wood, concrete, or macadam. Some 128 miles of sidewalks were built, and 3,000 gas lamps and a system of sewers were installed. Old Tiber Creek was filled in. Scores of new parks were graded and beautified with fountains. A special park commission planted 6,000 trees.

Soon there were more paved streets in Washington than in any other city in the country. And President Ulysses S. Grant declared in a message to Congress, "Washington is rapidly becoming a city worthy of the nation's capital." At the moment, Grant temporarily swept a few facts about the grand public works under the rug—like the whopping $20 million bill for the improvements.

Alexander Shepherd was a handsome, strapping man with blustery charm. He'd been a successful plumber, an alderman, newspaper owner, and president of the City Reform Association. He was a natural to become governor of the territorial government. Once installed in office, though, he ignored budgets and followed a bankruptcy course to beautify his domain. Before long Congress reacted, and Shepherd was nearly booed out of town. In 1874 the territorial form of government gave way to a trio of commissioners. Shepherd took his family to Mexico. But when he returned to the United States in 1887, he was acclaimed as the man who had made Washington a showplace. And he certainly had.

The nation's Centennial Celebration of 1876 in Philadelphia and the Chicago Exposition brought about a cultural awakening throughout the country. Following that period the Corcoran Art Gallery was built in Washington, the Metropolitan Museum in New York, and the Museum of Fine Arts in Boston. In 1884 the Washington Monument was completed. And in 1897 the Library of Congress, which took 11 years to build, also was completed. During the following year, 1898, L'Enfant's plan was dusted off again, and adjustments were made to suit the District to the motor age.

But the capital of the United States was 100 years old and home to 300,000 before the plan for development and improvement known as the McMillan Park Commission was enacted in 1901.

The principal thrust of the commission's plan was to develop the Mall, since 1872 little more than a pasture traversed by the tracks of the Pennsylvania Railroad. The company agreed to remove its tracks in return for funding in order to construct Union Station in cooperation with the Baltimore & Ohio Railroad, fronting on Massachusetts Avenue and the Capitol, "yet not too near that building."

The Mall, in addition to housing the National Gallery of Art and the Smithsonian Institution, was to become the site for the Freer Gallery, the National Museum, the Department of Agriculture, and other important structures. When finished, it would extend one mile in length, 300 feet in width, from the Capitol through the Washington Monument, beyond to the Lincoln Memorial. Projected plans also included several public buildings—office buildings for members of the House, Senate, and the Supreme Court (which had met in the Capitol until then).

This also was a time for highway construction. Built under the plan were the Rock Creek Parkway, the Anacostia Park Development, Fort Drive along the Palisades of the Potomac, and the Mount Vernon Parkway.

Esthetics came into play in 1910, when the National Commission of Fine Arts was created, its duty to advise on fountains, statues, and monuments in public squares, streets, and parks throughout the District of Columbia. According to most reports, this is when the commission fixed the 110-foot maximum rooftop height limit for buildings in the downtown district, so that the Capitol dome might be seen from everywhere.

WASHINGTON TODAY: Until Franklin D. Roosevelt came along, only President Grant had really changed Washington—and Grant only got the credit because Boss Shepherd had spent too much! During the Great Depression in the '30s, FDR's Works Progress Administration—*WPA, We Do Our Part*—put the unemployed to work erecting public buildings and artists to work beautifying them.

More recently (1971), the John F. Kennedy Center for the Performing Arts, on the Potomac's East Bank, gave Washington four great theaters, filling a longtime need for a cultural haven.

In 1974 the opening of the new Hirshhorn Museum and Sculpture Garden on the Mall provided a much-needed major museum of modern art. Another storehouse of art treasures is the magnificent East Building of the National Gallery of Art, which opened in 1978. It was built to handle the overflow of the gallery's burgeoning collection and to accommodate exclusive shows like the King Tut exhibit and the Dresden china displays.

In time for the Bicentennial, the National Air and Space Museum opened its splendid new quarters to house everything from *The Spirit of St. Louis* to the latest space capsule. Also in time for the nation's big birthday party, the first leg of the capital's much-needed subway system, Metro, was completed. The 45 acres between the Washington Monument and the Lincoln Memorial were transformed into Constitution Gardens, and in 1982 the park became the site of the Vietnam Veterans Memorial. And the Bicentennial itself, which everybody in town fretted about for years—not enough funds, not enough facilities, doubts about logistics, and whether too few or too many visitors would show up—turned out to be a fabulous, year-long birthday party that has permanently affected the look and feel of the city.

The most recent major development (1987) was the $75 million Smithsonian complex on the Mall, housing the Arthur M. Sackler Gallery of Art, the relocated National Museum of African Art, the International Center, and the Enid A. Haupt Garden.

The capital has changed for the better, and the people are changing too. Washingtonians are becoming much more sophisticated and much more demanding. Today, D.C. can hold its own as a great town for theater, dining, shopping, concert-going, and other metropolitan pleasures.

So it's no wonder Washington attracts 19 million tourists each year. History and heritage, art and politics, cuisine and culture combine to make this a vital and beautiful city—a fitting capital for a great nation.

CHAPTER II

GETTING AROUND THE CAPITAL

□ □ □

Pierre Charles L'Enfant designed Washington's great, sweeping avenues crossed by numbered and lettered streets. At key intersections he placed spacious circles. Although the circles are enhanced with monuments, statuary, and fountains, L'Enfant planned them with a dual motive—they were also designed to serve as strategic command posts to ward off invaders or marauding mobs. After what had happened in Paris during the French Revolution—and remember, that was current history at the time—his design views were most practical.

GETTING ORIENTED

AN OVERVIEW: Viewing L'Enfant's Washington as a whole, you can see that the primary artery is **Pennsylvania Avenue,** scene of parades, inaugurations, and other splashy events. Pennsylvania runs on a direct line between the Capitol and the White House. In the original plan the president was supposed to be able to see the Capitol Building from the White House at all times—an uninterrupted view. But, for unexplained reasons, Andrew Jackson placed the **Treasury Building** between the White House and the Capitol, blocking off the presidential vista. Pennsylvania Avenue continues on a northwest angle to **Georgetown** from the White House.

Washington's longest avenue, **Massachusetts Avenue,** runs parallel to Pennsylvania. Along the way you'll find **Dupont Circle,** central to the area known as **Embassy Row.** Farther out are the **Naval Observatory** (the vice-president's residence is on the premises), **Washington National Cathedral,** and **American University.** Then Massachusetts Avenue just keeps going, right into Maryland.

Connecticut Avenue, running more directly north, starts at **Lafayette Square** directly facing the White House. It's the city's Fifth Avenue, the boulevard with elegant eateries, posh boutiques, and expensive hotels.

Wisconsin Avenue, from the point where it crosses M Street, is downtown Georgetown. Antique shops, trendy boutiques, discos, restaurants, and pubs all vie for attention. Yet somehow Georgetown manages to keep its almost-European charm.

THE STREET PLAN: Once you understand the city's layout, it's very easy to find your way around. You'll find it helpful, when reading this, to have a map handy.

The city is divided into four basic segments—**Northwest, Northeast, Southwest, and Southeast.** If you look at your map, you'll see that some addresses—for instance, the corner of G and 7th Streets—can appear in four different places. Hence you must observe the quadrant designation (NW, NE, SW, or SE) when looking for an address.

The **Capitol Building** dome is the center bull's-eye for the District of Columbia—the dividing point for the four quadrants: each of the four corners of the District of Columbia is exactly the same distance from the Capitol dome. The White House and most government buildings and important monuments are west of the Capitol Building (in the Northwest and Southwest quadrants). So are important hotels and tourist facilities.

Numbered streets run north-south, beginning on either side of the Capitol with East 1st Street and West 1st Street. **Lettered streets** run east-west.

Avenues, named for states, run at angles across the grid pattern and often intersect at traffic circles. For example, New Hampshire, Connecticut, and Massachusetts Avenues intersect at Dupont Circle.

FINDING AN ADDRESS: It's a cinch. On **lettered streets** the address tells you exactly where to go. For instance, 1776 K St. NW is between 17th and 18th Streets (the first two digits of 1776 tell you that) in the Northwest quadrant (NW). Note that I Street is often written as "Eye" Street to prevent confusion with 1st Street.

To find an address on **numbered streets** you'll probably have to use your fingers. For instance, 623 8th St. SE is between F and G Streets (the 6th and 7th letters of the alphabet; the first digit of 623 tells you that) in the Southeast quadrant (SE). One thing to remember though—there's no J Street (we've heard that skipping the letter J was meant as a slap in the face to unpopular Chief Justice John Jay). So when counting, remember that K becomes the tenth letter.

As you go farther out—beyond Washington's original layout —the **alphabetical system** exhausts itself. But it continues in still

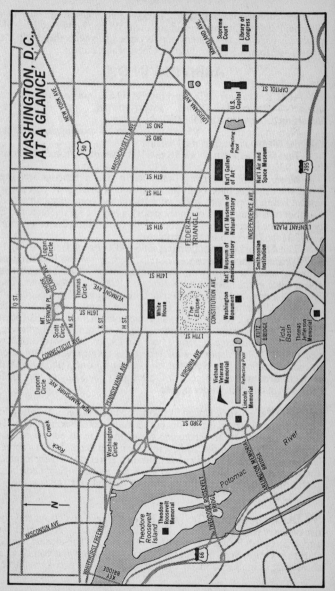

WASHINGTON, D.C., AT A GLANCE

another alphabetical pattern. Two-syllable names are used—Adams, Bryant, Channing, and so forth. When the two-syllable alphabet is used up, the system begins once again with three-syllable names—Albemarle, Brandywine, Chesapeake, etc.

ARRIVING IN D.C.

BY AIR: You can arrive in Washington, D.C., by air at any of three airports—**National, Dulles International,** or **Baltimore-Washington International (BWI) Airports.**

National is closest to the center of town; if your luggage is light, take the **Metro** right into the District.

Taxi fares will run about $8 to $10 between National and your hotel, $35 to/from Dulles, and $40 to/from BWI.

Note: There have been incidents in which tourists arriving from the airports have been gouged by taxi drivers. If you think you're being ripped off, make sure to get the company name and number of the cab (they're on the door), a receipt for the fare, and if possible, the license plate number of the cab and the driver's name. Call 331-1671 to report any problems.

The **Airport Connection** (tel. 685-1400, or toll free 800/431-5477) runs buses between two hotels (the Capitol and Washington Hiltons) and the Baltimore-Washington Airport, with departures about once every hour in each direction. Call for exact times. The fare is $12 one way, $20 round trip; children under 6 travel free.

The **Washington Flyer,** run by the same company (same phone numbers), operates buses between eight D.C. hotels (both Hiltons, the Sheraton Washington, the Shoreham, the Mayflower, the Hotel Washington, Grand Hyatt, and J. W. Marriott) and National and Dulles Airports, with departures about every 30 minutes in each direction. For National, the fare is $5 one way, $9 round trip; children under 6, free. For Dulles, you pay $12 one way, $20 round trip; children under 6, free.

BY TRAIN: Historic **Union Station,** at Massachusetts Avenue and North Capitol Street, is the Amtrak terminal here. Recently the 81-year-old Beaux-Arts structure was handsomely restored at a cost of more than $160 million, and eventually it will expand with a three-level marketplace of shops and restaurants. It's conveniently located and connects with Metro service. There are also plenty of taxis here at all times. For rail reservations, contact Amtrak (tel. toll free 800/USA-RAIL).

BY BUS: Greyhound/Trailways buses connect just about the entire country with Washington, D.C. They pull in at a terminal at 1st and L Streets NE (tel. 737-5800 or 565-2662). The closest Metro station is Union Station, four blocks away. It's not what you'd call a showplace neighborhood, so if you arrive at night, a taxi is advisable.

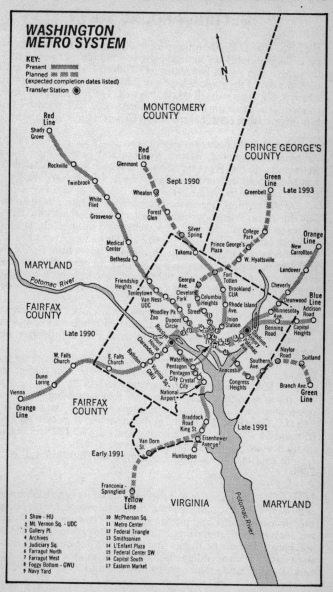

WASHINGTON METRO SYSTEM

KEY:
Present
Planned
(expected completion dates listed)
● Transfer Station

MONTGOMERY COUNTY

PRINCE GEORGE'S COUNTY

Red Line
Shady Grove
Rockville
Twinbrook
White Flint
Grosvenor
Medical Center
Bethesda

Red Line
Glenmont
Sept. 1990
Wheaton
Forest Glen
Silver Spring
Takoma

Green Line
Greenbelt   Late 1993

College Park
Prince George's Plaza
W. Hyattsville

Orange Line
New Carrollton
Landover
Cheverly

MARYLAND

Potomac River

FAIRFAX COUNTY

Friendship Heights
Tenleytown
Van Ness UDC
Woodley Pk Zoo
Dupont Circle
Rosslyn

Georgia Ave.
Cleveland Park
Columbia Heights
U Street

Fort Totten
Brookland - CUA
Rhode Island Ave.
Union Station

Deanwood
Minnesota Ave.
Benning Road

Blue Line
Addison Road
Capitol Heights

Late 1990

Court House
Clarendon
Virginia Sq.
GMU
Ballston

W. Falls Church
E. Falls Church

Dunn Loring

Vienna

Orange Line

FAIRFAX COUNTY

Waterfront
Pentagon
Pentagon City
Crystal City

National Airport

Anacostia

Southern Ave.
Naylor Road   Suitland

Congress Heights

Branch Ave.
Green Line

Late 1991

Braddock Road
King St.
Eisenhower Avenue

Van Dorn St.

Early 1991

Huntington

Franconia - Springfield

Yellow Line

VIRGINIA

Potomac River

MARYLAND

1 Shaw - HU
2 Mt. Vernon Sq. - UDC
3 Gallery Pl.
4 Archives
5 Judiciary Sq.
6 Farragut North
7 Farragut West
8 Foggy Bottom - GWU
9 Navy Yard
10 McPherson Sq.
11 Metro Center
12 Federal Triangle
13 Smithsonian
14 L'Enfant Plaza
15 Federal Center SW
16 Capitol South
17 Eastern Market

GETTING AROUND TOWN

BUSES: The D.C. Metrobus people describe the system as complex. They're right! If you need help, you can obtain free information about bus routes by calling 637-7000 from 6 a.m. to 11:30 p.m. any day of the week. If a subway (Metro) route would be more efficient, the agent will tell you that as well. The line is usually busy, though; don't wait until the last minute to call. There's also a full **bus information center** at the Metro Center station, at 12th and F Streets, NW.

Metrobuses operate on all main arteries of the city and out to Arlington, Alexandria, Mount Vernon, and other Virginia and Maryland suburbs. Free timetables are available from the **Washington Metropolitan Transit Authority,** 600 5th St. NW, Washington, DC 20001 (tel. 962-1261).

At this writing, fares in the District are 80¢ during rush hours, 75¢ during non-rush hours, and transfers are free; there's no charge for up to two children under 5 accompanied by an adult. During nonpeak hours the fare is $1.60 to $2.50 into Virginia and $1.25 to $1.65 into Maryland, more during rush hours (6 to 9:30 a.m. and 3 to 6:30 p.m.). You can pay your fare in exact change (drivers do not make change), tickets, or tokens, which are sold in over 150 Metrobus Ticket Outlets (phone 962-1328 for locations).

Buses operate just about around the clock, seven days a week. Weekday service, especially during rush hours, is very comprehensive; weekend and late-night service is a little less frequent.

With ID, disabled persons and senior citizens may ride the buses for half of the peak fare (or less) at all times. The former can call 962-1245 for information; the latter, 962-1179.

If you're going to be in Washington for an extended stay—and you plan to travel a lot by bus—consider a two-week pass such as the $15 **D.C. Only Pass,** good for unlimited Metrobus rides in the District and $4 worth of Metrorail rides. And call 962-1328 for details on money-saving **weekend family passes.**

To find out about Metrobus **fringe parking lots,** call 637-7000.

METRO: Washington is justifiably proud of its superb Metrorail subway system. The trains are modern in every respect, with carpeting, air conditioning, and picture windows. The stations are attractive, complete with attendants in glass kiosks to provide information and keep a close eye on things. You purchase a fare-card upon entering a station from a vending machine that records the time and location. Keep it handy. You have to insert it into a fare gate, which automatically computes the cost of your ride, as you leave the station.

The Metro runs from 5:30 a.m. to midnight Monday through Friday, from 8 a.m. until midnight on Saturday, and from 10 a.m. to midnight on Sunday. The fare is determined by distance traveled. During non-rush hours a ride can cost from 80¢ to $1.10; during peak hours fares range from 80¢ to $2.40. Peak hours are 5:30 to 9:30 a.m. and 3 to 6:30 p.m.

There are four lines—Red, Blue, Yellow, and Orange, converging at various stops. All but Yellow Line trains stop at Metro Center, all but Red Line trains at L'Enfant Plaza. All lines serve downtown Washington, making points of interest very accessible. Metro stations are marked by brown columns topped by the letter "M." Colored stripes indicate which lines the station serves.

The first time you use the Metro, pick up a copy of *All About Metro* from the kiosk attendant; it explains the system thoroughly. *Note:* If you plan to continue your travel via Metrobus, you must pick up a transfer at the station where you enter the subway, not at the transfer point. Look for the transfer machine.

TOURMOBILES: You can save on shoe leather and see most Washington landmarks in comfort aboard Tourmobiles—open-air, blue-and-white sightseeing trams that run on routes along the Mall and as far out as **Arlington Cemetery** and even **Mount Vernon.**

You may take either the Washington and Arlington Cemetery tour, or tour Arlington Cemetery only. The former visits 15 different sights on or near the Mall, and three sights at Arlington Cemetery: the gravesites of the Kennedy brothers, the Tomb of the Unknowns, and Arlington House. The cost is $7 for adults, $3.50 for children under 12. For Arlington only, adults pay $2.25; children, $1. Buses follow "Figure-8" circuits from the Capitol to Arlington and back.

Here's how the Tourmobile system works. You may board vehicles at 15 different locations:

The White House
The Washington Monument
The Arts & Industries Building
The National Air and Space Museum
Union Station
The Capitol
The National Gallery of Art
The Museum of Natural History
The Museum of American History
The Bureau of Engraving and Printing

The Jefferson Memorial
West Potomac Park (free parking here)
The Kennedy Center
The Lincoln Memorial
Arlington Cemetery

You pay the driver when you first board the bus. Along the route, you may get off at any stop to visit monuments or buildings. When you finish exploring each area, you step aboard the next Tourmobile that comes along without extra charge. The buses travel in both directions and serve each stop every 20 to 30 minutes. One fare allows you to use the buses for a full day. Between June 1 and Labor Day you can also buy a ticket after 4 p.m. good for the rest of the afternoon and the following day ($9 for adults, $4.50 for children); the rest of the year the same offer pertains after 2 p.m. Well-trained narrators give commentaries about sights along the route and will answer your questions.

Tourmobiles also run round trip to Mount Vernon from April to October. Coaches depart from the Arlington National Cemetery Visitors Center and the Washington Monument at 10 a.m., noon, and 2 p.m. The price is $13.50 for adults, $6.25 for children under 13, including admission to Mount Vernon. A combination tour of Washington, Arlington Cemetery, and Mount Vernon is $21 for adults, $10 for children—much cheaper than the Gray Line equivalent. Another offering is the **Frederick Douglass National-al Historic Site Tour,** including a guided tour of Douglass's home, Cedar Hill. Departures are from the same points as the Mount Vernon tour, at 10 a.m. and 1 p.m. Adults pay $5; children, $2.50. A two-day **Combination Frederick Douglass Tour and Washington-Arlington Cemetery Tour** is also available at $14 for adults, $7 for children. For both the Mount Vernon and Frederick Douglass tours you must reserve at least an hour in advance.

Tourmobiles operate year round on the following schedules. From June 15 through Labor Day, they ply the Mall between 9 a.m. and 6:30 p.m. After Labor Day, hours are 9:30 a.m. to 4:30 p.m. From Arlington, between October and March, they start at 8 a.m. and end at 5 p.m. April through September, it's 8 a.m. to 7 p.m.

For further Tourmobile information, call 554-7950.

OLD TOWN TROLLEY TOURS: A service similar to Tourmobile's is Old Town Trolleys, in operation since 1986. For a fixed price, you can get on and off these green and orange open-air vehicles as many times as you like at 16 locations (listed below) in the District. Most of the stops are at hotels, but they're hotels near almost all major sightseeing attractions, including Georgetown.

The trolleys operate seven days a week, between 9 a.m. and 4 p.m. Labor Day to Memorial Day, and until 8 p.m. the rest of the year. Cost is $11 for adults, $9 for students and seniors, free for children under 12 with an accompanying adult. The full tour, which is narrated, takes two hours, and trolleys come by every 30 minutes. The following stops are made:

> Hyatt Regency Hotel (near National Gallery, Union Station)
> Pavilion at the Old Post Office
> Grand Hyatt (near Ford's Theatre, Convention Center)
> J. W. Marriott (near National Theater)
> Hotel Washington (near White House, Renwick, Corcoran)
> Capital Hilton (near National Geographic Explorer's Hall)
> Holiday Inn (near Dupont Circle)
> Washington Hilton (near Phillips Collection)
> Sheraton Washington (near National Zoo)
> Washington Cathedral
> Georgetown Inn
> Marbury Hotel (near C&O Canal)
> Lincoln Memorial
> Loew's L'Enfant Plaza (near Mall museums)
> Holiday Inn Capitol Hill (near Mall museums)
> U.S. Capitol

Tickets can be purchased at all stops except the Lincoln Memorial. For details, call 269-3020.

TAXIS: It's pretty easy—and often inexpensive—to hail a cab in D.C. Taxis run on a zone basis—and if you stay within a zone (most tourist attractions are conveniently grouped in Zone 1), your individual cost is just $2.50; it can be even less ($2.20) within a subzone. But once you leave the initial zone, your fare goes up accordingly—$3.40 for a second zone, $4.30 for a third, $5.15 for a fourth, etc. Few trips go beyond three zones. Tip is not included. There's a $1 rush-hour surcharge Monday to Friday from 4 to 6:30 p.m. And if you're traveling with one or more other persons, regardless of how many zones you traverse, there's an extra charge of $1.25 for each individual, though one child under 5 can ride free. There are also snow emergency surcharges. A zone map is posted in taxis. Ask your driver in advance what the fare will be; it can add up.

Don't be surprised if your taxi stops to pick up other passengers on the way to your destination; it is legal, and sharing makes finding a taxi easier. The zone system is not used when your destination is an out-of-district address (like the airport); the fare is based on mileage covered. You can call 331-1671 to find out what the rate should be between any point in D.C. and an address in Virginia or Maryland. Call 767-8370 for inquiries about fares within the District.

CAR RENTALS: Within the city an automobile can be a frustrating handicap. Traffic is congested and slow during business hours, street parking is a nightmare, and parking lots put out "No Vacancy" signs early. So avoid in-city driving if you can. For such areas as Arlington, Alexandria, Mount Vernon, and Baltimore Harbor, however, a car is most welcome.

Most car-rental companies offer special promotional rates at different times of the year and on weekends. Ask about them, and you may save as much as 50% on listed rates.

Budget Rent-a-Car (tel. toll free 800/527-0700) claims the lowest prices at all three airports. In addition to airport locations, there's a Budget office at a convenient downtown address, 12th and K Streets NW (tel. 628-2750). The firm offers a good fleet mix, from luxurious Lincoln town cars to seven-passenger Dodge Caravans, to a full selection of economy cars—not to mention "specialty cars" like Porsches, BMWs, and Mercedes. And in any car you rent, a portable cellular phone is available for $3 a day plus 95¢ a minute for calls. At this writing Budget offers low weekend rates from Thursday noon to Monday noon—$22.95 to $26.50 with 100 free miles a day for an economy car. Cars rented in town can be dropped off at the airport at no extra charge, and vice versa.

Check the phone book for other car rental companies.

WASHINGTON'S WEATHER

Many a January presidential inaugural address has been delivered on the Capitol steps with the president's breath taking off in clouds on the frosty air. Washington can be pretty cold in winter, with lots of snow—except for those occasional times when it gets unexpectedly warm. Washington weather is a bit unpredictable. Advantages of winter visits are low hotel prices and no lines at attractions.

Springtime, especially in April when the cherry trees are in bloom, is the most popular season for visitors.

In summer, heat and humidity can be high, and if you aren't used to it, you'll feel limp. But most places are air-conditioned. Hotels with swimming pools make a summer vacation much more enjoyable.

Autumn in Washington is an unqualified delight. The weather is comfortable, the tourist throngs have abated, and we recommend it as the best time for a vacation visit.

Average Temperatures in Washington, D.C.					
	High		Medium		Low
	F	C	F	C	F	C
January	44.6°	(7°)	35.0°	(1.6°)	27.4°	(−2.6°)
February	44.4	(6.8)	36.2	(2.3)	28.0	(−2.2)
March	53.0	(11.6)	44.0	(6.7)	35.0	(1.6)
April	64.2	(17.8)	54.2	(12.3)	44.2	(6.8)
May	74.9	(23.8)	64.7	(18.2)	54.5	(12.5)
June	82.8	(28.2)	73.1	(22.8)	63.4	(17.4)
July	86.8	(30.4)	77.4	(25.2)	68.0	(20)
August	84.4	(29.1)	75.3	(24)	66.1	(18.9)
September	78.4	(25.7)	69.0	(20.5)	59.6	(15.3)
October	67.5	(19.7)	57.8	(14.3)	48.0	(8.8)
November	55.1	(12.8)	46.5	(8)	37.9	(3.3)
December	44.8	(7.1)	37.3	(2.9)	29.8	(−1.2)

ADVANCE PLANNING

A lot of what you'll want to see and do in the capital can be arranged after you arrive, but some things should be done in advance, while you're still back in Kansas—or wherever.

CHOOSE A HOTEL: Advance booking not only assures you a room (100% occupancy is no rarity here, especially in peak tourist seasons) but allows you to take advantage of amazingly low weekend rates at first-class hotels. For a free listing of 90 hotels offering special weekend deals, write or phone the **D.C. Committee to Promote Washington,** P.O. Box 27489, Washington, D.C. 20038-7489 (tel. toll free 800/422-8644), and request a copy of *Washington Weekends.* Generally, even if a longer stay includes a weekend, you can get the special rate for those nights if you ask.

Another good source for weekend rates is **Taj International Hotels,** 1315 16th St. NW, Washington, D.C. 20036 (tel. 202/462-7104, or toll free 800/ILUVTAJ or 800/DC-VISIT). Owners and operators of five Washington hostelries, Taj offers some of the most advantageous weekend rates and packages in town, and they extend those rates to include off-season weekdays (November to February and during July and August) as well. Contact them for details.

PLAN YOUR SIGHTSEEING ITINERARY: There's too much to do to play it by ear. Careful planning makes for a much more enjoyable trip. Read the sightseeing chapter in this book, decide on your priorities (you can't see everything, and it's more rewarding to see several attractions thoroughly than to breeze through dozens), then map out each vacation day. Take geographical proximity into account (no reason to wear yourself out traipsing from one end of town to the other), and include ample leisure time to make the experience enjoyable.

WRITE YOUR SENATOR OR CONGRESSPERSON: You always suspected that the folks on the Hill served some useful purpose, didn't you? Well—they can provide you with passes for VIP tours (they're more comprehensive and/or allow you to avoid long lines) of the Capitol, the White House, the Kennedy Center, and the FBI, if you write far enough in advance. Unfortunately, many people know about this (it's in the guidebooks), and ticket supplies are limited. Six months prior to your trip is not too soon to write. Address requests, including the exact dates of your vacation, to your representative, U.S. House of Representatives, Washington, D.C. 20515; or to your senator, U.S. Senate, Washington, D.C. 20510. Some members will also supply Visitor's Passes to view the House and/or Senate in action.

UTILIZE VISITOR INFORMATION SOURCES: The **Washington, D.C., Convention and Visitors Association,** 1212 New York Ave. NW, Sixth Floor, Washington, D.C. 20004 (tel. 202/789-7000), can answer all tourism-related questions. They also send out, upon request, free brochures detailing sights in and around the District, restaurant and hotel guides, and a map.

Also write to the **D.C. Department of Recreation,** 3149 16th St. NW, Washington, D.C. 20010 (tel. 202/673-7660), enclosing a stamped, self-addressed envelope, and request their calendar of events. It tells you about concerts, theater, free outdoor entertainment, cookouts, crafts shows, and other peak happenings.

And if you're interested in **touring the caverns** under the Lincoln Memorial, you have to make reservations months in advance. Details are in Chapter V.

IN-TOWN INFORMATION SOURCES

Washington's abundance of attractions can be mind-boggling, but, happily, the city has numerous services that make things easier, whether you need only routine information or emergency assistance.

INFORMATION FOR EVERYONE: The **Washington Visitor Information Center,** on Pennsylvania Avenue between 14th and 15th Streets NW, one block from the White House (tel. 789-7000),

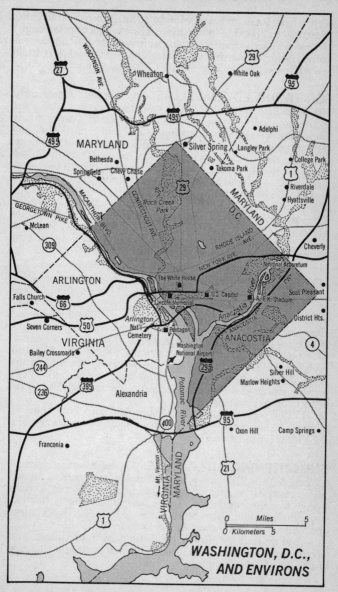

WASHINGTON, D.C., AND ENVIRONS

is open from 9 a.m. to 5 p.m. Monday to Saturday to field all visitor questions and provide information. There are racks of brochures and promotional literature, and maps are available. On hand are volunteers from the International Visitors Information Service (details below). It's well worth stopping by. Closed major holidays.

FOR TROUBLED TRAVELERS: The **Travelers Aid Society,** 1015 12th St. NW (tel. 347-0101), is a nationwide, nonprofit social service organization geared to helping travelers in difficult straits. Their services might include reuniting families separated while traveling, helping retrieve lost luggage, providing food and/or shelter to people stranded without cash, even emotional counseling. If you're in trouble, seek them out. The 12th Street office is open from 9 a.m. to 5 p.m. weekdays, and the phone number is manned by professionals 24 hours a day. Other offices are in the south baggage area of National Airport, open from 9 a.m. to 9 p.m. Sunday to Friday, to 6 p.m. on Saturday (tel. 684-3472); on the lower concourse at the west end of Dulles Airport, open from 10 a.m. to 9 p.m. Sunday to Friday, to 6 p.m. on Saturday (tel. 661-8636); and at Union Station, open seven days from 9:30 a.m. to 5:30 p.m. (tel. 347-0101).

FOR FOREIGN VISITORS: The **International Visitors Information Service (IVIS),** 733 15th St. NW, at H Street, Suite 300 (tel. 202/783-6540), is a nonprofit, community volunteer organization that provides special services to D.C.'s many visitors from abroad. Here you can obtain publications and brochures about Washington attractions in your own language, and staff members can answer your questions. No matter how obscure your dialect, IVIS can probably find someone to understand you (they have a Language Bank of volunteers who speak over 50 languages on call). They'll provide assistance with accommodations, sightseeing, dining, and other traditional tourist needs.

IVIS is open weekdays from 9 a.m. to 5 p.m., but phones are manned 24 hours a day. This organization can also be contacted at the Visitor Information Center (above).

ENLIGHTENING LITERATURE: *Washingtonian* magazine's "Where & When" section gives a full rundown of current happenings: music, dance, theater, films, museums, art galleries, lectures, poetry readings, workshops, sports, and special events (for kids too). Ofttimes you'll also get the latest on new eateries and nightspots here. Pick up a copy at any newsstand.

And do read the *Washington Post* for up-to-date information about what's doing in town. The "Weekend" section included in the Friday edition is especially helpful.

DIAL-A- . . . : The **Smithsonian** has a phone number (tel. 357-2020) for recorded daily information on all its museums' special programs and activities.

Dial 737-8866 for the **Tourist Information Center's** recording of events of interest to tourists.

To find the **correct time,** call 844-2525; 936-1212 for a **weather** report.

And while we're on the subject of phoning, you should know that the **area code** for Washington, D.C., is 202, most of Virginia is 703, and all of Maryland is 301. Many Virginia and Maryland numbers are local calls from the District, and you don't have to dial an area code. In this book, phone numbers listed without area codes are all local.

CHAPTER III

WHERE TO STAY IN WASHINGTON

□ □ □

Your first priority on a Washington visit is finding a place to stay. Luckily, with some 48,000 hotel and motel rooms in the District and surrounding metropolitan area, there is no shortage of rooms. They exist in every category, from super-luxurious accommodations befitting royalty to budget guesthouses—with many more, alas, in the upper bracket than the lower. Presented below are our choices of those establishments in all price categories that offer the best value for the money in Washington. Most of the recommendations are in the Northwest section, an area in which many major sightseeing attractions and good restaurants are located.

GETTING THE MOST FOR YOUR HOTEL DOLLAR: In-the-know travelers can save considerably on hotel rates. First, remember to avail yourself of **weekend rates** (see item 1 in "Advance Planning," Chapter II, and the box in this chapter). Hotels often slash tariffs 30% to 50% on weekends—and sometimes these reduced rates are carried over into the week as well.

But weekend rates aren't the whole story. Keep in mind the perspective of the hotelier, large or small. A hotel makes zero dollars per night on an empty room. Hence, though they don't bruit it about (for obvious reasons), most hotels are willing to **bargain on rates** rather than risk unoccupied rooms. For them, $50 a night for a $100-a-night room is better than nothing. Haggling probably won't work in spring when hotels are running close to 100% full; summer and holidays are the best times for bargains. But whenever a rate is quoted, it's always a good idea to ask, "Can I get a better deal?" If the desk clerk can't help you, ask to speak to the desk captain. We're not saying you won't risk a snub or two, but those who persevere can nurse wounded feelings all the way to the bank. An especially advantageous time to secure lower rates is late in the afternoon/early evening on your day of arrival, when a hotel's likelihood of filling up with full-price bookings is remote.

Of course, we know there are some of you who would sooner die than play Middle Eastern market with Marriott. If you get harried when you have to haggle, utilize a free service offered by **Capitol Reservations,** 1201 K St. NW, Washington, D.C. 20005 (tel. 202/842-4187, or toll free 800/VISIT-DC). They'll find you a hotel in the price bracket you desire that meets your specific requirements, and they'll do the bargaining for you. "Because of the high volume of room nights we book," explains owner Thom Hall, "many properties offer discounts available only through this service." Capitol Reservations listings begin at about $55 a night for a double, they've all been screened for cleanliness and other desirability factors, and they're all in safe neighborhoods.

Finally, everyone reserving a hotel room should inquire about **special packages.** And many hotels offer special rates as a matter of course to senior citizens, families, active-duty military personnel, and government workers.

Whatever rate you end up with, keep in mind that the hotel tax here is 10% of your total bill, and the occupancy tax is $2 per night. And if you have a car, look into the cost of parking when you reserve; some centrally located hotels charge as much as $15 a night!

FOR GROUPS ONLY: If you're planning a meeting, convention, or other group function (school, church, fraternal organization, corporate, etc.), you should know about a service called **U.S.A. Groups** (tel. toll free 800/USA-GRPS). Representing hotel rooms at almost every property in the Washington, D.C./Virginia/Maryland region—in categories from luxury to low cost—this organization works hard to locate a property that perfectly fits your group's needs and budget. Unlike a hotel sales office, geared to wooing business and filling rooms regardless of suitability, U.S.A. Groups makes finding your optimum accommodations its first priority. And it saves you dozens of phone calls seeking space, rate, and facility information. Best of all, the service is free.

THE GRAND HOTELS

Some are old and venerable, others are new, chic, and glamorous, but all hotels listed under this heading are plush hostelries providing abundant luxuries and gracious service to guests occupying their $175-a-night-and-up rooms. All have beautiful gourmet restaurants, most of which merit a visit even if you stay at a less elegant address.

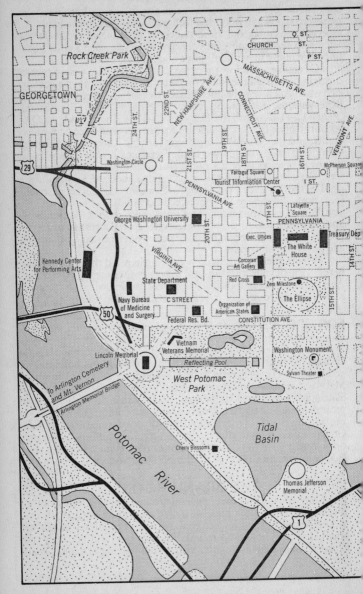

DOWNTOWN WASHINGTON, D.C.

RHODE ISLAND AVE.

O ST.

N ST.

M ST.

L ST.

NEW YORK AVE.

K ST.

Franklin Park

Washington Convention Center

MASSACHUSETTS AVE.

H ST.

G ST.

City Post Office

F ST.

Union Station

E ST.

J. Edgar Hoover Bldg.

D ST.

PENNSYLVANIA AVE.

C STREET

Internal Revenue

Justice Dept.

LOUISIANA AVE.

Senate Office Bldg.

CONSTITUTION AVE.

Museum of African Art

Museum of American History

Natural History Museum

National Gallery

Reflecting Pool

Supreme Court

MADISON DR.

E. CAPITOL ST.

The Mall

Hirshhorn Museum

National Air and Space Museum

JEFFERSON DR.

U.S. Capitol

Folger Library

Smithsonian

Freer Gallery

INDEPENDENCE AVE.

Botanic Garden

Library of Congress

Sackler Gallery

MARYLAND AVE.

VIRGINIA AVE.

195

395

G ST.

Washington Channel

I ST.

K ST.

L ST.

OHIO DR.

M ST.

The current trend is toward old-fashioned European-style services and traditions. You can leave your shoes outside the door at night and find them polished in the morning. Afternoon tea, complete with fresh-baked scones and Devonshire cream, is a likely option; another is comprehensive concierge service—often around the clock—to provide whatever the pampered guest might desire, be it a private Lear jet or beluga caviar at 3 a.m. "Anything legal supplied" might be their motto. One is tempted to see how outrageous a request will be honored, but we leave that to you. At this price level, you can count on twice-daily maid service, with gourmet chocolates or other treat when your bed is turned down for the night. Some hotels listed in this section even supply a butler.

Billed as the "crown jewel of Pennsylvania Avenue," the newly renovated **Willard Inter-Continental,** 1401 Pennsylvania Ave. NW, Washington, DC 20004 (tel. 202/628-9100, or toll free 800/327-0200), is actually the crown jewel of all Washington hotels. Reopened in 1986, it was built in 1901 as the grandest of grand hotels on the site of an even earlier hostelry built by Henry Willard in 1850.

The Willard's history is inextricably intertwined with the history of Washington. It flourished from pre-Civil War days (at one time there were separate entrances and floors for pro-Union and secessionist factions) through just after World War II. In the 1860s Nathaniel Hawthorne said of the Willard, "You exchange nods with governors of sovereign States; you elbow illustrious men, and tread on the toes of generals. . . . You are mixed up with office seekers, wire pullers, inventors, artists, poets, prosers . . . until your identity is lost among them." Brought to the capital by her lover and manager, P. T. Barnum, the "Swedish Nightingale," Jenny Lind, received a steady stream of distinguished visitors during her stay here, among them Daniel Webster and President Millard Fillmore. On the day Jefferson Davis was sworn in as president of the Confederacy, a group of statesmen met in Willard Hall in an unsuccessful last-ditch attempt to avert full-scale civil war. And Lincoln spent not only the eve of his inaugural here, but sometimes held staff meetings in front of the lobby fireplace. It was at the Willard that Julia Ward Howe penned the words to the "Battle Hymn of the Republic."

In 1901 Henry Willard's nephew, Joseph Willard, hired Henry Janeway Hardenbergh—architect of New York's Waldorf Astoria and Plaza Hotels—to design the French Second Empire beaux arts palace that is still standing today. The hotel continued as a "residence of presidents." Calvin Coolidge conducted affairs of state from the Willard for a month while waiting for Harding's widow to vacate the White House. But in the late 1940s the neighborhood began to decline, and by the time the Willard finally closed its doors in 1968, the hotel had considerably deteriorated.

Happily, preservationists blocked efforts to demolish the property. It became a national landmark in 1974, and in the 1980s restoration began and a new building, designed to harmonize with the old, was constructed. This addition consists of a series of four pavilions around an interior fountained plaza, with dormer windows and curved mansard rooflines. In the original building, the exquisite plasterwork and scagliola marble were repaired or replicated, along with marble mosaic tile floors, carpeting, and chandeliers. By analyzing paint scrapings, restorers—including artisans from Italy and Greece—created a palette of colors close to those that adorned the original interior. Public areas were given the most meticulous attention. The colonnaded main lobby is again an awesome entranceway, with vast marble columns ascending to a lofty ceiling decorated with 48 state seals and hung with huge globe chandeliers. The original front desk, a petal-shaped structure of ochre marble, glass, and polished wood, now serves as the concierge desk. Peacock Alley is once again a plush potted-palmed promenade lined with exclusive boutiques. And the Willard Room (the term "power lunch" originated here) is simply stunning with its intricately carved oak paneling and plaster ceiling, gilt-topped scagliola columns, and stately floor-to-ceiling windows. It's the setting for new American cuisine meals, with piano music provided during dinner. (Details in Chapter IV.) Another facility is the circular Round Robin Bar, once an all-male precinct wherein Henry Clay mixed the first mint julep in Washington.

There's also the newly created Espresso Café, featuring Italian hi-tech decor and serving croissant sandwiches, pastries, and vintage wines by the glass.

The 365 rooms are suitably sumptuous, decorated in Egyptian earth tones or sea and sky blues. Furnishings are Edwardian and Federalist reproductions, and walls are hung with beautiful gilt-framed French prints. Cable color TVs (with remote control, movie channels, plus video message and video checkout) are concealed in armoires, and all rooms offer settes or armchairs with hassocks, desks, refrigerators/stocked mini-bars, beside control of room lights and TV, full-length mirrors, and closets with raised sections for the hanging of formal gowns. In the bath you'll find a hair dryer, scale, phone, TV speaker, makeup mirror, and possibly even a bidet. And as a Willard guest, you'll be pampered with twice-daily maid service, nightly bed turndown, complimentary shoe-shine, 24-hour room service, and European-style concierge service.

Since its reopening, the hotel has already hosted 17 heads of state, including Prime Ministers Nakasone of Japan, Peres of Israel, Gandhi of India, and Chirac of France. The sixth floor of the hotel is specially designed to offer top security to such visitors as require it.

The Willard is one of several Washington hotels that offers a smashing afternoon tea, from 3 to 5 p.m. on weekends, in The Nest, a charming lounge (once a ladies' sitting room) up an oval wrought-iron staircase. A full tea for $11.50 includes a choice of freshly brewed teas, tea sandwiches filled with good things like smoked chicken and fruit chutney, watercress and English cheddar, and roast beef with creamed horseradish, a freshly baked scone with Devonshire cream and strawberry preserves, and a fresh fruit tartlet.

The rates: $185 to $260 single, $210 to $285 double, the differential indicative of factors like room size, location, and configuration. An additional person pays $25, and children under 12 stay free in their parents' room. Reduced weekend rates (just $145 a night, single or double, at this writing) and packages are available. Suites begin at $425.

Esquire magazine calls the **Jefferson,** 1200 16th St. NW (at M Street), Washington, DC 20036 (tel. 202/347-2200, or toll free 800/368-5966), "one of the ten best hotels in the world." Opened in 1923 just four blocks from the White House, it has served as the Washington home of political personages, royalty, actors, writers, and other notables. Among those who've enjoyed the Jefferson's discreet small-hotel hospitality are Edward R. Murrow (he stayed here for months while house hunting when he was appointed director of the USIA), the Caspar Weinbergers (they moved in with their collie, Mr. Buffington, after Reagan took office), Helen Hayes, Robert Frost, Katherine Anne Porter, Leonard Bernstein, and H. L. Mencken (his room was lined with shelves of his favorite books). With just 100 rooms, and a very high staff-to-guest ratio, the Jefferson puts utmost emphasis on service. It's evocative of an earlier era when only the rich traveled and did so with servants in tow. A butler is available around the clock; if you like, he'll unpack your luggage and press any clothes that were wrinkled in transit. Scuffed shoes are shined gratis overnight, laundry is hand-ironed and returned to you in a wicker basket wrapped in tissue paper, beds are turned down and rooms freshened every evening, and a newspaper (discuss your preference with the concierge, also on 24-hour duty) is delivered to your room each morning. Staff members will greet you by name, and, should you return, your preferences will be remembered.

The Jefferson is impressive from the minute you set foot in the sedately elegant lobby. Beautiful Persian rugs adorn marble floors, Italian turn-of-the-century crystal chandeliers are suspended from a carved-plaster rosette-motif Adams ceiling, big bouquets of roses adorn 18th-century tables and the manager's Louis XV desk, and rose-and-gold silk-covered Chippendale sofas face a Georgian reproduction fireplace. A Thomas Jefferson grandfather clock chimes the hours in dulcet tones. A very fine art collection graces public areas, rooms, and hallways.

Off the lobby is the Hunt Club, handsomely decorated in Roman ochre and forest green, its oak-wainscotted walls hung with hunting prints. Chippendale furnishings, Federalist and Chinoiserie mirrors, intricately carved moldings, and exquisitely appointed tables are the backdrop for haute cuisine luncheons and dinners. The room is a warren-like arrangement of intimate dining areas, and baroque music further enhances the cozy ambience. Every afternoon from 3 to 5 p.m. a full afternoon tea—complete with scones, finger sandwiches, pastries, and fresh fruits—is served here. Typical dinner entrees (in the $20 to $25 range) are a classic steak au poivre in brandy and cream sauce, rack of lamb with roast parsley and rosemary sauce, and breast of duck in sweet hazelnut sauce with a crisp hazelnut-ginger crust. Breakfast is served in the Monticello Room, also off the lobby, a delightful setting with white lace-curtained windows, pale-yellow watered-silk wall coverings, and floor-length aqua floral-print cotton chintz tablecloths.

Each of the guest rooms at the Jefferson is uniquely decorated. Yours might have a four-poster bed with plump eyelet-trimmed comforter and pillow shams (many offer canopy beds), a cherry-wood bibliothèque from the Napoleonic period filled with rare books, a French Empire Louis XVI bureau, French doors, or a red-lacquer Chinoiserie case filled with objets d'art. All are lovely, and all are equipped with color TV, AM/FM radio, and in the bath, a terry robe, a tub with brass spigots and a silk shower curtain, a telephone, and fine Spanish toiletries.

Rates at the Jefferson are $150 to $235 single, $160 to $255 double, $20 for an additional person, free for children under 12 in the same room with their parents. A luxurious weekend package, priced at $125 single, $145 double, per room, per night, includes a welcome bottle of champagne and chocolates in your room, continental breakfast on Saturday, brunch Sunday morning, cocktails for two in the Hunt Club, valet parking, tax, and service.

Few hotels have a more aristocratic air than the **Hay-Adams,** 16th and H Streets NW (overlooking Lafayette Square), Washington, DC 20006 (tel. 202/638-6600, or toll free 800/424-5054). It stands on the site of the 19th-century homes of John Hay (Lincoln's private secretary and later Theodore Roosevelt's secretary of state) and historian Henry Adams (great-grandson of John Adams). Adams found the property and coaxed his close friend Hay to become a neighbor. ("I need not say how eager I am to spend your money to have you next door. I would sacrifice your last dollar.")

In 1927 famed Washington builder Harry Wardman created the Hay-Adams "to provide for the socially elite as well as men who loom large in the country's life." Styled after an Italian palazzo with Doric, Ionic, and Corinthian orders and intricate ceiling motifs, it had such modern miracles as circulating ice water and the first air-conditioned restaurant in town. Among the early guests were Amelia Earhart, Sinclair Lewis, Ethel Barrymore, and Charles Lindbergh.

In the 1980s the hotel is as elegant as ever. A limousine for guest use and 24-hour butler service (you can have a suit pressed at 2 a.m.) are among the amenities. Homemade chocolates and petits-fours are provided with nightly turndown, closets have old-fashioned shoe racks (and real hangers), and shoeshine is complimentary.

The oak-paneled lobby is festooned with art and antiques—17th-century Medici tapestries, French Empire candelabras, 19th-century Chinese gouaches, and Regency furnishings.

The sunny Adams Room, one of several food and beverage facilities, may be D.C.'s prettiest dining room. Bounded by a wall of windows overlooking Lafayette Square and the White House, it has a French country breakfast-room ambience with Louis XV-style chairs (upholstered in red fabric with a delicate yellow floral print), pale-yellow silk wall coverings, and plush celadon rugs on oak floors. It's open for breakfast, Sunday brunch, and lunch only.

The counterpart to the Adams Room is the richly appointed Tudor-style John Hay Room, its oak-paneled walls hung with framed reproductions of Hans Holbein drawings from the Windsor Castle collection and a reproduction of a 17th-century French tapestry. Large brass chandeliers are suspended from a vaulted Moorish ceiling. Classic French cuisine is featured. Dinner here might consist of an hors d'oeuvre of escargots de Bourgogne, followed by poached Maine lobster with hazelnut/herb-butter sauce and a selection from the pastry cart. Plan on a tab of at least $100 for two, with tax and tip, more if you opt for a bottle of wine.

In the alcove of the John Hay Room is the charming Tea Room with a 17th-century *Portrait of Charlemagne* over the sofa. Its plush furnishings include a William IV mahogany drum table and a George III inlaid mahogany game table. It adjoins the lounge, which contains additional antiques and Holbein reproductions. The former is the setting for formal afternoon teas complete with finger sandwiches and fresh-from-the-oven scones and pastries; sherries are also served. The latter features nightly piano-bar entertainment.

Finally, there's the clubby downstairs English Grill Room with Tudor ceiling, plank oak floors, and bookcases filled with works about Hay and Adams. Drinks and an English menu are featured.

The 143 rooms are individually furnished with antiques and appointments far superior to those usually found in today's hotels. Though each is different, a typical accommodation might feature 18th-century-style furnishings, silk wall coverings hung with botanical prints and well-chosen original art, a gorgeous molded plaster ceiling, and French silk floral-print bedspreads, upholstery, and curtains. About 30% have fireplaces (ornamental only); others have French doors that open on views of Lafayette Square and the White House. Among the frills: full-length mirrors on the doors of your ample closet (usually offering a three-way view); magnifying cosmetic mirrors, fine English soaps, terrycloth robes, hair dryers, and phones in the bath; and remote-control TVs with HBO, congressional, sports, and news channels.

Rates run a wide gamut—$180 to $275 single, $200 to $300 double; the higher end is for a White House view. An additional person pays $25 a night. Children under 12 stay free in their parents' room. A reduced-rate weekend package is available. Also, you'll be interested to know that there are eight smaller rooms at the Hay-Adams (they were originally for servants traveling with guests, but they're delightfully decorated today) that go for just $150 a night, single or double. You can request one of these when you reserve.

The 24-hour room service from the Jockey Club may be the reason Julia Child and Craig Claiborne elect to stay at the **Ritz-Carlton,** 2100 Massachusetts Ave. NW, Washington, DC 20008 (tel. 202/ 293-2100, or toll free 800/424-8008), when visiting D.C. But easy access to a great restaurant is only one of this hotel's assets. The Ritz-Carlton is a gem—from its charming Federal-style lobby to its pristine hallways (with Oriental carpets on the floors), to its 230 rooms (24 are suites) the residential decor of which a local writer has described as "unostentatious quality."

It's always a treat to find hotel rooms that live up to the promise of plush public areas—ditto interiors that flout the current decorator mode. Rooms at the Ritz are all one could hope for on both counts. Forest-green carpeting complements exquisite English linen chintz floral-print bedspread, curtain, and upholstery fabrics. Framed botanical prints adorn walls covered in Laura Ashley or similar tiny-patterned English wallpaper. Drexel Heritage armoires house honor bars, color TVs, alarm-clock AM/FM radios, and locked drawers, and additional furnishings include comfortable sofas, Regency chairs, and handsome desks. The effect is strikingly attractive. Your phone at the Ritz has two lines. Your bath is equipped with a full-length mirror, makeup lights, a heat lamp, an extra phone, a small TV, fine toiletries on a brass-fixtured sink, and fluffy oversized towels. The *Washington Post* is delivered to your door each morning, and nightly turndown brings an imported chocolate. Guests also enjoy full concierge service and complimentary shoeshine.

We've already mentioned the Jockey Club, one of Washington's most fashionable restaurants, and you'll find more about it in Chapter IV. Adjoining the Jockey Club is the cozy Fairfax Bar, its decor inspired by the famous London nightclub, Anabel's. Here you can sink into plush velvet sofas with pretty throw pillows—or a comfortable burgundy-leather club chair—before a blazing fire (there are two working fireplaces). The furnishings are so arranged that an intimate conversation is possible. Like the Jockey Club, the Fairfax has wood-paneled walls (here of polished knotty pine), random-oak plank floors, and horse-themed paintings on the walls. A yellow rose in a glass flask adorns each table. The Fairfax is a romantic setting for afternoon tea or sherry, cocktails, and after-dinner drinks. It's also open for light lunches, and there's nightly piano bar.

Rates at the Ritz-Carlton are $170 to $220 single (the difference reflects room size and location), $195 to $245 double, $30 for each additional person, no charge for children under 12. However, on Friday and/or Saturday night tariffs plummet to $145 per night, single or double occupancy. Other weekend packages—with luxury frills like champagne and chauffeured limos—are also available.

The **Four Seasons**, 2800 Pennsylvania Ave. NW, Washington, DC 20007 (tel. 202/342-0444, or toll free 800/828-1188, 800/462-1150 in New York), is glamorous. Since its opening in 1979 guests have included Richard Simmons (he did jumping jacks in the lobby), Rodney Dangerfield (when he came to D.C. to donate his tie to the Smithsonian), Larry Hagman (he donated his hat), and Michael Jackson (they set up a special dance floor in his room), not to mention King Hussein of Jordan, the prime minister of the Netherlands, and Ronald Reagan.

The Four Seasons is lovely. Open the front door and you enter a lush garden lobby where thousands of tropical plants and palm trees grow and large floral arrangements at either end further the garden ambience. Classical music enhances the setting.

The Four Seasons offers a standard of luxury and sumptuous service that harks back to the Grand Hotel era. Guests are preregistered and escorted directly to their rooms on arrival. The concierge staff, on duty 24 hours, can get your suit pressed in ten minutes (even at 3 a.m.), make reservations at a Paris restaurant, arrange a private Lear jet, or provide anything from an exercise bike to a mink stole. From room service (24 hours, of course) you can order the likes of pâté de foie gras and beluga caviar. Put your shoes outside the door at night and they'll be shined (gratis) by the morning. There's nightly turndown, and if you've taken an afternoon nap the sheets will be changed. When your car is parked, the windows are washed. And speaking of cars, there's a limousine for complimentary guest use.

Of course the rooms are fittingly elegant. Many offer views of Rock Creek Park or the C&O Canal (both of which are conveniently adjacent for jogging); the others face on the hotel's courtyard. All are equipped with color TVs (with movie and other cable channels plus remote control), digital clock radios, mini-bars, and refrigerators. In the marble-paneled bath you'll find a full-length mirror, a fluffy terrycloth robe, a makeup mirror, a hair dryer, an additional phone, a single flower in a vase, and, if you're a woman traveling alone, a basket of fine bath products. Rooms are residential in feel. They feature four different color schemes—peach, gray, carnation, and peony—and contain large oval leather-topped mahogany desks, comfortable reclining armchairs with footstools, Hepplewhite-reproduction chairs, and handsome mahogany armoires. Walls are covered in moiré silk.

Aux Beaux Champs, the hotel's major restaurant, is renowned throughout Washington for its delightful interior and fine French cuisine. Windows all around make for sun-drenched breakfasts and lunches and provide canal and park views. Like other public areas, it has a garden (or "beautiful fields") motif with indoor trees, a muted green carpet, and beautiful flower arrangements. All is elegance: the liqueurs displayed on a Queen Anne tea table next to a case of exquisite desserts, the Austrian ash-paneled walls hung with early 19th-century English engravings of India, and the tables set with white linen and Canton Royal Doulton. A la carte entrees here average about $20 for dinner; complete prix fixe dinners are $60.

Lush plantings—trees, ferns, and shrubbery—and so many flowers in bloom that the air is perfumed, characterize another Four Seasons dining facility, the Garden Terrace. As at Aux Beaux Champs, a wall of floor-to-ceiling windows makes for lots of light and canal views. Seating is cocktail lounge style (plush velvet sofas and armchairs at glass-topped tables), and a pianist entertains from about 4 p.m. on. The Garden Terrace serves lunch, light fare throughout the day, cocktails, a New Orleans jazz brunch, and a classic English afternoon tea with finger sandwiches, fresh-baked scones, Devonshire cream, homemade preserves, and pots of your favorite tea. It also features a special vodka and caviar menu.

Finally, there's Desirée, a private nightclub/disco which extends temporary membership to hotel guests.

Rates range from about $185 to $215 single, $215 to $245 double. An extra person pays $30; children under 18 stay free in a room with their parents. A reduced-price weekend package is offered.

Billing itself as "Washington's correct address," the **Madison,** at the corner of M and 15th Streets NW, Washington, DC 20005 (tel. 202/862-1600, or toll free 800/424-8577), has hosted such prestigious guests in recent years as Egyptian President Mubarak, Chinese Premier Zhao Ziyang, and Japanese Prime Minister A. W. Yasuhiro Nakasone. Even Raisa and Mikhail Gorbachev stayed here during their U.S. visit. But it's not just heads of state who opt for the Madison—Elizabeth Taylor, Pearl Bailey, Robert Redford, Frank Sinatra, and Bob Hope have all graced the guest roster.

Though it was built in 1963, the Madison has the aura of a gracious grande-dame hotel. You'll feel it the moment you enter the plush antique-filled lobby, which contains many pieces from the vast collection of owner Marshall B. Coyne. Among the objets d'art gracing the lobby are a Chinese Imperial altar table; a Louis XVI palace commode, cartel clock, and gold-leaf girandole mirror with Sevres plaques; an 18th-century Georgian breakfront used to display a fine collection of Boehm porcelains, and an English Regency mantel clock.

Like the public areas, the rooms are beautifully appointed. They're individually furnished and contain antiques or Chinese rugs from Coyne's collection and/or display cabinets filled with objets d'art. Decor might be Oriental, with Thai silk curtains and bedspreads, or French provincial. All guests receive a welcome note with a small packet of gourmet chocolates on arrival. In-room facilities include remote-control color TV with HBO movies and other cable stations, a well-stocked mini-bar, and a bath equipped with a full-length mirror, makeup mirror, hair dryer, terrycloth robes, a refrigerator with ice, phone, fine bath products, a scale, and heated towel racks. At night your bed is turned down and additional chocolates are left upon the pillow.

The Madison's French haute-cuisine restaurant—named for the Virginia homestead of James Madison—is the Montpelier, its entrance flanked by a 19th-century English oil by Charles Clair and rare Boehm porcelains (a replica of the Boehm swans Nixon brought to Mao on his visit to China). Each morning gratis newspapers—everything from the *Wall Street Journal* to *Le Monde* —are available to diners. The Montpelier offers a luxe Federal-style setting with gilt-framed mirrors and oil paintings adorning rosewood-paneled walls. Adjoining the restaurant is the similarly furnished Montpelier Lounge for cocktails and hors d'oeuvres. For less formal dining, there's a pubby eatery with candlelit oak tables, Tudor-style stained-glass windows, and green-leather chairs. In addition, the cozy Hideaway serves light fare and drinks.

The Madison specializes in service with a 24-hour concierge on duty to assist guests in every way. Room service is also round the clock.

Rates are $195 to $235 single, $25 for each additional person. The weekend rate is $110 single or double (parking included), with a two-night minimum stay required.

Designed by the architectural firm whose beaux arts masterpieces include Grand Central Terminal in New York, the Stouffer-owned **Mayflower,** 1127 Connecticut Ave. NW (between L and M Streets), Washington, DC 20036 (tel. 202/347-3000, or toll free 800/HOTELS-1), is the grande dame of Washington hotels. It's even listed on the National Register of Historic Places.

Every president since Coolidge has held his inaugural ball in the gilded Grand Ballroom. FDR—who lived at the Mayflower between his election and inauguration—penned the words "The only thing we have to fear is fear itself" in suite 776. Both Lyndon Johnson and John F. Kennedy called the hotel home as young congressmen, and famous guests have included everyone from Winston Churchill to John Wayne. For 20 years before his death, J. Edgar

Hoover ate the same lunch at the same table in the Grille Room every day—chicken soup, grapefruit, and cottage cheese. One day he spotted Public Enemy No. 3 at an adjoining table and nabbed him. One could go on forever with Mayflower lore.

A major restoration has uncovered large skylights in the lobby and the Café Promenade (both covered for blackout reasons during World War II). The lobby's pink marble bas-relief frieze and mezzanine balconies—obscured during previous renovations—have also been restored, along with the spectacular block-long Promenade. Ceilings and columns have been regilded, Italianate murals rediscovered, and thousands of yards of new carpeting and marble installed. The Mayflower's classic beauty and grace evoke an earlier era.

In the 724 graciously appointed guest rooms hardwood crown moldings adorn high ceilings. Color schemes are either soft pink/beige or muted green; furnishings are Federal style in mahogany, cherry, and oak; and baths have luxuries like built-in hair dryers, phones, and marble vanities with solid-brass fixtures. Your color TV and radio are discreetly concealed in an armoire, and clocks, minibars, and full-length mirrors are in-room amenities. Complimentary coffee and a newspaper are delivered to your room each morning if you ask for a wake-up call.

The hotel's premier restaurant—much acclaimed by critics—is Nicholas, featuring new American cuisine in a gem-like setting. Ecru-colored walls are hung with traditional gilt-framed French oil paintings, while potted palms, richly appointed tables, crystal chandeliers, shaded sconces, and lush floral arrangements are reflected in gleaming beveled mirrors. Menus change frequently. A typical Nicholas dinner (about $100 for two, tax and tip included): goat cheese with basil and pine nuts baked in phyllo dough; medallions of veal sautéed with wild mushrooms, roasted peppers, shallots, and marjoram; and a dessert of hot chestnut-and-ginger soufflé. Lunch prices are about 20% lower. An extensive wine list complements the menu.

Washington lawyers and lobbyists gather for early-morning meetings at the Café Promenade off the lobby. It's a posh spot for lunches and dinners too, with white wicker chairs and tables under a beautiful domed skylight. Edward Laning's murals adorn the walls, and there are crystal chandeliers, trees, marble columns, and lovely flower arrangements. At dinner, it's romantic; a harpist entertains in the musician's balcony from teatime on. The room originally was, in fact, a tea room where Madame Mishtowt, wife of a naval attaché of the Russian Embassy, presided over *thé dansants*. When Prohibition ended, it became a cocktail lounge. At lunch you might opt for a lavish buffet, including a selection from the dessert display table that centers on a chocolate sculpture of the *Mayflower*.

Rooms at the Mayflower begin at $184 single, $204 double;

it's $20 for an extra adult, free for children under 18. Weekend rates are much lower (close to 50% less), and June 15 to September 15 "summer value rates" are in effect. In fact, for some reason, rates quoted when you call the 800 number are often considerably lower than the "official" rates we've provided. It's definitely worth a call.

Henley Park, 926 Massachusetts Ave. NW (at 10 St.), Washington, DC 20001 (tel. 202/638-5200, or toll free 800/222-8474), is an intimate, 96-room, British-style hostelry that puts the emphasis on service and comfort. Heavy staff-to-guest ratio includes 24-hour comprehensive concierge service, room service is also round the clock, a free copy of the *Washington Post* is delivered to your door each weekday a.m., and a gourmet chocolate is left on your pillow when your bed is turned down at night.

Named for the quaint British town Henley-on-Thames (where the Henley Rowing Regatta takes place every July), the hotel replaced a 1918 seven-story Tudor apartment house that was stripped bare in 1982–1983. New electrical wiring, plumbing, and interior walls were installed, but the charming Tudor exterior and other period elements were preserved, including 119 gargoyles on the façade. The lobby, with its original paneling, rough-set terracotta tile floor, exquisite Tudor ceiling, archways, and leaded windows, is particularly evocative of the period. A floral centerpiece on a marble-topped stone pedestal is always gorgeous.

The room decor is residential in the English country-house mode. Furnishings are 18th-century styles—Hepplewhite, Chippendale, and Queen Anne—with lovely period beds (you might get a four-poster). There are four color schemes—burgundy/cream, powder blue/soft brown, apricot, and coral/off-white. The floral-print bedspreads and drapes are charming, and the walls are hung with framed botanical prints; crown moldings harmonize with the carpet color. Amenities include refrigerator mini-bars plus HBO and other movie options on your color TV, these including VCRs; a wide choice of movie cassettes is available at the front desk. Baths offer beautiful brass fixtures, heat lamps, phones, makeup mirrors, full-length mirrors, and luxury soaps and toiletries.

In keeping with the British theme, the hotel's posh French restaurant is fittingly named Coeur de Lion (for Richard the Lionhearted, an English king of French descent). A lovely dining room, its walls of weathered brick and mirror are adorned with English oil paintings and a Bacchanal-themed allegorical mural; sunlight is filtered through mauve multipaned windows; a glittering crystal chandelier is suspended from a skylight; and planters and potted palms add a touch of green. At night the flower-bedecked tables are enhanced by long tapered candles. The menu features French cuisine, highlighting seafood, and an excellent wine list is offered. Adjoining the Coeur de Lion is Marley's, a delightful cocktail lounge with art nouveau lighting fixtures over a marble-topped bar, floral tapestry-upholstered banquettes, antique maps on the walls, and, once again, mauve leaded-glass windows. It's the setting for nightly jazz entertainment.

And this being a "veddy British" hotel, there is, of course, a charming tea parlor—the octagonal Wilkes Room, with cushioned paisley love seats, comfortable mauve wing and arm chairs, a Persian rug on the highly polished oak floors, and a working fireplace. The wainscotted coffee-colored walls are hung with equestrian prints. Finger sandwiches, pastries, fresh-baked scones with clotted Devonshire cream, and a variety of teas and sherries are served here every afternoon. It's a marvelously cozy place, stocked with magazines and newspapers for your leisurely perusal.

Singles at Henley Park are $115 to $175; doubles, $135 to $195. Children under 14 stay free in their parents' room. Weekend rates are substantially reduced, and holiday packages are available. A great value here: in summer (mid-June through Labor Day) you can stay at the Henley Park for just $69 a night, single or double, that rate including free parking. Parking is usually $12 a night.

The **Sheraton Carlton,** 923 16th St. NW (at K St.), Washington, DC 20036 (tel. 202/638-2626, or toll free 800/325-3535), dates to 1926. It was designed to resemble an Italian Renaissance palazzo and "put an end to the question as to whether the ultimate in luxury and comfort are really found outside the homes of preeminent wealth." The hotel was the pet project of Harry Wardman, an English immigrant of humble parentage who went to seek his fortune in Australia in the 1880s. Harry boarded the wrong boat and wound up in America. He became a fabulously successful Washington builder/contractor, but he was still snubbed by Washington high society. So he built the "uncompromisingly exclusive" Carlton—a sumptuous setting to lure titled diplomats, senators, socialites, and screen stars to his door. And in this he was successful. The Carlton has always attracted luminaries, from the Sultan of Oman to Charlie Chaplin, not to mention the King of Yugoslavia, Katharine Hepburn (in slacks when that was risqué), Joan Crawford, the Duke of Windsor, U.S. presidents (all since Coolidge have at least attended functions here), and, in recent years, stars like Mick Jagger and Robert Redford. General John F. Pershing lived at the Carlton during Prohibition, often ostentatiously bringing his own flask to the dining room and mixing an old-fashioned at his table. And Harry Truman held his state dinners in the Carlton Room.

Wardman's social sense, however, may have been better than his business sense. He lost all in the 1929 crash, and the Carlton reverted to his creditors. The property has been a Sheraton since 1953.

In the 1970s a $6.3-million renovation restored the public areas to their former grandeur. The Carlton's lobby, extending the entire length of the hotel, is one of the most opulent in town. Six floor-to-ceiling Palladian windows are framed by rose velvet drapes, furnishings mirror the original pieces that Wardman collected from Italian palaces and villas, and the exquisite carved beamed ceiling is hung with crystal candelabra chandeliers.

In 1988, another $16 million renovation took place, and the entire hotel was closed. Accommodations were expanded in size by reducing the 250 rooms to 200; all of them were completely recarpeted, repapered, and refurnished. Residential in feel, they're decorated in soft earth tones (muted gray, rose, and sand) with traditional mahogany pieces and marble-topped tables. Every luxury has been provided: mini-bars and color TVs (with HBO and other cable stations) in handsome mirror-façaded armoires; three phones (desk, bath, and bedside) with two lines to allow for simultaneous calls; digital alarm clocks; writing desks; private safes; and baths offering cosmetic and full-length mirrors plus fine toiletries. Butler and concierge service is available—just press a button in your room to summon either. You'll also enjoy the nightly bed turndown.

The renovation also added a new exercise room, but if you'd prefer to work out in privacy, a rowing machine or stationary bicycle will be brought to your room. The swimming pool at the Sheraton Washington and the Washington Squash Club can also be used by Carlton guests.

Allegro is the Sheraton's new restaurant, offering Northern Italian cuisine and nightly piano music in a deluxe setting with Palladian windows and a stenciled ceiling. A handsome oak-paneled lounge adjoins. On the lower level, gentlemen might make an appointment to have their hair coiffed by Milton Pitts, "first barber" to Ronald Reagan; his shop is located here. Pitts also clipped the Nixon and Ford locks during those presidential terms.

Rates are $180 to $230 single, $200 to $250 double. Children under 17 stay free in their parents' room. Reduced weekend rates are offered.

LUXURY HOTELS

The distinction between the above-described grand hotels and those listed below is subtle. Rates for the latter are in the same high-priced category (or a tad lower), but their aims are different. Listed here are properties of the major hotel chains—Hiltons, Sheratons, and Marriotts—whose numerous facilities and services (like car-rental desks, airline desks, shops, several restaurants, and hair salons) are geared more to the business than the leisure traveler. Some are primarily convention hotels. The chains have been touched by grand hotel trends (you probably won't get Ivory soap in the bath), and they also compete in other areas—health-club facilities and swimming pools, locations adjoining shopping malls, plush lobbies where entertainment is offered during cocktail hour, and in-room movies (plus special cable stations), alarm clocks, AM/FM radios, and mini-bars. Room service is often available around the clock.

The latest fad—one that's caught on tremendously and is likely to stay—is the concierge floor. It's a special area of the hotel set aside for guests who pay a little bit more. They get larger rooms with additional amenities, special concierge and housekeeping service, a private lounge where complimentary continental breakfast and cocktail-hour hors d'oeuvres are served, and in most cases, daily newspaper delivery and nightly turndown. People traveling alone on business especially enjoy concierge levels, which provide a congenial setting in which to meet others.

Another category covered under this heading is the small luxury hotel offering grand-hotel services in a more intimate setting.

Set on 14 acres adjacent to Rock Creek Park (an additional 1,800 green acres), the **OMNI Shoreham,** 2500 Calvert St. NW (at Connecticut Avenue), Washington, DC 20008 (tel. 202/234-0700, or toll free 800/228-2121), is a resort hotel right in the heart of the city. And what a hotel it is! Built in 1930 as one of the nation's most deluxe hostelries, it has been the scene of inaugural balls for every president since FDR. In the early years, prominent socialites like Perle Mesta and Alice Roosevelt Longworth held private parties here, and such stars as Rudy Vallee, Lena Horne, Bob Hope, Maurice Chevalier, Frank Sinatra, and Judy Garland performed in the Blue Room—today a meeting facility. A special ramp was built to accommodate frequent visitor FDR and his wheelchair in 1932. Truman held private poker games in room D-106 while his limousine waited outside. And the most ostentatious guest ever was King Saud who, traveling with a full complement of armed guards and 32 limos, dispensed solid-gold watches as tips. In later years JFK courted Jackie over drinks in the Blue Room, and Richard Nixon introduced his entire cabinet-to-be over network television at a dinner here.

Some years back the OMNI Shoreham completed a $30-million restoration to its original luxe appearance and grand-hotel ambience. The vast Renaissance lobby regained its former stateliness. Chinese carpets were laid on the marble floors, the exquisite stenciled artwork on the vaulted ceilings was restored, clerestory windows were fitted with new glass, and opulent crystal chandeliers and wall sconces cleaned and repaired. Potted palms and plush sofas upholstered in moss-green velvet complete the picture.

Potted palms also figure prominently in the decor of the delightful Garden Court, as do ficus trees and tropical plantings, all of which greenery is reflected in beveled mirror walls. Like the adjoining lobby, the Garden Court has 35-foot vaulted ceilings. Rock Creek Park provides a fitting backdrop for this very popular cocktail lounge. The hotel's excellent restaurant, the Monique Café et

Brasserie, is reminiscent of the famed La Coupole in Paris—a convivial enclave of polished brass, dark woodwork, simulated marble columns, Oriental mirrors, and, once again, potted palms. Traditional brasserie fare is served—choucroûte and saucissons, steak au poivre, couscous, etc.—along with a selection of traditional American choices (this is, after all, a hotel with a substantial convention clientele). Most dinner entrees are in the $10 to $16 range. Lunch and Sunday brunch are less pricey repasts.

The guest rooms—there are 800 of them on eight floors—have also been completely renovated to match the elegance of the public areas. They're all very large (that's the way they built 'em in the '30s) and beautifully decorated in muted colors—soft burgundies, subtle grays, and chalky blues. All have baths with travertine marble floors and full-length mirrors, big roomy closets, and large beds (king-size, queen-size, or double). In-room movies are offered on your color TV, which also contains an AM/FM clock radio.

The OMNI Shoreham is a great place for the physical-fitness crowd. Rock Creek Park offers ten miles of jogging, hiking, and bicycle trails (including a 1.5-mile Perrier parcourse with 18 exercise stations) just outside your door. (See Chapter V for additional Rock Creek Park facilities.) There are three lighted Har-tru tennis courts behind the hotel and two outdoor pools—a large one for swimming laps and a kiddie pool.

The hotel has always been famous for nightlife, today centered in the art deco Marquee Cabaret, a beautiful facility with a classic molded cove ceiling, Louis XV-style dusty-rose velvet chairs and moss-green banquettes, and Lalique-like frosted lamps flickering on marble tables. For many years the Marquee was the showcase for political satirist Mark Russell. These days the entertainment runs to comedy revues.

A few additional facilities: a number of shops, a newsstand, a travel/sightseeing desk, and a parking garage for 600 cars.

Rates are $140 to $180 single, $160 to $200 double, $10 for an extra person, free for children under 18 in their parents' room.

Named for the chain's founder and chairman, the 774-room **J. W. Marriott,** 1331 Pennsylvania Ave. NW, Washington, DC 20004 (tel. 202/393-2000, or toll free 800/228-9290), opened in 1984. Designed as Marriott's flagship property, it is also an important element in the master plan to renovate historic Pennsylvania Avenue.

Like other Marriott properties, the J. W. combines futuristic architecture with warmly traditional decorator color schemes to create an exciting but very livable environment. The imposing rectangular lobby, with expanses of marble flooring and gigantic crystal chandeliers overhead, surrounds two levels of marquee-lit stairwells. The traditional touch includes ficus trees, many plants, and arrangements of fresh flowers. It's a comfortable space, with many intimate areas for private conversations.

Of course there are numerous services and facilities at this convention-seeking hostelry. A health club contains an indoor swimming pool, exercise room (with Universal equipment), hydrotherapy pool, and sundeck (kids can amuse themselves in the adjoining video arcade while you do your workout). There's indoor (valet) parking for 450 cars, and on the premises are car-rental/airline/travel desks and a gift shop. The hotel also connects with The Shops of National Place, a 65,000-square-foot, multilevel open-atrium mall with over 85 shops and restaurants.

Speaking of restaurants, there's no lack of dining facilities here, and since you're so close to the National Theatre, don't be surprised to see stars from the shows at adjoining tables. The most elegant facility is Celadon, a unique French/Chinese gourmet restaurant. The decor favors the East with Chinese Chippendale chairs (like the walls upholstered in celadon green) and Oriental vases, dinnerware, and screens. Lovely flower arrangements brighten things up as does the taped music, which ranges from Vivaldi to show tunes. Lunch and dinner menus offer Occidental/Oriental options ranging from filet mignon to Hunan sea bass in ginger sauce.

The very pretty National Cafe utilizes a pink-and-peach Victorian/art nouveau motif, along with azalea-filled planters, bamboo and rattan upholstered furnishings, many mirrors, and crystal chandeliers overhead. Lunch or dinner, the fare ranges from simple burgers and salads to heartier entrees. A full à la carte dinner for $20 to $25 is easily managed here, and a prix-fixe buffet is just $13.95. The National has outdoor seating at umbrella tables when weather permits.

Al fresco dining is also a feature of SRO (for Standing Room Only), a New-York-style deli. And for piano entertainment and jazz bands nightly there's the Garden Terrace. Ficus trees flourish under this club's skylight ceiling, and much of the seating provides a view of Pennsylvania Avenue and Pershing Park.

So much for facilities. There *are* rooms here, too. They're decorated in muted pink/peach/beige or soft green color schemes and are equipped with double-double or king-size beds, color TVs (with HBO and other cable channels), clocks, desks, and live plants. Each bath has a full-length mirror, heat lamp, and complete amenities basket.

The 14th and 15th floors comprise the concierge level with a private lounge for guests (it offers a gorgeous view of the city). Frills for these floors include complimentary continental breakfast and cocktail-hour hors d'oeuvres, additional toiletries, nightly turndown with a Godiva chocolate, and an electric shoe shiner. And rooms on these floors are larger.

WEEKENDS WERE MADE FOR WASHINGTON: Weekends, and sometimes off-season weekdays as well, D.C. hotel prices at properties ranging from budget to five star are slashed. Expect to pay just a little over half the usual price for accommodations. That means you can stay at a top luxury establishment and pay the tariff of a medium-priced hotel—or stay at a budget hotel for peanuts and spend your extra cash on good restaurants. Write or call the **D.C. Committee to Promote Washington,** P.O. Box 27489, Washington, DC 20038-7489 (tel. toll free 800/422-8644), and request a copy of *Washington Weekends*. It lists weekend rates at 90 hotels in all price ranges.

Taj International Hotels, 1315 16th St. NW, Washington, DC 20036 (tel. 202/462-7104, or toll free 800/ILUVTAJ or 800/DC-VISIT), are the owners of 22 ultra-luxury properties in India, including the famed Taj Mahal Hotel in Bombay and the Lake Palace in Udaipur (the latter was the sumptuous backdrop for the James Bond movie *Octopussy*). About a decade ago the firm expanded operations to the U.S., and they now own and/or manage five Washington, D.C., hotels, all of which are described in this chapter—the Hampshire Hotel, the Canterbury, the Marbury, the Quality Hotel, and the Ramada Inn. Their weekend rates, also available weekdays November through February and during July and August, begin at just $55 per room. And they also offer marvelous weekend packages with extras like champagne and chocolates upon arrival, among other perks. Write or call (it's toll free) for details.

Caveat: When you make reservations, always inquire about weekend, off-season, and other special rates and packages. Be sure to verify that your reservation has been made at weekend rates before hanging up, and check on it again when you register. At many hotels, you can't suddenly turn up at the desk Monday morning and expect to get weekend rates; you have to be so registered in advance.

Rates at the J. W. are $185 single, $205 double, $10 additional on the concierge level. An extra person pays $20. Children under 18 stay free in their parents' room. Weekend rates are $99, single or double, on Friday or Saturday night.

Don't let the Virginia address scare you. The **Marriott Crystal Gateway Hotel,** 1700 Jefferson Davis Hwy., Arlington, VA 22202 (tel. 703/920-3230, or toll free 800/228-9290), has a Metro stop right on the premises that puts you within minutes of Mall museums, the Capitol, Georgetown, Alexandria, and all other D.C.-area attractions. It's also five minutes from National Airport (complimentary shuttle service is provided), and connects via a short passageway to the Underground, a subterranean mall of 200 quaint "shoppes" and modern emporia, restaurants, and services (a post office, Ticketron office, bank, and unisex hair salon). Tennis and racquetball courts are also located below stairs.

But Underground offerings and the Metro aren't the only pluses at this beautifully designed property. From its six-story atrium skylight lobby adorned with Oriental objets d'art (there's piano music here at cocktail hour) to its lovely and spacious pastel-hued rooms (pale pinks and muted greens are the predominant decor colors), the Gateway is a winner. All 700 guest rooms are equipped with every amenity (color TV, in-room movies, AM/FM radio, and alarm clock), and special features include nightly turndown (upon request) and almost round-the-clock room service.

A well-equipped health club offers an exercise room and saunas adjoining an indoor/outdoor pool and hydrotherapy pool. And in addition to over a dozen restaurants in the Underground, there are three hotel dining facilities. Most plush is Veronique's, for romantic dinners under the stars (there's a skylight) to the strains of harp music. The fare is classic French cuisine. Not quite as posh but still rather elegant is the Terrace, wherein cushioned wicker furnishings and more lush greenery. It's open for all meals, serving American fare. It's lovely to lunch here—or enjoy a lavish Sunday brunch buffet—at a table overlooking the pool. Light buffet fare (lunch and dinner) is featured at the Atrium Cafe, right off the lobby. And at night there's dancing at Crystal's, a very simpático bar/lounge/disco with comfortable furnishings, potted palms, gleaming brass, and sparkling glass.

The 16th floor of the Gateway's Capitol Tower is the concierge level. The private lounge for guests is especially nice for business people traveling alone. Most 16th-floor residents amble in every morning for complimentary breakfast (fresh-squeezed juice, fresh-baked pastries, a selection of teas or coffee, and fresh fruit). It's a pleasure to have someone to watch the "Today" show with, but if you're not in the mood you can curl up on a comfy sofa in the corner and read the *Washington Post*. Honor bar cocktails and quite bountiful hors d'oeuvres are also served here from 5 to 7 p.m., and cordials from 9 to 11 p.m. A concierge is on duty from 7 a.m. to 11 p.m. to assist you in every way. Additional in-room amenities for concierge level guests include nightly turndown, bathroom scales, electric shoe polishers, and magazines.

Rates are $170 single, $190 double, $185 single and $210 double on the concierge level. An extra person pays $25. Children under 18 stay free in their parents' room. A weekend family plan for Friday, Saturday, and Sunday nights, subject to availability, allows up to five people to occupy a room for just $95 a night.

The **Capital Hilton,** on 16th Street NW (between K and L

Streets), Washington, DC 20036 (tel. 202/393-1000, or toll free 800/HILTONS), should be called the new-and-improved Capital Hilton. A five-year, $55-million renovation was completed in 1987, earning the hotel a four-star rating from Mobil as well as the AAA Four Diamond Award. The 549 guest rooms were totally redecorated in stunning contemporary style. Color schemes utilize understated monochromatic tones (camel, mauve, charcoal gray) with bone and ebony lacquer furnishings. Each room contains two comfortable chairs, a sofa, a cocktail table, a desk, refrigerator/mini-bar, two extra-long double beds or a California king-size, three phones —desk, bath, and bedside—and a color TV with digital alarm clock, remote control, AM/FM radio, cable stations, and a choice of six current movies. In your spiffy marble bath you'll find Neutrogena and Vidal Sassoon products, a mini black-and-white TV, a hair dryer, and a three-sided mirror that tells all (for better or worse). A terry robe is available on request. Further room enhancements include a live plant and very attractive art. One-of-a-kind suites are furnished in antiques.

Floors 10 to 14 contain the hotel's 70 Towers (concierge-level) accommodations. Here, guests enjoy in-room VCRs (movie tapes are available), nightly bed turndown with gourmet chocolates, private registration and checkout, the services of a personal concierge, and complimentary continental breakfast and afternoon tea (there's also an honor bar) in a plush private lounge.

Public areas were also upgraded in the renovation, and a fifth-floor fitness center features a wide range of Nautilus equipment and a tanning room, plus steam and sauna, with separate areas for men and women.

Hilton restaurants include a very handsome Trader Vic's with oak-paneled walls and ceilings, tufted red-leather booths, and subdued lighting from gleaming brass ship lanterns. Nautical art and ship models tastefully replace the usual Polynesian clutter, though one room does have a thatched ceiling. The food here is excellent. Don't pass up the cosmo tidbits pupu platter of fried prawns, spareribs, crab Rangoon, and sliced pork—a memorable appetizer. Luncheon entrees are in the $10 to $15 range; dinner entrees, mostly $15 to $22. Another terrific Hilton dining room is Twigs, offering "nouvelle American" gourmet fare such as grilled lamb chops with mint jelly, sauteed pork loin with apples and prune sauce (served with potato pancakes), and grilled fresh West Virginia river trout with tomatillo chutney. There's a marvelous crème brûlée topped with caramelized pecans for dessert. Lunch and dinner entrees in the main room are mostly in the $7 to $11 range and include sandwiches, omelets, and other light fare, along with more substantial selections. Grill Room dinner entrees are priced from $15 to $20. But Twigs' most glorious meal is its lavish Sunday brunch (about $20 per person), including free-flowing coffee and champagne and unlimited selections from an abundant buffet. In addition to gorgeous salads, fresh cold salmon, an omelet bar, breads, fresh fruits, a carvery station, and an abundance of fresh-baked cakes and pastries, hot dishes might include New York sirloin with eggs, baked sole stuffed with crabmeat, and stir-fried chicken. There's live entertainment, and it takes a while to plow through all that food, so relax and make a day of it.

Complientary tapas are served in The Bar, a plushly furnished lobby lounge, weekdays from 5 to 7 p.m., and a pianist entertains there all evening.

Further Hilton pluses. The hotel is two blocks from the White House. A complimentary newspaper is delivered to your door each weekday morning. Buses to all airports leave from the premises. There are shops (hairdressers, a gift shop, a florist, newsstand, shoe-shine stand, and jeweler) and airline desks (American, United, Northwest Orient, and Eastern/Continental) in the lobby. And all big-hotel services (secretarial, audio-visual, computer rental, over-night mail, concierge, tour and ticket desk, etc.) are available.

Despite all the renovation, the 45-year-old Hilton has a proud history in this town. In the '40s, big-name entertainers like Edith Piaf and Xavier Cugat played the Embassy Room. Many movies—from *Born Yesterday* to *All the President's Men*—have been filmed in the suites and lobby. All American presidents since FDR have at-tended functions here, and Truman lived at the Hilton while the White House was being remodeled (the baby grand piano he played is still here in the Constitution Suite). During President Kennedy's inaugural festivities, Frank Sinatra and the Rat Pack took over a doz-en connecting rooms on the tenth floor so they could visit each other without being confronted by autograph seekers in the halls. And, of course, the annual Gridiron Club Dinner and political roast is held in the Ballroom each year.

Rates at the Capital Hilton range (depending on size, view, and location) from $150 to $200 single, $175 to $225 double. Chil-dren stay free with their parents. An extra person pays $25. Tower rooms are $220 single, $245 double. A weekend package is $79 per room per night on Friday and Saturday nights, subject to availabil-ity.

Its two semicircular concrete-and-glass wings make the **Wash-ington Hilton and Towers,** 1919 Connecticut Ave. NW (at T Street), Washington, DC 20009 (tel. 202/483-3000, or toll free 800/HILTONS), appear like an oversize bird in flight from the air. This is a kind of super-hotel, with 1,150 rooms and every possible amenity. In 1988, $27 million was spent totally renovating rooms and corridors, so accommodations here are looking great. The property hosts numerous conventions and functions in its meeting rooms and International Ballroom—scene of inaugural balls, debu-tante cotillions, state banquets, and society shindigs. Spring through fall, you might sauna with a senator at the Racquet Club (many lawmakers are members), which also offers a large heated outdoor pool, children's wading pool, three Har-tru tennis courts, tennis and swimming classes, a Jacuzzi, sun room, weight rooms, massage, shuffleboard, bike rental, pro/swim shop, and video games to keep the kids occupied while you work out. There's plenty of room for jogging, too, at this resort-like property.

Rooms are cheerful and attractively furnished in a variety of color schemes (such as pale mauve, cinnamon, and muted jade). All have color TVs with a choice of Spectravision movies, mini-bar/refrigerators, and full-length mirrors in the bath. And because the hotel sits atop a small hill, you're sure to enjoy a panoramic view.

The tenth floor is called the Towers. It is a VIP hotel-within-a-hotel featuring a beautifully furnished lounge (with a gorgeous view) for Towers guests only. Here a concierge is on duty from 7 a.m. to 11 p.m. to attend to all your needs (dinner or theater reservations, checking up on lost luggage, special services, etc.). You can relax on plush velvet-upholstered with the morning paper (several are provided), watch your favorite shows on a large-screen projection TV, and enjoy a complimentary continental breakfast. Afternoon tea is served from 3 to 5 p.m., and you can wind down after a busy day with cocktails from the honor bar. Special in-room amenities for Towers guests include nightly turndown service with a cordial and a mint, fancy soaps and other such products in the bath, bathroom scales, alarm clocks, and AM/FM radios. Many Towers rooms offer panoramic Washington views.

The Hilton's dining facilities include Colonial's, a coffeeshop featuring Early American decor; the Gazebo, for al fresco lunches and light fare under a yellow-and-white-striped tent top by the pool; and Ashby's, a plush turn-of-the-century-motif dining room with gold walls, gaslight-style chandeliers, and tufted banquettes. The latter features gourmet continental fare with dinner entrees like fresh lump crabmeat baked with cream and seasonings, veal sauteed with wild mushrooms, and Dover sole. Entrees are mostly in the $18 to $23 range. At lunch you can enjoy Ashby's ambience and cuisine for considerably less. Ashby's Club, the adjoining lounge, features live entertainment and dancing in an Edwardian billiard-room setting. There's also nightly piano bar music at the Pointe Lounge overlooking the lobby.

Limousine service is available to all airports, and there's indoor parking for 600 cars. The bustling lobby offers the full complement of shops and services.

Rates are $140 to $160 single, $160 to $180 double, $20 for each additional person; children stay free in their parents' room. Towers rooms cost $180 single, $200 double. Inquire about money-saving weekend packages.

The **Sheraton Washington,** 2660 Woodley Rd. NW (at Connecticut Avenue), Washington, DC 20008 (tel. 202/328-2000, or toll free 800/325-3535), is a hotel with a split personality. The original section, Wardman Towers, was considered "Wardman's Folly" when it opened in 1928, because it was so far out in the suburbs. However, the city has grown up around it, and the Towers have been home to three presidents (Hoover, Eisenhower, and Johnson), Supreme Court justices, diplomats, military leaders, and Washington socialties. Today a Metro (Woodley Park-Zoo) is on the premises, and chic Adams Morgan restaurants are in easy walking distance. The Towers' public areas still retain the gracious feel of an earlier era, from the lovely peach-colored lobby with its antique furnishings and crystal chandeliers to the substantially proportioned rooms traditionally furnished and painted in soft pastel colors. All accommodations have sitting areas, desks, and large closets; some also have kitchens (sink only) and bay windows. In this section is the pink-hued suite occupied by Perle Mesta during her heyday as Washington's top hostess.

In dramatic contrast is the modern Main Building, which, when completed in 1980, brought total room count to 1,505 and made the Sheraton one of the largest luxury convention hotels on the East Coast. It has an immense, bustling, multilevel lobby with gleaming stainless-steel columns, stylized escalators, and a skylit atrium under which ficus trees flourish. The sunken Lobby Lounge contains plush green-velvet furnishings grouped around a gurgling fountain. In addition to shops, you'll find a beauty salon and barbershop, a pastry/ice cream shop, a copy center, and a post office. Other facilities include the Courtyard Cafe, an ultracontemporary eatery with seating in "pods" and marquee-like lighting; umbrella tables and many, many plants create an al fresco feel. Classic American fare—from Maryland crabcakes to Texas chili—is featured; you can even have peach cobbler with homemade ice cream for dessert.

The hotel's premier restaurant is Americus, a lavish dining room decorated in mauve and burgundy tones with Tiffany-style lighting fixtures. New American cuisine highlights fresh fish and seafood dishes. There's a Raw Bar area, the scene of nightly piano entertainment. And every Sunday Americus is the setting for the most elaborate Sunday brunch in town, with over 100 items including unlimited complimentary champagne and fresh-squeezed orange juice. On our last visit the buffet tables were laden with raw oysters, shrimp, smoked meats, waffles and egg dishes, smoked salmon, beef Wellington, strawberry fritters, dozens of salads, softshell crab, a wide array of desserts, fresh-baked breads, and much more. The price is just $20.95 per person, $10.95 for children under 12. Here, too, a pianist entertains. After an Americus dinner, adjourn to Early Light (featuring a modernistic glass-and-chrome setting) for dancing to live music. L'Expresso—a snack shop—and the Twentieth Century—an attractive cafeteria—round out the Sheraton's food and beverage facilities.

Rooms in the newer section feature modern decor with built-in furnishings and navy, sand, or rust color schemes. Closets have full-length folding mirror doors that leave you no secrets from yourself. Throughout the hotel, old and new rooms feature clocks and TVs with HBO and Spectravision pay movies. Personally, we greatly favor the Wardman Tower rooms over the newer wing accommodations.

Two outdoor 30- by 60-foot heated pools are additional amenities, and a Perrier Parcourse Circuit in adjacent Rock Creek Park is a treat for joggers. There's also a workout room with exercise equipment.

Singles pay $145 to $165 a night; doubles, $170 to $190. An extra person is $30; children under 18 stay free in their parents' room. Inquire about low weekend rates and frill-filled weekend packages.

One of 144 prestigious Hilton International hotels in 46 countries (everywhere from Abu Dhabi to Zurich), the **Vista International,** 1400 M St. NW, Washington, DC 20005 (tel. 202/429-1700, or toll free 800/VISTA-DC), is one of the most architecturally innovative properties in town. "With guest rooms surrounding the atrium," says architect Wayne Williams, "we've designed the hotel as a cityscape centered around a living stage where all activity takes place." The atrium in question soars 14 stories and is capped by a 7,000-square-foot glass dome that floods the lobby interior with natural light. Architecturally varied towers housing the rooms overlook the atrium, their balconies hung with lush foliage to enhance the suggestion of private residences facing a city square. Victorian-style street lamps, a clock tower, numerous plants and flower arrangements, and a cobblestone-like floor further the illusion. Lunch, dinner, afternoon tea, and cocktails are served "al fresco" in the Lobby Court, an elevated octagonal area just off the atrium. And a string quartet plays nightly on the balcony from 5 to 9 p.m.

Americana is the predominant theme at the Vista. Thus the hotel's gourmet restaurant, the Harvest, highlights mid-Atlantic recipes, especially local ones, such as authentic Maryland crab cakes and U.S. Senate bean soup. The menu changes seasonally, so the freshest fare can be presented at all times. The Harvest's decor is fittingly American. Its five intimate dining areas resemble rooms in an old Georgetown mansion. They feature original American art (including changing exhibits from New York's Museum of Folk Art); Chippendale, Georgian, and Duncan Phyfe furnishings; area rugs of American stencil design; and raw white oak paneling. It's all very charming, and the food is excellent. On our last visit (in spring) the menu offered a full dinner for $30 (one of many choices plus à la carte listings) that began with pickled baby vegetables, then proceeded to asparagus and smoked salmon with a potato pancake, Maryland spring onion soup, crisply roasted Long Island duckling with red and black currants, three accompanying vegetables (perhaps snow peas and water chestnuts, buttered carrots with chives, and stir-fried asparagus with sesame seeds), a salad of raddicchio and Bibb lettuce in citrus dressing, white chocolate ice cream with raspberry sauce, and a pot of Colombian coffee. Similar table d'-hôte meals are offered at lunch in the $15 to $21 range.

American fare, accompanied by domestic and imported wines, is also the specialty at the Verandah Restaurant, styled after a gracious Victorian veranda of an old Southern plantation. Premium wines are offered by the glass.

Sip rare sherries, ports, cognacs, and fine champagnes (available by the glass) in the Tower Lounge. Overlooking the central atrium from the first floor of the Givenchy Tower (it contains six suites decorated by the famed French designer), this elegant lounge under an ivory canvas awning centers on an oval marble bar.

Rounding out the facilities is the clubby Federal Bar for nightly piano entertainment. The Federal is a handsome facility with a square oak verde marble-topped bar, polished brass, and turn-of-the-century etched mirrors. Oak-paneled and green-felt walls are adorned with political caricatures from *Puck* and *Judge Magazine* (1840–1910). The all-day menu, served from 11:30 a.m. to 11 p.m., features pot pies, salads, sandwiches, burgers, chili, etc.

Additional on-premises facilities include shops (the lobby also connects to the Prudential Building with its own arcade of shops and services), a fine pastry shop, a Business Center with secretarial services and communications equipment, a fitness center (exercise machines, sauna, and massage room), underground parking for 165 cars, and all big-hotel services (24-hour room service, babysitters, concierge, etc.). All guests enjoy nightly turndown service, complimentary shoe shine (leave your shoes outside the door at night), and early morning tea or coffee on the day of departure.

The 413 rooms and suites are decorated in earth tones, coral, forest green, and sky gray. Rattan and oak furnishings are upholstered in shades of apricot, mauve, and green. Every room has a marble-topped desk, two dressers, several large mirrors, a refrigerator and fully stocked mini-bar, color TV with a choice of eight movies, and bedside TV and light controls. The optimum in privacy, service, and comfort is offered in rooms on the Executive Floor (12). Here guests have their own manager, concierge, and housekeeping staff (on duty from 6 a.m. to midnight). In an elegant private lounge, complimentary continental breakfast, afternoon tea and pastries, and evening cocktails and hors d'oeuvres are served. Backgammon and chess tables are provided, and the TV has special news and congressional stations. Services here include chocolates with nightly turndown, fresh flowers and fruit in your room, terry-cloth robes, Givenchy products for men and women in the bath, and complimentary daily paper with wake-up tea or coffee.

Rates are $140 single, $155 double, $175 single and $195 double on the Executive Floor. Children of any age stay free in a room with their parents. An extra adult pays $20. The weekend rate is $79 single, $89 double.

The exquisite **Canterbury Hotel,** 1733 N St. NW, Washington, DC 20036 (tel. 202/393-3000, or toll free 800/424-2950), is a small European-style property. Its prestigious address was once the home of Theodore Roosevelt, and Franklin D. Roosevelt resided at 1733 N St. between 1913 and 1917 while serving as secretary of the navy during World War I. The building housing the hotel is not the original town house the Roosevelts occupied. However, it does attempt to recapture the elegance of that era. One travel magazine called this hotel "the intimate alternative to high-rise indifference and chrome confines."

Upon entering the Canterbury you step into a graciously appointed lobby where classical music is always softly playing (ditto in the elevators and restaurants—a welcome change from hotel Muzak). In this tranquil setting you can sit comfortably before the fireplace and plan your day's itinerary. Evenings, the adjoining Union Jack Pub, complete with dart board and a menu featuring items like fish and chips, is the perfect place to relax after a busy day on the town. A complimentary drink is served to guests here at cocktail hour, and English beers on tap are served in pint mugs.

Each of the 99 guest rooms is actually a junior suite with a sofa/sitting area, dressing room, mini-bar, and kitchenette or full kitchen. All have rich mahogany 18th-century English reproduction furnishings and king- or queen-size beds, some of them four-posters with canopies and Early American–style quilt bedspreads. A recent refurbishment added attractive pink-and-gray-striped wallpaper and burgundy velvet-upholstered chairs. Floors were also recarpeted in burgundy. A live plant and an objet d'art such as a brass duck on the dresser are residential touches. Gilt-framed art reproductions and mirrors grace the walls. Guests are pampered with containers of scrumptious chocolates, fresh fruit, and champagne upon check-in, these goodies replenished at nightly turndown. A complimentary copy of the *Washington Post* is delivered to the door each morning, and the *Wall Street Journal* is available free in the lobby and restaurant. Baths are supplied with cosmetic mirrors, hair dryers, phones, thick towels, and baskets filled with fine toiletries. Amenities include remote-control color TVs with HBO movies, AM/FM clock radios, and refrigerators stocked with soft drinks and Lindt candy bars.

The Canterbury has a first-rate restaurant on the premises, the richly oak-paneled Chaucer's. Whether you stay here or not, it's worth coming by for a meal. The food, service, and ambience are all superb. An especially good buy is the $12.95 prix-fixe dinner offered from 5:30 to 7 p.m. It includes a choice of soup of the day, pâté or salad, an entree (like breast of chicken diablo, roast prime rib with Yorkshire pudding, or fresh fish of the day), a selection from the pastry cart, and tea or coffee. À la carte, the same meal (depending on your choices) might cost more than twice that amount. Further details on Chaucer's are in Chapter IV. Speaking of meals, your rates at the Canterbury include a complimentary continental breakfast served in the guest lounge each morning—juices, a selection of breads and croissants with butter and marmalade, and tea, coffee, or hot chocolate. Also gratis: use of the Office Health Center, a fully equipped health club a few blocks away.

Single rooms range from $135 to $175; doubles, from $155 to $195 (room size and location account for the spread). An extra person pays $20 per night; children under 12 stay free in their parents' room. Low weekend rates are available.

We love the **Hampshire Hotel,** 1310 New Hampshire **Ave.** NW (at N Street), Washington, DC 20036 (tel. 202/296-7600, or toll free 800/368-5691), an elegant residential property with 82 charming rooms and a first-rate restaurant. Accommodations include 54 spacious suites equipped with one king-size or two double beds, sofas, full kitchens, and mini-bars stocked with drinks, cheeses, nuts, crackers, and chocolates. The 36 front-facing rooms have balconies, and most accommodations provide lovely rooftop/treetop views. All offer attractive mahogany furnishings in 18th-century styles, leather-topped desks, hair dryers and full-length mirrors in the bath, full dressing rooms, color TVs with HBO movies, and AM/FM alarm-clock radios. Cream/teal-blue paisley bedspreads, drapes, and sofa upholstery are complemented by chocolate-brown carpeting, pale-blue or grasspaper wall coverings, and Oriental artworks in gilt bamboo frames. On arrival you'll find a small box of Godiva chocolates (always most welcome), a coffee maker with complimentary packets of tea and coffee, and a basket of designer toiletries. A live plant in the room is a nice residential touch. You'll be treated to a cocktail in the restaurant the first night of your stay and a nightly gourmet chocolate wafer when your bed is turned down. Each morning the *Washington Post* is delivered to your door. And all concierge services are provided by the front desk.

Like its sister hotel, the Canterbury (both are Taj International properties), the Hampshire soothes the soul with classical music in public areas. And it, too, has a much-acclaimed on-premises restaurant, Lafitte, serving the best Créole fare in town. (See Chapter IV for a full description.) It's a big plus for guests, as is the free use of the nearby Office Health Center—a full spa offering Universal equipment, weights, steambath, whirlpool, and more. Ditto the hotel's location—within walking distance of Georgetown and two blocks from the Dupont Circle Metro station, providing easy access to the rest of town. Though the Hampshire's on a quiet street, nightspots and restaurants abound in the area.

Rates are $109 to $149 single, $124 to $164 double, free for children under 12 in their parents' room, $15 per extra person. The weekend rate here (offered Thursday through Sunday, subject to availability) is just $34 per person per night.

If you'd like to stay right in the heart of Georgetown, an excellent choice is the **Marbury Hotel,** 3000 M St. NW, Washington, DC 20007 (tel. 202/726-5000, or toll free 800/368-5922). Its location is at the very hub of Washington's chicest nightlife/ restaurant/shopping scene, but its accommodations are in a seven-story building set back from the street. Hence none of the noise of nighttime revelers reaches your room. Though the Marbury was built in 1982, its quaint charm evokes an earlier era. Its arcaded two-story brick façade, with white flower boxes at every window, occupies an entire city block. The hotel is entered via a pleasantly traditional lobby, furnished with French provincial pieces. It serves as a depot for the Old Town Trolley Line (details in Chapter II) and also houses the Marbury Shoppes—a handful of boutiques featuring women's designer fashions, fine crafts, antiques, and imported leatherware and brassware. On a lighter note, there's a gourmet popcorn shop. Complimentary coffee (with cookies or danish) is set out in the lobby each morning, and there's a guest-services desk to help you plan a sightseeing itinerary, make travel arrangements or restaurant reservations, etc.

The Marbury's 164 rooms are residential in feel, decorated in shades of ecru/gray and forest green, with Oriental accents, such as some very nice Chinese screens and prints adorning the walls. They're equipped with double or king-size beds, comfortable armchairs upholstered in pretty cotton chintz fabrics, desks, full-length mirrors, and color TVs with HBO and bedside remote control. A big plus: A fully stocked mini-bar in each room and a refrigerator and cabinet filled with munchies like crackers, pâté, cheeses, macadamia nuts, and gourmet chocolates. There are also larger junior suites with sofa beds and coffee tables, and nine duplex carriage suites that can accommodate up to four people.

The hotel has a very pretty oak-floored dining room with Palladian mirrors built into burgundy lacquer walls. Its crisply white-linened tables are always set with arrangements of fresh flowers and aglow with candles. Especially nice here is a Sunday buffet brunch ($16.95 for adults, half price for children under 14) enhanced by piano entertainment and unlimited champagne. On our last visit a sumptuous spread included smoked salmon, pâtés, cheeses, sushi, deviled eggs, waffle and omelet stations, eggs, bacon, sausage, potatoes, fresh orange juice, about ten salads, an array of fruits and desserts, breads and rolls, and chafing dishes brimming with beef bourguignon, filet of sole in garlic cream sauce, and roast duck with fresh raspberry sauce. Of course you can also enjoy all other meals here, plus room service. Fare ranges from burgers and salads to gourmet regional American cuisine entrees. Prices are always reasonable, but table d'hôte lunches and dinners represent especially good values. This being Georgetown, the Marbury also features occasional nighttime entertainment in its spacious Lions Gate Taverne—a singer or pianist. This "olde English" pub is the scene of nightly happy hour revelry weekdays from 5 to 8 p.m. when lavish internationally themed buffets (everything from sushi to souvlaki) are complimentary with your drink. And it's the only hotel in the heart of Georgetown with a swimming pool, this one on the fifth floor with a two-level sundeck overlooking a small park and the canal.

Rates are $110 to $150 single, $130 to $170 double; suites begin at $159 single, $170 double; an extra person pays $10, and children under 12 stay free in their parents' room. The weekend rate is $79 to $119, single or double, and it's offered Friday through Sunday *and* selected weekdays throughout the year! Inquire when you reserve.

MODERATELY PRICED HOTELS

Establishments listed in this category charge an average of $70 to $130 for a double room. Some are at the higher end, some at the lower, and some include fully equipped kitchens.

On a quiet residential street near Dupont Circle—the kind of street with a neat little garden and a shady tree in front of each house —**Carlyle Suites,** 1731 New Hampshire Ave. NW (between R and S Streets), Washington, DC 20009 (tel. 202/234-3200), occupies a converted landmark art deco building. Its exterior art deco elements are complemented by similarly styled silver moldings, deco light fixtures, and cove ceilings.

Only the 170 suites (on eight floors) eschew the art deco motif. Cheerfully decorated in pastel shades (mauve, grape, and ice gray), they have oak beds, white stucco walls, brand-new gray drapes and charcoal carpeting, and cheerful print bedspreads with matching pillow cushions on the sofa. All accommodations are equipped with huge closets, color TVs with Spectravision movie choices, and AM/FM radios. The reason we call them suites is because they also offer small but complete kitchens (stoves, refrigerators, and sinks; cookware, cutlery, and china available on request), and seating areas with sofas and dining tables. Many are extremely spacious. There's a shopping service for guests and a huge Safeway store is just two blocks away.

The Carlyle puts a lot of emphasis on service. The front desk offers 24-hour concierge-like assistance and employees are given "everybody's-a-concierge" training. There's a coin-op washer/ dryer on the premises, and parking is free.

The hotel belongs to the Office Health Center on 19th and M Streets, which guests can use gratis. This fully equipped health club offers Nautilus and Universal exercise equipment, Lifecycles, exercise bikes, treadmills, whirlpool, sauna, steam, and much more.

Jimmy K's, the Carlyle's restaurant, is one of its great assets. It is decorated in shades of gray, black, and grape, with accents of neon-purple tubing. Jimmy further enhances the ambience by playing music from the '30s and '40s. Quality trendy/continental fare is served; entrees run the gamut from tortellini with pesto to Maryland crabcakes, though deli sandwiches, salads, and haute gourmet items like veal Oscar are also available.

Carlyle Suites has very competitive rates. Singles are $59 to $89, doubles are $69 to $99, and an extra person pays $10 a night. Children under 18 stay free in their parents' room. One-bedroom suites begin at $125 a night. Reduced weekend rates begin at just $19.95 per person, based on double occupancy.

The **Georgetown Dutch Inn,** 1075 Thomas Jefferson St. NW (just below M Street), Washington, DC 20007 (tel. 202/337-0900), is superbly located in the very heart of Georgetown, just a half block from the C&O Canal (many rooms offer canal views), on a charming brick-paved street lined with maple trees.

Since taking over the inn's management in 1987, SBS International has been continually upgrading the premises. They combed District antique shops for beautiful furnishings to enhance room decor, adorned the walls with framed historic prints of Washington, and added live plants for a nice homey touch. The inn has built a reputation as a comfortable home away from home, drawing a celebrity clientele. Nell Carter stayed here during *Ain't Misbehavin'*'s revival at the National, as did many *Les Misérables* cast members. Ditto George Shearing, Dizzy Gillespie, and the Smothers Brothers when playing local engagements.

All of the inn's "rooms" are actually very spacious one- and two-bedroom suites, nine of them ultraluxurious duplex penthouses. Even a "standard" accommodation here includes, in addition to your bedroom, a living room with a convertible sofa, dining area, and desk, plus a complete kitchen (stove, refrigerator, sink, dishwasher, and mini-bar) that is stocked with dishes and cutlery; cookware and microwave ovens are available on request. There are color TVs and phones in every living room and bedroom (even phones in the baths). The suites are pleasantly residential in feel, individually decorated with antiques and period reproductions; you might find a Victorian or Sheraton sideboard in your living room, perhaps a bombé (rounded) dresser in the bedchamber.

Amenities here include on-premises free parking (a real boon in Georgetown), nightly bed turndown with little chocolate "wooden" shoes on your pillow (remember, this is the *Dutch* Inn), and a complimentary continental breakfast served in the lobby each morning. There's a shopping service as well as plenty of nearby food stores. And, on request, the newspaper of your choice is delivered to your door each morning.

The inn boasts an excellent restaurant that is patronized by locals as well as hotel guests. Leo and Linda's—run by Leo and Linda Speros, who owned the acclaimed Normandy Farms in Potomac, Maryland, for over a quarter of a century—is a delightful little place. Featuring a California-style decor with cherry blossom–pink walls, it has candlelit, pink-clothed tables and Casablanca fan/chandeliers overhead with matching frosted-glass wall sconces. Dinner here might begin with a creamy shrimp bisque followed by Maryland crabcakes, blackened redfish, or herbed veal chop on a bed of linguine. Homemade desserts include a great crème brûlée. Dinner entrees are in the $14 to $18 range, lunch options much less expensive at $5 to $9.

Rates at the Dutch Inn: $95 to $125 for one person in a two-room suite, $110 to $140 for two people, with $15 for each additional occupant. Two-bedroom duplex penthouses are $190 to $250 for up to four people, again charging $15 for each additional occupant (they can sleep up to eight). Weekend rates are reduced to $70 to $85 single or double in a two-room suite, $140 to $170 in a penthouse suite (both suites subject to availability).

The **Quality Hotel Downtown,** 1315 16th St. NW (at Scott Circle), Washington, DC 20036 (tel. 202/232-8000, or toll free 800/368-5689), recently underwent a total renovation from a homey, family-style hotel to a rather luxurious hostelry. The good news is that despite its plush new look, the Quality's still charging very moderate rates. And, in fact, it's still a good bet for families.

For openers, each of the 135 rooms here is actually a large suite, with a complete kitchen containing sink, stove, and full-sized refrigerator; pots, pans, cutlery, and china are provided on request. And the new decorator schemes are lovely. Done up in pastel shades like muted teal blue and pale rose/mauve, the rooms feature Chippendale-style mahogany, pecan, and cherrywood furnishings. Walls covered in raw silk are hung with gilt-framed Chinese prints, bedspreads are pretty cotton chintz florals, and ceilings are embellished with decorative moldings. Each room has a dining area, sofa, 19-inch color TV (with HBO movies) concealed in an armoire, radio, large walk-in closet, and dressing room. And baths, fitted out with shiny new brass fixtures, offer hair dryers, phones, and fancy toiletries. Some rooms have handsome desks, and a few feature Murphy beds—an innovation much appreciated by people who conduct business in their hotel rooms. Deluxe suites at the Quality are in Oriental or traditional French motifs, the latter with bombé dressers and other pieces evocative of provincial châteaux. Even the public areas of the hotel have been attractively upgraded. Hallways on every floor have new raw-silk beige wall coverings and flower-bordered forest-green carpeting, and the lobby is furnished with silk- and velvet-upholstered Louis XVI-style chairs.

The Quality's restaurant, Bleeker's, is pleasant and pretty. Flower-bedecked tables are clothed in cheery coral linen, Oriental and floral prints adorn cream-colored walls, and numerous plants flourish in the sunlight from a wall of windows. At night Bleeker's is cozy, lit by candles in cut-glass holders. The menu is American, highlighting regional specialties from a Tex-Mex burrito to shrimp Créole to Maryland crabcakes. Prices are very reasonable.

An underground parking garage, a coin-op basement laundry, free use of the swimming pool at a nearby hotel, and a location that puts you in easy walking distance of Dupont Circle, K Street restaurants, Georgetown nightlife, the White House, and the Metro, are additional pluses.

Rates are $78 to $98 single, $88 to $118 double, $10 for an additional person, and children under 16 stay free in their parents' room. Much lower weekend rates are available.

On a tranquil tree-lined street close to Mall attractions, Dupont Circle, and the White House, the **Ramada Inn Central,** 1430 Rhode Island Ave. NW, Washington, DC 20005 (tel. 202/462-7777, or toll free 800/368-5690), is popular with government employees, business people, and families. The latter, especially, appreciate the rooftop pool and sundeck and the full kitchens (in all but 20 of the 186 rooms at this all-suite hotel), with dishes, pots and pans, and cutlery available on request. The rooms are warm and homey in appearance. Hints of rust and blue complement brown wall-to-wall carpeting, and beige walls are hung with cheerful, framed prints of green plants. The large walk-in closets have louver doors, and bedspreads feature nice floral prints. All rooms have one or two double beds. Amenities include a color TV with HBO movies, an AM/FM radio, direct-dial phone, and, in many cases, an extra phone in the bath. And there are dining room areas with tables under Tiffany-style lamps.

Eighteen one-bedroom suites additionally offer a full living room with a sofa bed plus a bedroom with a king-size bed. There are phones and TVs in both rooms.

Other facilities at the Ramada include a coin-op laundry in the basement and indoor parking ($5.60 a day). Irons and ironing boards are available free upon request.

Off the lobby is the Kitchen Cabinet, an unpretentious and rather pretty restaurant with lots of leafy green plants, rust carpeting, tables set with rust cloths and adorned with fresh flowers, and lighting from brass candelabras and wall sconces. Open for all meals, it features moderately priced American fare and a special menu for children.

Guests gather for cocktails in the Civil Servant Lounge, a cozy low-ceilinged pub with shelves of books and sofas grouped around a fireplace. Framed historic prints and photos line the walls, and low lighting emanates from candles and wall sconces.

Rates at the Ramada are $69 to $99 single, $79 to $109 double. One-bedroom suites are $110 to $130, single or double. The weekend package is just $55 per room, single or double; it's also available weekdays during off-season (November through February and July and August).

Fronted by an elegant gray awning, the **Hotel Anthony,** 1823 L St. NW, Washington, DC 20036 (tel. 202/223-4320, or toll free 800/424-2970), offers 99 rooms in the heart of the downtown business/shopping/restaurant area. It's just five blocks from the White House and one block from the Metro, putting guests within easy reach of all other major sightseeing attractions.

The Anthony's large and comfortable rooms are done up in three basic period styles—contemporary (mauve/peach/gray color schemes), art deco, and Colonial Williamsburg. All have kitchens with sinks and refrigerators, and in some cases, microwave ovens or stoves. Coffee makers, cutlery, china, and cookware are provided. Other in-room features are color TVs with HBO movie channels, AM/FM radios, extensive closet space, and baths equipped with Water Pik shower massages and stocked with Vidal Sassoon toiletries. Typical art deco colors—glossy pinks and grays—are featured throughout the public areas, as is a shell motif.

There are dozens of restaurants in the surrounding streets, but in the hotel itself is the cozy Samantha's, a plush Yuppie watering hole with art nouveau wall sconces, a working fireplace, and lots of stained glass. Reasonably priced deli sandwiches, burgers, quiches, salads, and omelets are featured, along with daily specials like steamed mussels in garlic and white wine sauce or smoked chicken with pasta pesto.

Anthony extras include a copy of the *Washington Post* each morning, complimentary continental breakfast, and gratis use of the nearby Office Health Center, a fully equipped fitness spa. A unisex hairstyling salon (it also offers manicures, facials, and pedicures) is on the premises.

Rates are $87 to $107 single, $97 to $117 double, $10 for an extra person, free for children under 16 in their parents' room. Weekend rates are available.

About six blocks from the White House, the **Hotel Lombardy,** 2019 I St. NW, Washington, DC 20006 (tel. 202/828-2600, or toll free 800/424-5486), offers 126 tastefully appointed rooms and suites. Because they were previously apartments, all but 20 of the Lombardy's rooms have full kitchens, large walk-in closets, and dining nooks. Like the public areas here, the rooms are very charmingly decorated. Entered via pedimented louver doors, they have attractive cherrywood furnishings (including nice-sized desks), cotton chintz floral bedspreads and drapes and cream-colored walls hung with ornate gilt-framed mirrors and well-chosen artworks. You'll find fine toiletries and a full-length mirror in your brass-fixtured bath. Other amenities are a color TV (VCRs and rental tapes are available), and AM/FM radio. A free newspaper is delivered to your room each morning, shoes are shined gratis overnight, and a washing machine and dryer are located in the basement.

The Cafe Lombardy, a sunny, glass-enclosed dining room/bar/lounge, serves all meals. And very good meals they are—mostly quiches, salads, and deli sandwiches at lunch; daily gourmet specials like roast lamb with fresh mint and shrimp wrapped in bacon and lime at dinner. Yummy desserts here, too. From its richly wood-paneled lobby with carved Tudor ceiling to its appealing restaurant and rooms, the Lombardy offers a lot of luxury for the price.

Rates are $85 to $130 single, $10 for each additional person, free for children under 16 in their parents' room. One-bedroom suites with full parlor are $110 to $140 single, $10 for each additional person. Weekend rates are much lower.

We were charmed by the **State Plaza Hotel,** 2117 E St. NW, Washington, DC 20037 (tel. 202/861-8200 or toll free 800/424-2859), from the moment we entered its antique-furnished lobby—a setting enhanced by beautiful floral arrangements and the soft strains of classical music. This all-suite property, converted from an eight-story apartment building several years back, is popular with performers from the nearby Kennedy Center—so there are usually ballet troupes and cast members in residence along with a sparkling of stars, like David Copperfield or Patti LaBelle.

All of the 215 accommodations are spacious and offer fully equipped kitchens, stocked mini-bars, and large closets. Spectravision movie options are offered on your color TV. Especially lovely are the newly redecorated suites (this is an ongoing process, with about a third of the accommodations revamped at this writing). These are done up in pale pink, periwinkle, and mauve color schemes, furnished with Federal-style mahogany beds and Queen Anne chests. Drapes and bedspreads utilize pretty cotton chintz fabrics, and framed botanical prints embellish the walls. Most have nice dressing rooms with skirted chintz vanities. And kitchens have been fitted with shuttered windows and louver doors. Don't worry, though, if you don't snag a renovated suite; the original decor is pleasant and homey, featuring 18th-century-motif bedspreads and drapes. Plaza suites, the most expensive, offer full living rooms and dining nooks.

Big pluses here include a coin-op laundry on the lower level; a grocery-shopping service (as well as a Safeway and gourmet shops nearby); and a great location—an easy walk to the Foggy Bottom Metro stop, Kennedy Center, the Lincoln/Vietnam Veteran's Memorials, Georgetown, the White House, and many other sightseeing attractions.

The Garden is an excellent on-premises restaurant with an adjoining awning-shaded flagstone patio for al fresco dining. Like most of the hotel's public areas, the Garden walls are pristinely painted in white-trimmed cream and hung with framed historic prints. Light and cheerful during the day, at night this oak-floored restaurant becomes rather elegant with candlelit white-linen tables. The menu features classic and new American cuisine, highlighting market-fresh fare and regional specialties. Fresh grilled seafood, salads, green pizzas topped with smoked duck, chicken breast, and homemade pastas are among the specialties. Lunch entrees are $8 to $14, dinner entrees $9 to $18. Even breakfast here is a treat, offering fresh-squeezed juices and entrees like an omelet filled with Tillamook (Oregon's finest) cheddar with applewood-smoked bacon, served with freshly made fries, and homemade applesauce. Premium wines are offered by the glass. Weekdays from 4 to 7 p.m., visit the Garden for complimentary hors d'oeuvres and two-for-one-priced drinks.

Rates range from $90 to $120 single, $110 to $150 double ($110 to $140 single, $130 to $170 double for the larger Plaza suites). An extra person pays $20 a night. Children under 16 stay free. Weekend rate is just $69 per room, based on double occupancy, including free indoor parking subject to available space. At other times parking costs $10 a night.

The **Comfort Inn**, 500 H St. NW, Washington, DC 20001 (tel. 202/289-5959 or toll free 800/228-5150), is a budget offshoot of the Quality Inn chain. The theory behind the Inns is that a low-cost hotel needn't be a no-frills hotel. Here the 197 rooms are attractively decorated and have a table with two chairs, full bath, color TV (with cable stations), a digital alarm clock, direct-dial phone, and an AM/FM radio. Oriental nuances—such as the Chinese motif in the hallway carpeting—reflect the property's Chinatown location (near numerous good Chinese restaurants, of course). But you needn't leave to eat. The Cafe Express offers reasonably priced home-cooked fare. A Metro stop is located a little over a block away, and many sightseeing attractions—including the Smithsonian museums—are within easy walking distance. On-premises facilities include a coin-op laundry, parking (just $5 a day), and a sunny exercise room with Universal equipment and a sauna.

Regular rates are $70 to $80 single, $80 to $90 double, $10 for an extra person, and children under 18 free. But the weekend rate—offered Friday through Sunday nights—plummets to just $50 per person for up to four adults, including complimentary parking. Reserve as far in advance as possible.

The 214-room, nine-story **Holiday Inn Central**, 1501 Rhode Island Ave. NW, Washington, DC 20005 (tel. 202/483-2000, or toll free 800/HOLIDAY), built in the 1960s, is the typical "no sur- prises" property this chain prides itself on offering. You'll find a sundries/souvenir shop and video game room off the lobby, a medium-sized pool and sundeck (nice views of the city here) on the roof, and a pleasant plant-filled on-premises restaurant called Mortimer's, decorated in ski-lodgey fashion with slanted oak panel- ing and a brown/rust color scheme. Mortimer's features competi- tively priced American fare such as barbecued chicken and ribs, steaks, and seafood. In fact, the food is so good, we often stop by to eat here even when we're not staying at the hotel. In addition to meals, a nice buffet of complimentary hors d'oeuvres—ribs, sau- sage, nachos, crudités, cheeses—is set out in the adjoining lounge from 5 to 7 p.m. weekdays for the happy hour crowd.

Rooms have grasspaper-covered walls hung with Early Ameri- can folk art, color-coordinated cotton chintz bedspreads and drapes, and beds with bamboo-framed backboards. All offer color TVs with Showtime movies, and some have clock radios. Beds are king-size or double-doubles. You'll find soda/ice machines and Metro maps in the hallways on every floor. Other pluses here are coin-op washers and dryers, free indoor self-parking, and room serv- ice.

Rates are $89 to $107 single, $99 to $117 double, $10 for an extra person, free for children 18 and under in their parents' room. The range depends on room size; the high end is for king-size leisure rooms, some with balconies. Friday, Saturday, and Sunday nights the Holiday Inn charges just $66, single or double.

A second **Holiday Inn** is centrally located at Thomas Circle, 1155 14th St. NW, at Massachusetts Ave., Washington, DC 20005 (tel. 202/737-1200, or toll free 800/HOLIDAY), and it, too, is a good choice in the moderate price category. Its 208 spacious and newly renovated rooms, on 14 stories, are attractively decorated in earth tones and equipped with satellite TVs (with ESPN, CNN, and movie stations) and AM/FM clock radios. We noted with apprecia- tion two soap dishes in the bath, one high up for showering. There's a fairly large rooftop swimming pool and sundeck, offering nice views of the city. Guests can order room-service meals from the ho- tel's restaurant/lounge, Filibuster's, a pleasant precinct whose menu cover provides a few fascinating facts on Senate filibustering (for instance, in 1935 Sen. Huey Long obstructed a bill by rambling on about his favorite southern recipes, including instructions for making "potlikker"). And inside, the bill of fare is as American as the U.S. Senate, featuring steak, ribs, burgers, seafood, and apple pie à la mode for dessert. Prices are moderate, and there's a full lunch buffet. The Holiday Inn has a washer/dryer for guest use and a spe- cial parking lot for oversize vehicles. Valet parking here costs $3 a night. The hotel is just five blocks from the White House.

Rates are $83 single, $95 double, $10 per night for an additional person; children under 12, free in their parents' room. And at this writing all Holiday Inns are featuring a "Great Rates" promotion; reserve more than seven days (but less than four months) in advance and you save 20% or more. Inquire if this, or other advance-booking promotions, are available when you reserve.

The **Normandy Inn,** 2118 Wyoming Ave. NW, Washington, DC 20008 (tel. 202/483-1350, or toll free 800/424-3729), is a gracious, small hotel that blends in perfectly with neighboring embassies. The 74 rooms—though a bit on the small side—have a European charm. They're rather pretty with teal blue or mocha carpeting, floral-motif brown-and-pink bedspreads with matching tie-back curtains, and beige walls hung with attractive prints. All rooms have two twins or one queen-size bed, color TVs, and direct-dial phones. About half offer refrigerators and small writing desks. And there are full-length mirrors on every bathroom door.

Continental breakfast (juices, tea or coffee, croissants, English muffins, toast, and cold cereals) is available in your room or in the Tea Room off the lobby for $3.50. The Tea Room is comfortably furnished—a pleasant place to read the paper (available gratis at the desk), write a letter, or chat. Coffee and tea are available throughout the day from an antique oak sideboard, and cookies are put out at 3 p.m. In nice weather you can take these snacks outside to umbrella tables on a garden patio. Tuesday nights complimentary wine and cheese are served to guests.

Numerous restaurants, subways, and buses are located nearby; underground parking is $4 a day.

Rates are $75 single, $85 double, $160 for one-bedroom suites, free for children under 12 in their parents' room. A weekend package, including a welcome bottle of wine, free parking, and continental breakfast, is just $27.50 per person per night, based on double occupancy; you must stay both Friday and Saturday nights.

The **Days Inn Downtown,** 1201 K St. NW, Washington, DC 20005 (tel. 202/842-1020, or toll free 800/562-3350), is conveniently located near the Convention Center, just three blocks from the Metro Center subway station. It's easy to rent a car here too: four auto-rental agencies vie for your business at 12th and K, one on each corner.

Here's great news! Days Inns throughout the country are offering a Super Saver rate of just $39 a night, any night, single or double —if you reserve 30 days in advance via the toll free number above. That just can't be beat.

A big plus at this particular Days Inn is its restaurant, Buckley's Grill, on the second floor. Very competitively priced, it offers excellent new American fare plus Créole specialties, fresh seafood, and baby back ribs. Great desserts here too. The setting's simpático: cream-colored walls with knotty-pine wainscotting are hung with nautical paintings, and tropical fish tanks further the marine motif.

The adjoining Buckley's Lounge is the scene of happy hour buffets served from 5 to 8 p.m. every Tuesday and Thursday. A small rooftop pool with sundeck and video game room makes this a good choice for families with young children.

The 220 rooms are cheerfully decorated in blue or rust color schemes and equipped with AM/FM radios and satellite TVs (with a movie channel and an in-house station for airing tourism information). And the public areas are clean and pleasant, like the rooms, looking sharp after a recent total renovation that included much fresh paint and the installation of new wallpaper, carpets, bedspreads, drapes, and fixtures.

Regular rates here are $70 to $80 single, $80 to $90 double, $6 for an extra person, free for children under 18 in their parents' room. On Friday, Saturday, and Sunday nights singles or doubles pay $60. Valet parking is $5 a night.

If you don't mind a 10- to 15-minute Metro or bus ride into the heart of town, you can do very nicely in the north Washington/ upper Connecticut Avenue area, in itself a very pleasant neighborhood. About three miles from the White House is the attractive **Connecticut Avenue Days Inn,** 4400 Connecticut Ave. NW (between Yuma and Albemarle Streets), Washington, DC 20008 (tel. 202/244-5600, or toll free 800/325-2525). Its 155 rooms were totally renovated just a few years back, and they're all kept in tip-top condition. Furnished in teak Danish modern pieces, with brass-framed art prints on grasspaper-covered walls, they offer color TVs with cable stations, AM/FM radios, and all the other expected amenities. Families can book a parlor suite which includes an extra room (and an extra TV) for the kids. Complimentary continental breakfast is served in the rather plush lobby each morning—coffee, juice, and doughnuts. And you can park free on the premises. However, if you have no car, the Van Ness Metro stop is only a block away. A coin-op laundry and many restaurants are close by.

Rates are $75 to $76 single, $80 to $81 double, $85 for a suite accommodating four people, $7 for an additional person; children under 16, free in their parents' room. The weekend rate is $65 to $75, single or double. If you're 55 or older, inquire about senior citizen rates.

A bit farther north is the **Walter Reed Hospitality House,** 6711 Georgia Ave. NW (at Aspen Street), Washington, DC 20012 (tel. 202/722-1600, or toll free 800/222-8388); however, a bus you can catch right across the street will whisk you into the center of the District in just 15 minutes. The closest Metro station (Takoma Park) is about eight blocks away. This is a delightful hotel, with reassuringly spiffy public areas—a plant-filled, oak-paneled lobby and well-lit hallways. Mr. Chan's Szechuan Restaurant, on the premises, offers a low-priced American/Chinese menu in a striking modern setting; walls are covered in Ultrasuede, carpeting is grass green, and seating is in chrome-framed sienna chairs. Complimentary morning coffee and the *Washington Post* are delivered to your door on weekday mornings. Rooms are furnished in handsome oak pieces, and the drapes and bedspreads are pleasingly pretty. Some rooms have sofas or "cuddle couches," and/or balconies. All the expected amenities are present, including color TVs with HBO movies and AM/FM radios. An outdoor swimming pool and sundeck make this a good bet for families, and proximity to Rock Creek Park is a lure for joggers. Parking is free.

Rates are $49 to $59 single, $59 to $69 double, $5 for an additional person; under-16s stay free in their parents' room. Weekend rates and off-season reduced-price promotional packages are available.

Just two blocks from the Kennedy Center is a **Howard Johnson's Motor Lodge**, 2601 Virginia Ave. NW, Washington, DC 20037 (tel. 202/965-2700, or toll free 800/654-2000), with a nicely landscaped façade where rose bushes bloom in season. It has 192 modern rooms, attractively furnished and decorated with grasspaper wall coverings and taupe or rust carpeting. Each is equipped with a color TV, AM/FM radio, desk, and small refrigerator. Some rooms have sofas, and over half have balconies. There's a Bob's Big Boy restaurant on the premises, offering typical American fare, including very attractively priced all-you-can-eat buffets at lunch and dinner. A coin-op laundry, free parking, a large L-shaped pool (big enough for laps) with adjoining sundeck and Ping-Pong room, a large gift/sundry shop, and a video game room are additional amenities.

Rates vary seasonally. They run the gamut from $58 to $81 single, $66 to $89 double, $5 for an additional person year round, free for children under 12 in their parents' room. Weekend rates are offered subject to availability.

The **Channel Inn**, 650 Water St. SW, Washington, DC 20024 (tel. 202/554-2400, or toll free 800/368-5668), is the only hotel in town that gives you a chance to live on the waterfront. It was built in 1973 as part of the waterfront renovation, which brought a marina, urban housing, and a row of seafood restaurants to the area. It's a simple modern building with 100 rooms, 60 of them offering a nice view of the Washington Channel and the marina; the others overlook the Washington Monument.

All rooms are identically furnished with painted off-white beds and dressers, paisley bedspreads in autumnal colors, brown carpeting, beige drapes, and grasspaper-covered walls hung with attractive floral silkscreens. They're not decorator-fancy, but they are large, homey, and comfortable—equipped with a table and two armchairs, direct-dial phone, color TV, and two sinks in the bath. Some have high cathedral ceilings, and all have balconies. Rooms are due for redecoration during the course of this edition, so they may look different by the time you arrive.

There are several advantages to a stay at the Channel Inn. The waterfront is an ideal place for jogging, there's a pool and sundeck out front, a golf course and indoor/outdoor tennis courts are within easy walking distance, and on-premises indoor parking is free.

The inn also has a fine seafood restaurant, Pier 7, in which most seats offer marina views. Under a peaked, beamed ceiling—from which are suspended immense wrought-iron and rope chandeliers with ship lantern fixtures—it offers seating in comfortable red-leather chairs and banquettes at red-clothed tables. Pier 7 is popular with local business people at lunch and with the after-theater crowd from the nearby Arena Stage. Across the way is a coffeeshop serving cafeteria-style breakfasts. And adjoining Pier 7 is the immense Engine Room lounge, featuring nautical decor (brass ship gauges, historic photographs of ships, and an actual ship's steering engine), beautiful water views, dark mahogany paneling, and tufted black-leather chairs and banquettes. At happy hour there's a buffet of free hors d'oeuvres and a low-priced raw bar; nightly except Sunday stop by for live jazz and dancing till 1 a.m.

Singles are $80 to $105, doubles are $90 to $115; children under 12 stay free in their parents' room. Weekend and group rates are offered subject to availability.

BUDGET HOTELS

The majority of these listings are in the $50-for-two range, some a bit more, some even less. Especially good rates are available if you're willing to forgo a private bath. Check out bed-and-breakfast accommodations (next category) for excellent low-priced lodgings, too.

Do keep in mind the two **Days Inns** listed above under the "Moderately Priced Hotels" category. Days Inns around the country feature, at this writing, a Super-Saver rate of just $39 a night, single or double, if you reserve 30 days in advance via the toll free number 800/562-3350. That can't be beat if you know you'll be traveling to Washington that far in advance.

The best news in years on the budget hotel scene is the spiffy **Washington International Youth Hostel**, 1009 11th St. NW, at K St., Washington, DC 20001 (tel. 202/737-2333), that opened in late 1987. In a fully renovated eight-story brick building, the hostel offers freshly painted dorm rooms (with 4 to 14 beds) and clean baths down the hall. Though the accommodations are basic, the facility itself provides a lot of features you won't find at a hotel. These include a huge self-service kitchen (stoves, refrigerators, and sinks) where you can cook your own meals (a supermarket is two blocks away), a dining room where you can eat what you've prepared, a comfortable lounge with armchairs and sofas, coin-op laundry machines, storage lockers, and indoor parking for bicycles. A restaurant is in the works for the future.

Upon registering, you'll be given a free guidebook written especially for hostelers detailing local sights and activities. WIYH offers special activities for guests—volleyball games, cookouts, lectures, movies, travel seminars, international nights, and more. And near the entrance, knowledgeable volunteers staff an information desk to help guests with sightseeing and other travel questions; maps and brochures can be obtained here as well.

The hostel's location is excellent—just three blocks from Metro Center Station, six blocks from the Mall. And the clientele is monitored, so you won't encounter the seedy types oft seen at other budget properties. It's a perfectly safe place to send your college-age kids, or, for that matter, your mother.

Rates are just $10 a night for AYH members; everyone else pays an additional temporary membership fee (one time only) of three dollars. An annual membership in AYH is $20. Anyone can stay, but since dorms are for men or women only, couples are, of course, separated. Maximum stay is three nights, but that limit may be extended with permission, subject to available space. You must supply your own linens, towels, and soap (blankets and pillows are provided); sleeping bags are not allowed. You can rent the requisite sleep sheet here for $1 a night or buy one. Call as far in advance as possible to reserve (there are only 250 beds and they go fast), and guarantee your reservation with a 50% deposit. *Note:* There is a midnight curfew here.

The **Braxton Hotel,** 1440 Rhode Island Avenue NW, Washington, DC 20005 (tel. 202/232-7800), represents the kind of development we'd love to see more of in this town. Baltimore developers Sam and Nancy Cheng have renovated a down-at-the-heels hotel and turned it into a clean and pleasant budget-priced property. The Braxton has 62 rooms, housed in a four-story yellow-brick building on a tree-lined residential street in the Dupont Circle area. They've planted a neat little garden out front, put up a snazzy burgundy awning, and furnished the lobby with comfortable white satin–upholstered sofas.

The rooms also have been revamped. Though short on frills, they have newly painted white stucco walls with Chinese red trim, Levolor-style blinds on the windows, and new mauve carpeting with matching bedspreads. All are air-conditioned and equipped with color TVs (with HBO cable) and direct-dial phones. The 20 singles contain one twin bed, the others have one or two doubles. And a nice feature is a gratis complimentary breakfast of coffee, danish, doughnuts, juice, etc., served in the lobby each morning. The Braxton has made sure to employ a pleasant and friendly staff.

The location is very central, within walking distance of Mall attractions, a Metro station, the White House, and numerous restaurants. Rates are $48 single, $54 for one or two in a room with one double bed, $58 for a room with two double beds. Children under 16 stay free with parents. Lower rates are offered weekends and selected weekdays, subject to availability.

New York Avenue, which a little farther east becomes Hwy. 50, is the classic American strip lined with fast-food eateries, car lots, gas stations, and motels. It's not an esthetic setting, but it does offer low-priced lodgings and easy access to downtown attractions. And though the neighborhood doesn't look great, it's perfectly safe; the crime rate out here is one of the lowest in the District.

One very noteworthy property here is the AAA-approved **Master Hosts Inn,** 1917 Bladensburg Rd. NE (corner of New York Avenue), Washington, DC 20002 (tel. 202/832-8600, or toll free 800/251-1962), with 150 rooms in three two-story motel buildings. All of the upstairs rooms have high sloped ceilings (there's a pointed roof), and about half the accommodations overlook the pool. A largish pool it is—big enough for swimming healthful laps —and it's surrounded by an expanse of lawn. Here, in a tranquil enclosed courtyard you can relax on chaise longues in the sunshine or under the shade of crabapple trees, maples, and pines. Or feed Willie, the resident squirrel and inn mascot. There are umbrella tables out here too, as there are in the flower-bordered courtyard of the on-premises restaurant, the New China Inn. The latter is an attractive little eatery with Chinese art and red-tasseled lanterns adorning the walls, comfortable leather booths, and a cozy bar. Here you can get low-priced Chinese or American meals. And both food and drinks can be enjoyed al fresco, weather permitting.

Speaking of restaurants, a short drive from the property is Berk Motley's (4321 Bladensburg Rd.), a very popular steakhouse in a rustic log cabin. Berk, a big-band leader of some renown, raises his own Angus cattle, so the beef is all fresh.

Meanwhile, back at the inn, the rooms are neat, clean, and well equipped. Some feature cocoa-rust color schemes, while others are done in mauve and light teal blue. All have one or two double beds, air conditioning, a dressing room, modern tub/shower bath, direct-dial phone, and color TV with two VCR movies offered nightly (groups can request a particular movie). All two-bedded rooms have an extra sink in the dressing room.

Some other pluses: a lobby vending machine area, sightseeing buses that depart from the lobby twice daily, all-night security patrol of the grounds, free parking, soda and ice machines in the halls, babysitting services, and a bus right across the street to the Mall. Best of all, the property adjoins the U.S. National Arboretum— 444 green acres of lawn, trees, flower gardens, shrubs (including 70,000 azaleas), wildflowers, and boxwoods. The Bonsai Collection here—53 miniature trees, some of which are over three centuries old—is on our not-to-be-missed list; it's exquisite. A stroll along Arboretum pathways is the perfect way to relax after a day of sightseeing or business.

Rates at Master Hosts Inn range from $44 to $53 for one person in a room with one double bed, $51 to $58 for two people in the same, $53 to $60 for one or two people in a room with two double beds. An extra person pays $5, a rollaway or crib is another $5, and children under 12 stay free in their parents' room. The above-quoted range depends on the season: rates are highest in summer, lowest in winter, middling in spring and fall. Show this book at the desk and you'll get a token for a free cocktail at the restaurant. Parking is free.

Also situated out this way is an **Econo Lodge,** 1600 New York Ave. NE (at Montana Avenue), Washington, DC 20002 (tel. 202/ 832-3200, or toll free 800/446-6900), with 136 modern rooms decorated in earth tones and equipped with all the expected amenities—color TV, direct-dial phone, air conditioning, and full bath. There's a nice-sized year-round indoor pool with adjacent sundeck, ice and soda machines are located on each floor, parking is free, and the on-premises coffeeshop serves inexpensive meals.

Rates are $43 for one person, $48 for two, $4 per additional person or rollaway, free for kids under 12 in their parents' room.

Two miles northwest of the White House, the **Connecticut-Woodley Guest House,** 2647 Woodley Rd. NW (between Connecticut Avenue and 27th Street), Washington, DC 20008 (tel. 202/ 667-0218), is located in a three-story, turn-of-the-century house amid luxurious private residences and foreign embassies. The above-mentioned Sheraton Washington is just across the street, chic Connecticut Avenue and Adams Morgan eateries are within easy walking distance, and the Woodley Park–Zoo Metro station is less than a block away.

There are 15 rooms at this hostelry, some with shared bath, others with private facilities. They're not fancy, but they are neat and clean, air-conditioned, and equipped with direct-dial phones. They don't have TVs, but there's a color set in the lounge, along with laundry facilities, comfortable furniture, and soft-drink machines. Parking is free, and daily maid service is provided. These low-priced accommodations are very popular, so reserve early. Rooms with shared baths cost $31 to $34 single, $37 to $39 double. With private bath you pay $40 to $43 single, $45 to $50 double. An extra person pays about $3 a night. Family rates are available.

BED-AND-BREAKFAST

B&B accommodations are a reasonably priced alternative to hotel living that can add an extra dimension to your travel experience. Going B&B allows you to meet locals and enjoy personalized attention from hosts who are generally well informed about area attractions and anxious to share their knowledge. Often B&B rooms are extremely charming as well.

In addition to specific B&B accommodations, we've listed several services under whose umbrellas are numerous homes renting out rooms on this basis. Reserve as early as possible to get the greatest selection of locations and lowest rates, and do specify your needs and preferences: discuss children, pets, preferred locations (do you require convenient public transportation), parking, availability of TV and/or phone, air conditioning, what the preferred breakfast consists of, how payment can be made, etc.

The **Kalorama Guest House,** 1854 Mintwood Pl. (between 19th Street and Columbia Road NW), Washington, DC 20009 (tel. 202/667-6369), is a San Francisco–style B&B guesthouse that has been so successful it has expanded in a short time from a six-bedroom Victorian town house (at 1854 Mintwood) to include four houses on Mintwood Place and two on Cathedral Avenue NW. A great effort is made throughout to create charming rooms and public areas. Owner Roberta Pieczenik regularly haunts antique stores, flea markets, and auctions to find beautiful furnishings and knickknacks that will enhance the decor.

Many rooms have brass beds, perhaps with lovely floral-print bedspreads and matching ruffled curtains. Other possibilities: Oriental throw rugs, a cane-backed rocking chair, an old Singer sewing machine table, an oak mirror shelf with a display of antique bottles, and turn-of-the-century artwork or very old framed family photos. Whatever you find, it will be a delight. Live plants and/or fresh flowers grace the rooms, and you're likely to get a dish of candy too. All rooms are heated, air-conditioned, and equipped with clock radios.

Over at 1854 is the cheerful breakfast room with shell-pink and exposed brick walls, plant-filled windows, and garden furnishings (park benches at marble tables). Breakfast consists of bagels, croissants, toast or English muffins, plus orange juice and tea or coffee. Adjoining amenities include a seldom-used TV, a phone (local calls are free), a coin phone for long-distance calls, a vending machine for soft drinks, a washing machine and dryer, and a refrigerator. Upstairs in the parlor, containing a working fireplace, there's a decanter of sherry on the buffet for complimentary afternoon apéritifs; magazines, games, and current newspapers are provided. There's a garden behind the house with umbrella tables, another simpático spot for breakfast, picnics, cocktails, or conversation. A barbecue grill is provided for guest use.

At 1859 Mintwood is another cozy parlor with two working fireplaces, Victorian oak furnishings, potted palms, and a ficus tree. A lower level here contains additional laundry-ironing facilities and a refrigerator.

Though the rooms have no phones, incoming calls are answered around the clock, so people can leave messages for you. Maid service is provided every three days.

The Mintwood Place location is very good—about halfway between Dupont Circle and Woodley Park–Zoo Metro stations, near dozens of restaurants, nightspots, and Connecticut Avenue shops. And the Cathedral Avenue houses, even closer to the Woodley Park–Zoo Metro, provide similarly wonderful amenities and facilities. Via the above phone number, you can make reservations at all Kalorama locations.

Rates are $30 to $60 single, $40 to $65 double, for a room with shared bath; $50 to $85 single, $55 to $90 double, for a room with private bath. A two-room suite with private bath costs $70 to $100 for up to six occupants. Weekend rate reductions are subject to availability.

Many B&B accommodations are decorator homey with rooms in *Architectural Digest* good taste. The **Adams Inn,** 1744 Lanier Pl. NW (between Calvert Street and Ontario Road), Washington, DC 20009 (tel. 202/745-3600), is down-to-earth, for-real homey, like the comfortable house of your Aunt Sonya. It offers 17 rooms and a carriage house. In a cozy parlor with a gas fireplace, floral-design carpet on oak floors, flowered wallpaper, and lace-curtained windows, maps, books, games, and magazines are provided for guests. White lace curtains also frame the windows of the dining room, wherein are a large mahogany table and a wood-burning fireplace. Continental breakfast—coffee or tea, doughnuts, muffins, a fruit cup, and orange juice—is served here each morning, though in good weather you can take this fare out to the front porch or the small flower-bordered garden patio with tables and chairs. Tea and coffee with doughnuts are available throughout the day.

Like the public areas, the rooms have a kitschy charm composed of furnishings selected from flea markets and auctions, matching ruffled curtains and bedspreads, and freshly painted or cheerfully papered walls. No TVs or phones here, but you do get a clock radio. One room has a decorative fireplace, and all have oak floors, some with carpets. Accommodations that share baths (these are kept nice and clean) have in-room sinks. Most attractive is the private carriage-house apartment across the garden, a light and sunny place with lots of windows, yellow/gold walls, printed patchwork drapes and bedspreads, and oak floors with scatter rugs. It has a fully equipped kitchen—pots, pans, cutlery, dishes, a toaster, etc.

All rooms are heated and air-conditioned. A coin-op washer/dryer for guest use is available in the basement, and there's limited on-premises parking ($5 a night). The location is quite convenient —four blocks from the Woodley Park–Zoo Metro station and close to Adams Morgan eateries. Carriage-house occupants can shop at a

Safeway supermarket just 100 feet away. Gene and Nancy Thompson are your genial—and very helpful—host and hostess, ably assisted by Dylyce Clark. They charge $35 single, $40 double, for rooms with shared bath; $50 single, $55 double with private bath; $10 per additional person; $70 for up to four people in the carriage house. And they promise to hold these rates for people presenting this book throughout 1989. All rates include the above-described continental breakfast. *Note:* No smoking is permitted on the premises. No pets. Children welcome.

The **Bed & Breakfast League, Ltd.,** 3639 Van Ness St. NW, Washington, DC 20008 (tel. 202/363-7767), is a referral service representing over 80 B&B accommodations in the District and adjoining Maryland and Virginia suburbs. Through the league you might find a room in a late-Victorian Capitol Hill mansion, a Georgetown home with a lovely garden, a turn-of-the-century Dupont Circle town house filled with period furnishings, a Woodley Park town house, or a Tudor-style duplex just off Wisconsin Avenue. Those are just a few of many possibilities. Rates for most accommodations range from $30 to $60 single, $40 to $75 double, $10 to $15 for an extra person. There's a two-night minimum-stay requirement and a booking fee of $10 (per reservation, not per night).

A similar service is Ellie Chastain's **Sweet Dreams & Toast,** P.O. Box 4835-0035, Washington, DC 20008 (tel. 202/483-9191). Ellie has about 100 listings—all of which she has personally scrutinized—in the D.C. area, ranging from a Victorian "wedding cake house" in the Cleveland Park area to a modern condo with resident small dog near Georgetown, to a restored home on Constitution Avenue with a "contemporary haphazard" decor, where guests are welcome to play the organ, beat the African drum, etc. Something for everyone! All are convenient to public transportation. A $50 deposit is required, and there's a two-night minimum stay. Rates range from $43 to $60 single, $55 to $75 double.

Finally, there's **Bed 'n' Breakfast Ltd. of Washington, D.C.,** P.O. Box 12011, Washington, DC 20005 (tel. 202/328-3510), with about 80 homes and unhosted furnished apartments on its roster. This organization specializes in historic District homes. Its current roster lists, among many others, a Romanesque Revival turn-of-the-century house near Dupont Circle, with original oak woodwork, red Georgia pine floors, and working fireplaces; an 1891 Colonial Revival town house on Capitol Hill; a beautiful Victorian residence in Logan Circle with a massive oak staircase, bay windows, and wood-burning fireplaces; and a Federal-style brick house in Friendship Heights with a walled-in garden and a heated outdoor swimming pool. Rates are $35 to $75 single, $45 to $95 double, $10 for an extra person, from $55 for a full apartment.

FOR STUDENT VISITORS

International Student House, 1825 R St. NW, Washington, DC 20009 (tel. 202/387-6445 or 232-4007), is for college-aged students of all nationalities, including Americans who are encouraged to room with foreigners. (ISH exists to "foster international understanding and promote cross-cultural interaction.") Housed in three adjacent buildings, one of them a magnificent Tudor mansion, just a few blocks from Dupont Circle, it offers a great deal for very little, though a month is the minimum stay permitted. Especially nice are the rooms in the Tudor building (they have leaded-glass windows); rooms in a newer wing have painted concrete walls and are larger but less charming. All are functionally furnished, air-conditioned, and equipped with switchboard phones for incoming calls. Linens, bedding, and towels are provided, but there's no maid service; students do—or don't do—their own cleaning.

An oak-paneled Tudor dining room with a working fireplace is the setting for daily meals (breakfast and dinner are included in the rates). Sunday tea is served in the oak-paneled Great Hall—an imposing room with a high, beamed Tudor ceiling, antique furnishings, Persian rugs, and a fireplace. Additional amenities include a laundry/ironing room, a rec room with table tennis and pool tables, a TV room, and a library.

Rates are $450 to $675 per person per month, the former for a bed in a four-person dorm with shared bath, the latter for a private room with bath. A bathless double is $475 to $560.

You can also try the **International Guest House** at 1441 Kennedy St. NW, Washington, DC 20011 (tel. 202/726-5808), just east of the Carter Barron Amphitheater in Rock Creek Park. It's run by the Mennonite Church and accommodates people from all walks of life not restricted to students, most of whom are from foreign countries. Americans (there's a quota of about 25%) are allowed to stay for a week only. Facilities are similar to the above listings, rooms are air-conditioned (no phones, but there are pay phones in the hall), and the location is reasonably convenient—about a 25-minute bus ride from downtown. Guests sometimes gather around the piano in the living/dining room. And the basement lounge offers Ping-Pong, TV, soda machines, and a refrigerator. There's an old-fashioned swing on the porch, and the back yard is equipped with playground equipment and a badminton net. Street parking is plentiful. There is an 11 p.m. curfew.

Rates, including a large continental breakfast (fresh-baked muffins, cold cereal, juice, and tea or coffee), are $15 per person nightly, $95 weekly. Children 6 to 16 pay half price; under-5s, free. Single guests are expected to share a room if the house is full. *Note:* No smoking or drinking is permitted indoors.

CHAPTER IV

WHERE TO EAT IN WASHINGTON

□ □ □

In the old days, visitors to Washington toured the historic sights and took their meals in government cafeterias or very ordinary restaurants. Washingtonians lived in a culinary boondocks. But all that is history. In the last decade or so Washington has discovered food. Today the District supports dozens of first-rate French restaurants, and all the latest West Coast trends are widely represented. Gourmet pizzas (topped with sun-dried tomatoes, goat cheese, and other exotica) and "new American cuisine" are the current rage—the latter essentially the old "nouvelle cuisine" highlighting regional specialties. Perhaps the patriotic Reagan era demanded a return to national nourishment. Artistic presentation of fare is still de rigueur, but those of you who starved during the nouvelle reign will be happy to note that portions have resumed normal size.

Washington seafood houses bring in fresh fish from the Chesapeake Bay. Crabcakes are on the majority of Washington menus. And in a city where former chefs of embassies often forget to go home and stay to open restaurants, the ethnic choices include Afghan, Moroccan, Thai, and Ethiopian fare. You can join the rich and powerful at select spots where historic decisions are made over gravlax and champagne. You can eat, as most Washingtonians do, at scores of medium-priced restaurants. And when you're watching your budget, you can still dine in amazingly good cafeterias.

THE TOP RESTAURANTS

These are the plush power-lunch locales where business decisions are made and policies finalized over haute cuisine. They're frequented by lobbyists courting politicians, journalists plying White

House staffers for information, and anyone else who can afford their hallowed precincts or write off $100-plus meals for two on expense accounts. If you want to hobnob with the movers and shakers in Washington, plan at least one meal at any of the following restaurants.

A jewel-like elegance characterizes **Le Pavillon,** 1050 Connecticut Ave. NW, at L Street, in the Washington Square Building (tel. 833-3846), a restaurant whose interior is designed around an exquisite Lalique crystal table (at the entrance) upon which large flower arrangements are displayed in a stunning hand-blown glass vase. Here, everything attains a degree of perfection that almost requires of diners a heightened esthetic awareness to appreciate the subtleties.

The setting is like the inside of a shell—pale peach and beige—with shimmery gold mesh curtains, etched-glass dividers, handtinted wallpaper from Italy, and tables beautifully appointed with Vuillermet silver, Limoges Haviland china, Sèvres crystal, and charmingly arranged flowers. Northern exposure ensures pure sunlight during the day; at night, candlelight creates a rosy glow.

Chef Yannick Cam's creations (he calls his style of cooking "cuisine personalisée") have been described as "alchemy." And his wife, Janet Lai Cam, is the most gracious maître d' in Washington. Under her discreet direction, service is efficient and courteous but never haughty.

Though you can order à la carte, prix-fixe meals allow you best to experience the harmony of courses Cam has created. Menus change daily to take advantage of worldwide seasonal specialties, ranging from Maine oysters to Scottish venison to Cavaillon melons flown in from the south of France. They're in advanced culinary French, but waiters patiently translate and enlarge upon complexities of preparation. An especially good way to experience Le Pavillon is to join in one of the restaurant's Winemaker's Dinners. At these affairs (about once a month; call to find out if there'll be one during your stay) a noted vintner selects about five of his most exquisite wines, and Cam designs a meal to harmonize with them. The cost is about $100 per person, including wine, tax, and tip.

A prix-fixe lunch ($24) might begin with a salad of watercress, avocado, and lobster tossed in a hazelnut oil Vinaigrette prepared with 25-year-old Jerez vinegar, this followed by an entree of squab roasted with anise and garnished with duck foie gras and vegetables. À la carte, you might add a cheese course (perhaps a firm ash-centered morbier) and/or a dessert of lemon curd galette with a coulis of strawberries and raspberries. That dessert, by the way, happens to be a favorite of Nancy Reagan's.

At dinner, prix-fixe meals start at $60 for four courses, with additional-course meals at $75, $90, and $100. The latter (which two can share) includes seven courses, perhaps beginning with shitaki mushrooms filled with mousse of chicken, duck, and foie gras, garnished with lobster, and "drizzled" with chive butter. That's followed by a warm salad of smoked salmon arranged over a confit of leeks; scallops from France with roe, pan-roasted with fava beans, tomato, and basil; a flan of rouget (red mullet from France), garnished with filet of turbot and served with sautéed oysters and zucchini; fresh foie gras served with purée of sweet red pepper and bacon garnish; breast of pheasant, roasted, sliced, arranged en aiguillette, with zucchini flowers, pheasant juices, and truffles; and for dessert, raspberry tartlets served afloat on crème anglaise flavored with apricot and marbleized with raspberry purée. Janet Cam describes such meals as "evolving poetry," and one food writer rhapsodized, "The tastes break in your mouth like waves lapping at a shore, gently, expressively." And that says it all.

Le Pavillon is open for lunch weekdays from 11:45 a.m. to 1:45 p.m., for dinner Monday to Saturday from 6:45 to 9:30 p.m., for desserts nightly until about 11 p.m. Reservations are essential.

We never realized, until we dined and danced at the **River Club,** 3223 K St. NW (tel. 333-8118), that we've spent our entire adult lives—from beads-and-jeans hippiedom to pre-chic yuppiedom—simply starved for glamor. We're talking about the kind of glamor you've glimpsed in old movies—stunningly attired men and women swigging champagne at posh supper clubs. The last place we ever expected to find it was in traditionally sedate and conservative Washington, D.C. But thanks to two trend-setting entrepreneurs—former rock-group manager Paul Cohn and partner Barry Silverman—we did.

This gorgeous restaurant and nightclub is the last word in art deco elegance. Softly lit and plushly carpeted, its exquisitely authentic $1.3 million interior features graceful etched-glass nudes (one of them a marble-framed panel under a cascading 10-foot waterfall), gleaming silver and black-lacquer columns, coved ceiling subtly aglow in pink neon, period-evocative murals and paintings, and a 70-food serpentine marble bar. Seating is in comfy-cozy alcoves at elegantly appointed tables ringing a sunken circular dance floor. An assemblage of young, charming, and highly skilled waiters are in black tie, and there's a roving "cigarette girl" with a large tray strapped around her neck.

Chef Jeff Tunk is a culinary wizard. The menu, which changes seasonally, offers tasting-size and full entree portions of most dishes, the former priced from about $8.50 to $13, the latter from $16 to $28. We elected to graze on sample portions—a multicourse banquet beginning with the best tuna sashimi we've ever tasted on a bed of spaghetti-shredded cucumber. Next, a salad of thinly sliced grilled quail tossed with five greens—red oak leaf, curly red lettuce, mache, endive, and radicchio—in a honey/mustard/port wine dressing; light-as-air spring rolls stuffed with smoked chicken,

Maryland lump crabmeat, and a julienne of vegetables served with pickled melon chutney; Chinese-style hacked smoked lobster, stir-fried with scallions in sesame oil and served over crisply fried spinach and julienned vegetables; and a filet of pinkly juicy salmon with crisp sesame-seed coating, pan-roasted in beurre blanc sauce flavored with papaya and opalescent basil. Did we skip dessert after all that? No siree Bob! We finished up with espresso, a crème brûlée in cookie-dough crust floating on strawberry coulis, and concord cake (don't miss it)—a marriage of ganache and dense chocolate mousse topped with sugared meringue rolls on crème à l'anglaise marble-ized with chocolate and raspberries. And, yes, dessert wines (we don't do things by halves). But not to worry; we spent hours working it all off on the dance floor.

Do take advantage of the River Club's marvelously knowledgeable and friendly sommelier, Peter Birmingham. The champagnes, wines, and dessert wines he recommends with ensuing courses will immensely enhance your meal. The club's list, though not inexpensive, is excellent. The River Club is the kind of place where you can manage to spend hundreds on caviar and champagne—or dine modestly at about $60 for two. Don your best duds and make an evening of it.

Open for dinner Sunday to Thursday from 6 to 11:30 p.m., Friday and Saturday till midnight. Dancing is until 2 a.m. on Friday, 3 a.m. on Saturday. Reservations essential.

Since the reopening of the magnificent Willard Inter-Continental Hotel in 1986, its premier restaurant, **The Willard Room,** 1401 Pennsylvania Ave. NW (tel. 637-7440), has become Washington's most prestigious see-and-be-seen dining room. This is nothing new. An 1880 guidebook to the city described the Willard Room as "a most agreeable and pleasing spectacle where refined people enjoy an unequaled table." Today that "refined" clientele includes upper-crust Washingtonians, visiting presidents and premiers, movie and sports stars, and often a king or two. To ensure the continuance of an "unequaled table," the restaurant shops the markets of the world to stock its larders, from the pâtés of Strasbourg to the finest mountain brook trout from West Virginia. Award-winning chefs and sommeliers have been assembled. And the room itself has been re-created to reflect its original turn-of-the-century splendor in every detail—the gorgeous carved oak paneling; the towering scagliola columns topped with gilded Ionic capitals; the brass and bronze torchères and chandeliers; the faux-bois beamed ceiling; and the gem-colored carpet have all been restored or faithfully reproduced.

Although the room is massive, its well-spaced tables (ideal for power-lunch privacy) seat only 72. They're softly lit by small shaded table lamps and exquisitely appointed with a Villeroy & Boch china pattern depicting a mosaic tile from the lobby. Floor-to-ceiling windows are framed by crimson velvet draperies. And lavish food displays grace beautiful flower-bedecked sideboards. A *Dossier* magazine article summed up the effect of all this magnificence rather neatly: "The Willard Room is so elegant," it said, "that one could eat a hot dog here and still think it was the dining experience of a lifetime."

The menus, highlighting East Coast cuisine, change frequently to offer seasonal specialties. On a recent visit, dinner appetizers ($8 to $20) included a Maryland crab and smoked salmon terrine in lemon chive sauce, and veal sweetbread with fresh truffles in a sauce of baked wild mushrooms. Among the entrees ($21 to $24) were loin of Delaware lamb in a piquant sauce of minted goat cheese with pine nuts and roasted garlic, poached Atlantic halibut with a panache of spring vegetables in a sauce of chamomile and juniper, and grilled salmon with Minnesota wild rice and fennel tarragon grapefruit sauce. Fresh seafood dishes are a house specialty—the panfried Chesapeake oysters with black caviar in champagne butter sauce moved us to rhapsodies. And speaking of rhapsodies, desserts such as pastry chef Dieter Schorner's white-and-dark chocolate mousse with raspberry sauce, superb crème brûlée, and chocolate Charlotte with caramel sauce are superlative.

Lunch entrees at the Willard Room are in the $16.50 to $19 range, Sunday brunch items a few dollars less. On all menus, items designed with low cholesterol and sodium levels are starred. If all of the above is too pricey for you, do come by for an $11.50 continental breakfast just for the experience; you could, however, order shad roe for your morning meal in the early spring, as Lincoln always did.

Open for breakfast Monday to Friday 7:30 a.m. to 10 p.m., weekends from 8 a.m.; for lunch 11:30 a.m. to 2 p.m. weekdays, from noon weekends; for dinner nightly from 6:30 to 10 p.m. when a pianist entertains. Reservations are essential.

Dubbed "the hottest room in town" by *Washingtonian* magazine in its very first year of operation, **Twenty-One Federal,** 1736 L St. NW (tel. 331-9771), has provided the District's power lunchers with yet another posh precinct. Art Buchwald has made the front corner table his own, and oftentimes seated nearby are Senator Edward Kennedy, Sargent Shriver, Jerry Rafshoon, Bill Regardie, Ben Bradlee, and Jack Valenti. Lynda Carter and Ethel Kennedy have thrown parties in the cleverly glass-enclosed private dining room (celebs can show off while other diners enjoy the view without being able to intrude).

What's all the excitement about? It's about first-rate new-American cuisine in a stunning setting. Owner/chef Bob Kinkead, who has a successful restaurant of the same name in Nantucket, is an award-winning and consistently excellent chef, much praised in publications like *Gourmet* and *Food & Wine*. His 150-seat dining room, divided into three major areas by gleaming openwork brass panels, features beautiful patterned Carrara marble floors framed in oak-paneled walls, and seating in charcoal suede banquettes and similarly upholstered black-lacquer chairs. Discreet lighting emanates from alabaster shell sconces, while a delicate pink glow from recessed ceiling lights flatters your complexion. The bar, scene of nightly piano entertainment (come by for gourmet munchies at cocktail hour), is separated from the dining rooms by a glass-enclosed wine room, wherein over 3,000 wine bottles are displayed on racks. Also glassed-in is an open rotisserie in the rear dining room, allowing diners a tantalizing view of food preparation.

Menus change seasonally. Depending on when you visit, you might begin with lobster and crabcakes that are bound with remoulade sauce spiced with chiles and jalapeños and served on a mustard crème fraîche sauce spiked with horseradish; corn/okra relish accompanies this dish. Another great starter is a delicately spiced, grilled vegetable salad—eggplant, zucchini, asparagus, red onions, and mushrooms—served with marinated tomatoes and grilled mozzarella wrapped in romaine leaves in a roasted yellow pepper vinaigrette. We've enjoyed such entrees as spit-roasted pork coated with Cajun spice mixture and served in a roasted chile/pork stock sauce with grilled red onions, poblano chile/coriander relish, and black bean/corn pudding; halibut sautéed in a light butter/chardonnay reduction sauce, served with paysan-cut vegetables, fresh oyster mushrooms, Nantucket bay scallops, and sautéed spinach; and a lamb trio—grilled leg and rack of lamb served in a merlot wine/rosemary/sweet-garlic sauce and a loin stuffed with veal and pistachio nuts, served with sautéed wild mushrooms, haricots verts, and potatoes gratinées dauphinoise (thinly sliced potatoes layered with garlic, cream, and parmesan). Portions are sizable, and the fresh-baked breads served with them are divine. Still, do loosen your belt and order dessert. Pastry chef Maeve Barnes turns out delights like a chocolate Bavarian cake dipped in hazelnut/chocolate ganache floated on hazelnut/chocolate crème anglaise and bread and butter pudding with bourbon/pecan sauce topped with whipped cream, custard, and sugared pecans.

Twenty-one Federal has a carefully chosen, largely (about 60%) American, reasonably priced wine list; ask your waiter to have the chef recommend the best wines for your meal. Friendly service (sans hauteur) by young waiters and charming distaff maitre d', Pat Miller, are further pluses here. Lunch entrees are in the $12 to $17 range, dinner entrees in the $16 to $26 range.

Open for lunch weekdays 11:30 a.m. to 2:30 p.m.; for dinner, Monday to Thursday 6 to 10 p.m., till 10:30 p.m. Friday and Saturday, with piano bar music till 11 p.m. on weekends. There's complimentary valet parking at dinner. Reservations essential.

Though it's technically located in Rosslyn, Virginia (a short and scenic walk across the Potomac from Georgetown), **Windows,** in the *USA Today* Building at 1000 Wilson Blvd. North (tel.

527-4430), was designated "the most significant new restaurant in Washington" by *Esquire* magazine and the city's "best new restaurant" by readers of *Washingtonian* when it opened in 1985. And geographical hair-splitting aside, owner/cuisinier Henry Dinardo has been called one of the 25 hottest chefs in America by *Food & Wine*. In fact, the food surpasses the view, which is less than the exceptional vista you might expect at a restaurant on a river with a name like Windows. It's pleasant enough, especially at night when lighted monuments form the backdrop, but during the day a wide ribbon of I-66 highway traffic is less than inspiring. We prefer not to sit at the curved window wall but in the raised area slightly back, from whence the highway is out of one's line of vision and the view consists of water, treetops, and blue sky. The interior view is lovely, whatever your vantage point. Subtly art deco in design, Windows has mauve lacquer walls and seating in comfortable chairs plushly upholstered in pale-rose raw silk. Beautifully appointed tables (Limoges china, Christofel silver, sprays of fresh flowers) are draped in floor-length white linen, and brass trim here and there adds a contemporary note. A cozy lounge area with a handsome mahogany bar adjoins.

Dinardo calls his style of cooking "creative American cuisine." That means you can expect the current West Coast trends like gourmet pizzas, Southwestern fare, and American regional specialties. It means he uses the freshest local ingredients (Virginia farmers raise fresh herbs, haricots verts, raspberries, beefsteak tomatoes, and poultry to the restaurant's specifications) and searches the world for sublime food sources. And it means the artistry of his food presentations (large white platters serve as "canvases" for culinary masterpieces) has been as carefully considered as the complexities of their preparation. But Dinardo's genius makes trendiness beside the point; he's simply an artist working in the current genre. He's catered to a prestigious clientele, including Presidents Carter and Reagan, Lady Bird Johnson's 75th birthday party, and Monaco's royal family.

On our last visit to Windows a glorious dinner began with appetizers of pastrami-smoked Norwegian salmon with honey mustard dressing and a warm duck pâté complemented by raspberry sauce and garnished with fresh raspberries. Other recommendables included Iowa corn and Maine lobster bisque with a purée of roasted red bell peppers and a wilted-spinach and arugula salad in a warm country-cured bacon/apple/onion dressing with New York state goat cheese.

The pizzas and pastas ($12.50 to $17) can be ordered as shared appetizers or entrees, and either way it would be a shame to pass them up. We had a rustic pizza topped with fresh morels and smoked duck, touched with a light pesto. Others were topped with exotica ranging from fennel sausage to barbecued chicken and chèvre. As for pastas, you might try a homemade angel-hair pasta with gulf shrimp, spring onions, and vine-ripened tomatoes in a fresh basil cream sauce. Some additional entrees ($15 to $24): roast rack of lamb with crisp potato cakes and snow pea pods in a rosemary/cassis sauce; farm-raised breast of chicken in a pool of mango nectar with California asparagus and sliced papaya, served with rice; grilled Menemsha swordfish served with fuji sprouts on a bed of crisp fried spinach with spicy black bean sauce; and peppersteak of farm-raised breast of Magret duck with sautéed pears and spinach in a pear and port wine sauce.

The wine list offers over 100 French and California vintages, some available each day by the glass, as are champagnes. And for dessert there's a scrumptious crème brûlée, among other temptations. Lunch entrees at Windows are in the $9 to $12 range, though for just $7.95 you could feast on a croissant sandwich filled with barbecued pork and served with coleslaw or, for $5.95, on a pizza topped with country-cured bacon, tomato, and mozzarella.

Open for lunch weekdays from 11:30 a.m. to 2:30 p.m., for dinner Monday to Thursday from 5:30 to 9:30 p.m., on Friday and Saturday till 11 p.m.

Under the creative and skillful direction of chef/owner Jean-Pierre Goyenvalle, **Le Lion d'Or**, 1150 Connecticut Ave. NW, at M Street (tel. 296-7972), has long been one of Washington's most esteemed French restaurants. It opened in 1976 to immediate acclaim, Goyenvalle having previously garnered a loyal following of gourmets at other area restaurants. And this talented chef continues to excel; in 1988 he received the prestigious Toque D'Argent award from the Maître Cuisiniers de France.

Here you forget you're underground (it's down a flight of stairs from the street), in a French country setting under a tented fabric ceiling. Walls are covered in cream-colored cotton and hung with French faïence platters from provincial France, copper implements, and gilt-framed paintings of pastoral scenes. Soft lighting emanates from brass chandeliers and wall sconces, seating is in tufted leather banquettes, and a single rose in a silver vase graces every pale-pink linen-clothed table. Big arrangements of country flowers in baskets complete the picture.

The food is beautifully presented and graciously served. Dinner features a selection of about two dozen hors d'oeuvres ($9.50 to $36), the latter price for beluga caviar. Other possible options are artichoke hearts with salmon mousse, duck foie gras with currants, and a salad of quail and truffles. The menu is in French only; we're translating. A wide array of entrees are also listed (most of them in the $20-and-up range). They include red snapper en croûte with beurre blanc, a filet of chicken with foie gras and morels, and a classic roast chicken flavored with tarragon. And the waiter will reel off a number of daily specials. Vegetables, such as spinach au gratin and a fricassee of wild mushrooms, are à la carte ($4.50 to $10). For dessert, the soufflés (orange, raspberry, pear, or chocolate) are not only superb but exquisitely presented on a silver tray with cookies, chocolate truffles, and pralines. Lunch entrees are mostly in the $13 to $16 range.

Open for lunch weekdays from noon to 2 p.m., for dinner Monday to Saturday from 6 to 10 p.m. Reservations are essential.

The **Jockey Club,** at the Ritz-Carlton Hotel, 2100 Massachusetts Ave. NW (tel. 659-8000), has perhaps been Washington's most "in" restaurant since its opening the night before JFK's inauguration. It immediately became—and has remained—a Kennedy-clan favorite (an exuberant Ethel once threw a cake in Andy Williams' face on his birthday), but has also caught on with subsequent Republican administrations; the Reagans even celebrated an anniversary here one year. Art Buchwald is another regular. And Supreme Court Justice Kennedy celebrated his appointment here as did Sandra Day O'Connor. The big surprise when you first visit this celeb-studded eatery is its total lack of pretension and crystal-chandeliered pomp. The Jockey Club is cheerful and pubby with bright red-leather banquettes and bentwood chairs, a random-plank oak floor, amber lanterns suspended from a low beamed ceiling (the subdued lighting is as cozy as the glow of a fireplace), and walls of stucco or aged oak paneling hung with pewter and English prints of hunting scenes, jockeys, etc. Tablecloths have red tattersall checks on white cotton, and a single red rose adorns every table.

The Jockey Club is open for breakfast, lunch, and dinner, and it is pricey. At a recent midday meal, with just one glass of wine apiece, we managed a tab of $93.65 before tip! Even at breakfast, scrambled eggs with sausage, toast, home-fries, a small glass of fresh-squeezed orange juice, and coffee, will run about $16. Of course, if you just want to see the place, you could squeak by with coffee and a toasted bagel and cream cheese for a mere $7. Crabmeat fanciers must try an appetizer of crabmeat cocktail, sauce dijonnaise, and/or an entree of the justifiably famous crabcakes Jockey Club, both available at lunch and dinner. The menu is of the traditional haute cuisine genre. Dinner here might comprise an appetizer of escargots bourguignon, followed by rack of lamb bouquetière, a wilted-spinach and mushroom salad, and a soufflé—Grand Marnier, raspberry, chocolate, lemon, or harlequin—for dessert. Lunch entrees range from about $13 to $19; dinner entrees, from $20 to $28. After dinner, consider a cognac before the fireplace in the adjoining Fairfax Bar.

Open for breakfast weekdays from 6:30 to 11 a.m. (till 11:30 a.m. on weekends), for lunch daily from noon to 2:30 p.m., for dinner nightly from 6 to 10:30 p.m. Reservations are required. Valet parking is available.

Morton's of Chicago, in the heart of Georgetown at 3251 Prospect St. NW (tel. 342-6258), is far and away the best steakhouse in town. In fact, it's matched by few others nationwide, save Arnie Morton's famed original Chicago eatery and branches like this one in Atlanta, Denver, and other cities. Morton, a flamboyant past executive vice-president of Playboy Enterprises, was instrumental in developing the Playboy Club concept. He left the bunny business in 1973 and went on to create a restaurant empire, everywhere attracting a celebrity-studded clientele. The Washington Morton's is no exception. You might spot Tip O'Neill or Ted Kennedy among the beef-eaters, not to mention performers playing the town (like Lena Horne or Dustin Hoffman), even visiting New York Mayor Ed Koch. It's also a favorite of athletes; the Washington Redskins served as waiters for a Special Olympics fundraiser here. And National Symphony conductor Mstislav Rostropovich dined here one night with a famous classical pianist, both wearing headphones! But, basically, one comes to eat, not gawk at the glitterati.

Those huge portions of succulent midwestern beef and scrumptious side dishes are the real attraction. Morton's has oft been called theatrical, and not the least dramatic of its elements is "menu" presentation. There's no written menu. A waiter (they're all aspiring-actor types) presents the entire menu visually. Laden with several cuts of steak, lamb and veal chops, a whole cooked chicken, and a lively lobster, he or she explains the entree options. What you see is what you get. Start off with an appetizer ($6.95 to $7.95), perhaps smoked salmon or a lump crabmeat cocktail. A Caesar salad ($3.75) is another possibility. Steaks ($18.95 for a double filet to $22.95 for a porterhouse or New York sirloin) are perfectly prepared to your specifications. Other entrees—a Sicilian veal chop, prime rib, lamb chops, fresh swordfish steak, oregano chicken, etc. —are $12.95 to $19.95. And lobster is priced according to the market. Side orders of items like flavorfully fresh al dente asparagus, a baked potato, or hash browns, are highly recommended. A loaf of onion bread on every table is complimentary. Consider taking home a doggy bag instead of doggedly finishing everything on your plate. It will save calories, give you a second at-home meal free, and leave room for dessert—perhaps a soufflé Grand Marnier or rich and creamy cheesecake.

Morton's interior is cozy and convivial—just right in every particular for its cuisine and clientele. Large framed LeRoy Neiman sports prints adorn wainscotted stucco walls. Seating is in comfortable cream-colored leather booths at white-linened tables, the latter adorned with flowers and lit by pewter oil lamps in the shape of donkeys or elephants. And shaded lamps here and there enhance the warmly intimate ambience. An open kitchen is hung with gleaming copper pots.

Open Monday to Saturday from 5:30 to 11 p.m. No reservations are taken after 7 p.m., but fans don't mind braving the lines.

Everyone who's anyone at the White House dines at **Maison Blanche/Rive Gauche,** 1725 F St. NW (tel. 842-0070). At this writing the lunchtime crowd is likely to include James Baker, Barbara Bush, Ed Meese, Nancy Reagan, and a mixed assortment of senators and staffers. Owner Tony Greco claims as many key policy decisions are made at Maison Blanche as at the White House, and Ronald Reagan scribbled across his photo the lament, "If only I could get your excellent reviews at my White House." Art Buchwald ("wherever I eat lunch is the in place") holds court at table no. 14.

Even when the administration changes (shortly after we go to press), Maison Blanche will probably retain its great popularity. It's a quick walk from the White House, and the French fare is excellent. The decor is plush—gold silk wall coverings hung with gilt-framed oil paintings, Belgian crystal chandeliers and wall sconces, tufted brown-leather banquettes and Louis XVI–style, brown velvet-upholstered chairs, etched-glass panels, and elegantly appointed tables. The adjoining lounge is called the Oval Room.

If your French is rusty—or nonexistent—you'll appreciate the comprehensive English translations of all menu items, which also provide additional details about preparation. For instance, an appetizer of les huitres en habits verts ($9.75) turns out to be oysters wrapped in spinach and fish mousse, steamed, and served with saffron butter sauce. Another tempting appetizer is la soupe Marius, an aromatic bouillabaisse brimming with chunks of fresh seafood, baked and served in a delicious pastry crust ($9). Dinner entrees (most hovering around the $25 mark, give or take a dollar or two) include tournedos of beef sautéed with five kinds of peppercorns in a cream sauce with a hint of mustard; prime veal chop with cognac, cream, and wild mushroom sauce; and lobster flan with jumbo lump crabmeat on a bed of spinach with chive and butter sauce. Tableside cart preparation is featured, there's an extensive wine cellar, and daily specials are offered at lunch and dinner.

Lunch prices are just a bit lower than the above-quoted, but stupendous savings are offered between 6 and 7 p.m., when a $19.95 multicourse prix-fixe dinner is served. This menu changes seasonally. On our last visit it was comprised of a choice of appetizers (squid salad with diced roast peppers, an avocado half served with diced scallops in a pastry shell, and terrine maison, among them); salad; a choice of entrees, e.g., rare breast and leg of duck with lingonberry sauce; a selection from the pastry cart; and tea or coffee.

Maison Blanche is open weekdays for lunch from 11:45 a.m. to 2:30 p.m., for dinner Monday to Saturday from 6 to 11 p.m. Reservations are essential.

A BUDGET BONUS: Under the same auspices and culinary supervision as the plush and expensive Maison Blanche/Rive Gauche is the adjoining **White House Connection Restaurant & Bar,** 1714 G St. NW (tel. 842-1777), a pleasant eatery with exposed brick and pine-paneled walls, cane-seated bentwood chairs at white-clothed tables, and windows overlooking a fountain. At lunch only, served weekdays from 11:15 a.m. to 2:30 p.m., you can order from an eclectic menu that runs the gamut from a pastrami on rye ($5.95) to filet mignon in black peppercorn sauce with potato and vegetable ($11.95), rainbow trout amandine ($9.50), or salad Niçoise ($7.95). A full lunch—soup or salad, entree, pastry, and beverage—is $11.95. Leave room for the pastry chef's exquisite desserts like white- and dark-chocolate mousse and nougat-filled amaretto cake spiked with almonds. You won't see power lunchers here, but power-aspirant lunchers—lower-echelon White House staffers.

Duke Zeibert's, 1050 Connecticut Ave. NW, at L Street, in the Washington Square Building (tel. 466-3730), is a reincarnated venerable on the D.C. dining scene. In existence for over 30 years, it closed in 1980 when the building it occupied was torn down, then reopened in 1983 in the new building that went up on the same spot. Washington legend and lore abound at Duke's. In the old days it was a Runyonesque hangout into which few women ventured ("Ladies go to Georgetown," said the *Washington Star.* "Macho Washington dines at Duke Zeibert's."). It was at a press conference here in 1975 that Sonny Jurgensen announced his retirement from the Redskins. Both Jimmy Hoffa and J. Edgar Hoover frequented the old Duke's, as did politicians, presidents, media types, and sports stars.

Though the new Duke's is less macho (he's selling ten times more wine, and orders of Perrier and lime are not unheard of), the old gang is still here in force. It's not unusual to note radio host Larry King, Red Auerbach, Howard Cosell, Art Buchwald, George McGovern, or even Jimmy the Greek among the lunchtime crowd. (In fact, it was at Duke's that the latter made his infamous remarks about the breeding of black athletes.) The staff—many of whom have been with Duke over three decades—has also been reassembled for the most part, and the hearty home-cooked American fare is as before. The decor, however, is different, and it no doubt plays a part in attracting distaff diners. The main dining room is under an eight-story atrium skylight. The ambience is light and airy opulence; it feels like you're dining in a crystal. Adornments include art deco lighting fixtures and numerous photos of sports figures and famous guests lining mahogany-paneled walls. Tables are placed far enough apart for discreet conversation, privacy being essential to the power lunch. Food is also served in the bar, and cocktails and light fare are offered on a terrace lined with trees that are lit by tiny lights after dark. Duke and his son, Randy, are always on hand to greet customers, many of whom are close friends.

On every table is a basket of assorted rolls and a silver bowl of New York pickles—a Zeibert trademark. The latter go well with overstuffed deli sandwiches ($9.50 to $10.50) made with fresh-cooked meats and served at lunch—breast of turkey, smoked tongue, Swiss cheese, onion, homemade coleslaw, and Russian dressing. In fact, you'll note many New York deli characteristics at Duke's, not the least of them the red-jacketed waiters who could fit in there, no-questions-asked. Furthermore, appetizers include matzoh-ball soup, chopped liver, and creamed herring. However, you could also—and wisely—begin your meal with a bluepoint oyster cocktail and follow up with feathery-light crabcakes served with mashed potatoes (heaven) and coleslaw. Another great treat here is an immense tender and juicy pork chop, also served with mashed potatoes. And if you want to feel like an insider, order a hamburger à la Duke—not on the menu—made with chopped onions mixed into the meat. Entrees are $10 to $15 at lunch, $15 to $22 at dinner, with daily specials priced a few dollars lower. For dessert, strawberry cheesecake—the rich Lindy's variety—is recommended.

Open Monday to Saturday from 11:30 a.m. to 11:30 p.m., on Sunday from 5 to 10 p.m. Reservations advised.

Washington Post restaurant critic Phyllis Richman calls the **Prime Rib**, 2020 K St. NW (tel. 466-8811), "Washington's most glamorous setting for plain old steak and roast beef." Modeled after Central Park South hotel restaurants, it is indeed glamorous—in a substantial, well-heeled fashion—with gold-trimmed black walls, comfortable black-leather chairs and banquettes, white-linened tables softly lit by shaded brass lamps, swagged white curtains, and large floral displays. Waiters are in black tie, a pianist at the baby grand plays show tunes, and the art on the walls merits a close look —it includes signed Picasso and Chagall prints and many gilt-framed Louis Icart art deco lithographs.

As for that "plain old" steak and roast beef, it's thick, tender, juicy, and prepared from meat of the best grain-fed steers that has been aged for four to five weeks. And it's served exactly the way you ordered it. An entree of roast prime rib with crisp vegetables and potato du jour is $11.95 at lunch; an eight-ounce serving of prime filet mignon wrapped in bacon and broiled, $13.50. At dinner portions are larger and prices higher: the prime rib is $19.50, filet mignon—18 ounces—is $20, and vegetables are à la carte. For less carnivorous diners there are about ten seafood entrees. A bountiful basket of fried potato skins with a big bowl of sour cream is a must.

Either meal might begin with an appetizer of smoked fresh trout with Dijon mustard sauce or creamy lobster bisque, and end with a gorgeous hot fudge sundae over Amaretto pound cake. Bar drinks here, by the way, are made with fresh-squeezed juices and Evian water.

Open for lunch weekdays from 11:30 a.m. to 3 p.m., dinner Monday to Saturday from 5 to 11:30 p.m. Reservations essential.

EXPENSIVE RESTAURANTS

Not all of the good and high-priced restaurants in Washington are haunts of power brokers. The following upper-bracket restaurants are—for the most part—more affordable than those detailed above, and more low key. They're distinguished by truly excellent cuisine and/or a beautiful setting in which to enjoy it. Dinner entrees at these places average about $11 to $18. Lunch prices, of course, are always lower.

AMERICAN: The **Old Ebbitt Grill,** two blocks from the White House at 675 15th St. NW, between F and G Streets (tel. 347-4801), is the city's oldest saloon, founded in 1856. Presidents McKinley, Grant, Johnson, Cleveland, Theodore Roosevelt, and Harding were patrons, and among its artifacts are Alexander Hamilton's wooden bears—one with a secret compartment in which it's said he hid whisky bottles from his wife. However, don't go expecting to find a fusty old tavern à la Williamsburg. The existing facility is a plush reconstruction around the corner from, and loosely based upon, the original. Fronted by the grandiose beaux arts façade of the defunct Keith-Albee Theater, it has Persian rugs on beautiful oak and marble floors, beveled mirrors, gas lighting, etched-glass panels, and other elements evocative of the Victorian atmosphere that characterized turn-of-the-century Washington saloons. Old Ebbitt heirlooms are scattered throughout—an antique clock above the revolving entrance doors, the Hamilton bears to the right, animal trophies bagged by Teddy Roosevelt in the Old Bar, etc. The street level comprises a dining area and three bars, all of which serve premium wines by the glass. The main dining room, hung with period oil paintings, has forest-green velvet banquettes and booths, lace-curtained windows, and beautifully appointed white linen-clothed tables with pink-shaded lamps. The Old Bar, the Ebbitt's famed collection of old beer steins on a ledge above it, is separated from the main dining room by a 6½-foot mahogany and glass partition. There's also an Oyster Bar, marble topped with brass stripping and a copper scupper. And behind the main dining room is Grant's Bar, complete with classic gilt-framed bar nude.

The Ebbitt is a stunning setting for meals, cocktails, or a romantic rendezvous. Menus change daily, but luncheon entrees (about $9 to $11) might include fettuccine tossed with spinach and walnuts in cream sauce, a fried oyster sandwich, or boneless chicken breast sautéed in butter with apricots and ginger, flamed in apricot brandy, and served with fresh vegetables and new potatoes. Typical dinner entrees ($11.50 to $14): Nantucket scallops broiled in white wine and butter, canneloni di casa (homemade pasta with spinach, mortadella, and four cheeses baked in a cream sauce), or softshell crab amandine. At either meal you can get a hamburger, thus enjoying the ambience at low cost, and you needn't sit at the oyster bar to order half a dozen raw oysters for $4.50 to $7.50, depending on whether they're Chincoteagues, Malapeques, Belons (the best), Pine Islands, or Long Islands. Desserts run the gamut from a hot fudge sundae made with homemade vanilla ice cream to Key lime mousse. These sumptuous surroundings are also accessible at breakfast—$4.50 for fresh fruit or juice, fresh-baked nut and fruit breads, and tea or coffee; $5.95 for eggs, hash browns, toast, bacon, fresh fruit or juice, and tea or coffee.

Open for breakfast from 7:30 to 11 a.m. weekdays and 8 to 11 a.m. on Saturday, for brunch on Sunday from 10 a.m. to 4 p.m. Lunch is served Monday to Saturday from 11 a.m. to 5 p.m.; dinner from 5 p.m. to midnight, except on Sunday when it begins at 4 p.m. The bars stay open until 2 a.m. Sunday to Thursday, till 3 a.m. on Friday and Saturday. Light fare is served till midnight and 1 a.m. respectively. Reservations essential.

CHINESE: The **Sichuan Pavilion,** 1820 K St. NW (tel. 466-7790), is unique in several ways. Though it is American-owned, its chefs are recruited from the highest ranks of the People's Republic of China's Chengdu Service Bureau, which operates luxurious hotels and restaurants for visiting dignitaries and prepares sumptuous state banquets. These chefs, supplied from home with special seasonings and spices not otherwise available in the U.S., are masters of Sichuan (usually spelled Szechuan) cuisine. The Chinese embassy sent their cook here for training, and when Premier Zhao Ziyang visited Washington, Sichuan Pavilion prepared special meals for him. We think this is the best—and most authentic—Chinese restaurant in Washington. The setting is unpretentious but elegant with white-linened tables, crystal chandeliers, and burgundy walls hung with paintings and calligraphy from the Chungking Institute of Fine Arts.

And the food is beautifully presented (these chefs are also trained in food sculpture and adorn platters with exquisite carrot and leek flowers). It's also light—never greasy—low in salt, and prepared without MSG.

Do begin with an appetizer of tangy Sichuan dumplings in spicy Sichuan red hot sauce or crispy but feather-light spring rolls. And keep in mind that though some of the dishes sound familiar— moo shu pork, Kung Pao chicken, twice-cooked shredded duck, etc. —their subtle flavors distinguish them from Sichuan fare you've had elsewhere. We'd love to work our way through the entire dinner menu, especially such chef's specialties as tinkling bells with ten ingredients (sliced shrimp, crab, beef, and chicken sautéed with vegetables and topped with Sichuan dumplings), a hot-and-mild lobster duet, Peking duck, and crispy fried sea bass in Sichuan sauce. Dinner entrees are in the $10 to $18 range for the most part; lunch entrees, mostly $10 or less. Each dish is a revelation; dining here is like discovering new colors on the spectrum. And as a concession to Western palates, there are dessert choices like rich white chocolate cake.

Sunday brunch, served noon to 4 p.m., features a prix fixe menu for just $9.95—an appetizer, soup, entree, and wine.

Open daily for lunch from 11:30 a.m. to 3 p.m., for dinner from 3 to 10:30 p.m. There's complimentary parking after 6 p.m. Reservations suggested.

CRÉOLE: Lafitte, in the Hampshire Hotel, 1310 New Hampshire Ave. NW, at N Street (tel. 296-7600), is the scene of many a fashionable Washington dinner party. Named for Jean Lafitte, the French pirate who fought on the American side in the Battle of New Orleans, it features authentic Créole cuisine.

The ambience is charming. Adobe peach stucco and exposed brick walls are adorned with oil paintings of New Orleans. And similarly evocative of the French Quarter is the restaurant's turn-of-the-century-style mahogany woodwork with sections of beveled mirror and ornate scrollwork. Soft lighting emanates from gaslight-style chandeliers and wall sconces, and candles in hurricane lamps create a romantic mood at night. Tables are clothed in cream linen and prettified with sprays of fresh flowers. Potted palms and shuttered windows add coziness, and the atmosphere is further enhanced Monday through Saturday night by a pianist; other times there's often player piano music, usually Dixieland.

The food is spicy and sumptuous. Begin your dinner with a nouvelle rendition of seafood gumbo ($4.75), escargots sauteed with mushroom caps and pecans ($6.05), or Mardi Gras boulets—shrimp and crabmeat cakes in étouffée sauce ($7.25). Like the appetizers, the entrees are all spectacular; it's quite difficult to choose. They include duck St. Ramon—smoked roast duckling breast and hindquarter, braised in red wine and served with fricassee sauce on a bed of wild rice ($16.95); blackened New Zealand lamb chops topped with Créole mustard sauce ($17.95); and smoked quail stuffed with andouille sausage and filet mignon served with wild rice ($18.95). Then again the fresh seafood dishes featuring plump, juicy shrimp (and crawfish in season) are also exquisite—e.g., large Louisiana shrimp sautéed in cream sauce thickened with sour cream and flavored with herbs and vegetables ($15.25). It's all so good, you'll just have to come back again. But before you leave, be sure to sample one of those luscious desserts displayed along with a lavish floral arrangement on the mahogany cabinet: perhaps ricotta and cream-cheese cake topped with fresh raspberries, a thickly frosted chocolate raspberry torte, or an even richer sweet-potato/pecan pie. We like to linger over coffee and dessert and/or a cognac in the adjoining lounge, the best vantage point from which to enjoy the piano music.

Much of the above is also offered at lunch, at which time most entrees range from $10 to $15. Full table d'hôte meals—appetizer, entree, and dessert—are available for about $12.50 to $16 at lunch, $16.50 to $23 at dinner. And this being a hotel restaurant, you can even come by for breakfast—pain perdue (New Orleans-style french toast) with sausage, pure maple syrup, one egg on Cajun hash, coffee, and fresh-squeezed orange juice ($6.95).

Lafitte serves breakfast weekdays from 7 to 10 a.m., on weekends from 8 to 10 a.m.; lunch Monday to Friday from 11:30 a.m. to 2:30 p.m.; Sunday brunch from 11 a.m. to 3 p.m.; and dinner Monday to Friday from 5:30 to 10:30 p.m., on Saturday from 6 to 11 p.m. Reservations suggested.

FRENCH, CONTINENTAL, AND AMERICAN NOUVEAU: Nora, 2132 Florida Ave. NW, at R Street (tel. 462-5143), features beautifully presented and healthful new American cuisine dishes in one of Washington's most charming settings. You enter via a cozy café-curtained bar where brick walls are hung with antique cooking utensils. Inside, fresh flowers and paraffin lamps adorn tables clothed in pale gray, and stark white walls display Amish patchwork crib quilts, ceramic dishes, and antique mirrors. Handmade Windsor chairs enhance the Early American feel, as does an immense coffee grinder from a turn-of-the-century Philadelphia general store in the center of the room. There's additional seating on a lovely brick-walled patio where plants flourish under a skylight ceiling.

The fare is extremely healthful (even Ralph Nader dines here), but not of the brown rice and bean sprout variety. Chemical-free and additive-free meats are used, vegetables and fruits are fresh and organically grown, and eggs are provided by a farm where the hens run free and their diet is pure. You'll taste the difference. The menu changes daily to utilize seasonal specialties and allow creative latitude to the chef. On a recent visit there were appetizers of chicken liver mousse with pistachios and smoked trout with creamed horseradish sauce, entrees ($13 to $18) ranging from Indonesian pork sate with rice pilaf and chili sauce, to softshell crab with basil sauce and pine nuts, to fettuccine mixed with home-cured ham, asparagus, herbs, and shitake mushrooms. A dessert of French bittersweet chocolate mousse with hazelnut cream sauce inspired rhapsodies, as did an equally good apple pie with peanut crunch ice cream.

Open for dinner Monday to Thursday from 6 to 10 p.m., on

Friday and Saturday to 10:30 p.m. Reservations are highly suggested. Nora does not take credit cards, but personal checks are accepted.

Chaucer's, 1733 N St. NW, at the Canterbury Hotel (tel. 393-3000), an oak-paneled below-street-level dining room that manages to be bright and cheerful, has garnered considerable critical acclaim. Noted the *Washington Post:* "From the exotic little sprays of flowers on the tables to the porcelain dish of mints brought with the check, Chaucer's goes that extra mile to make a diner know that this is a restaurant that intends to carve a special niche for itself." Another reviewer described Chaucer's as "more like a fine European Grill Room . . . than a restaurant in the classic American genre." It's a small, intimate eatery (there's seating for about 50) with a beamed ceiling, handsome gilt-framed mirrors, ecru linen-clothed tables, and crystal wall sconces. During the day, sunlight streams in through a high-ceilinged brick-walled atrium at one end; at night, candles glow on every table. And taped classical music is always played in the background.

The fare is American/Continental cuisine. Lunch or dinner, you might begin with an appetizer of grilled shitake mushrooms stuffed with three cheeses ($7). Lunch entrees, in the $10 to $13 range for the most part, include such tempting dishes as fettucine with shrimp and shitake mushrooms in tomato cream sauce and a brochette of shrimp and andouille sausage served with Créole rice and mustard sauce. Dinner choices ($15 to $20.50) run the gamut from shrimp sautéed in white wine/tarragon cream sauce with a hint of Pernod to prime ribs of beef au jus with Yorkshire pudding. For dessert, it's hard to beat the crème brûlée (available with fresh raspberries in season), though the Lindt chocolate cake also represents a major temptation. Order both and share. And if all this is above your budget, come by for the before-theater prix fixe ($12.95), served from 5:30 to 7 p.m.; it includes an appetizer, entree, dessert, and tea or coffee.

Chaucer's is also a lovely spot for your morning croissant and coffee, and there's a special Sunday brunch menu featuring items like an assorted smoked fish platter ($10.25) or a Boursin omelet ($6.95). For $14.95 you can get a three-course brunch (such as saucisson en brioche, poached eggs with smoked salmon and hollandaise, and a strawberry soufflé with Grand Marnier), including a complimentary drink, newspaper *(Washington Post* or *New York Times),* and tea or coffee.

Chaucer's is open for breakfast weekdays from 7 to 9:30 a.m., on weekends from 8 to 10:30 a.m.; for lunch Monday to Friday only, from 11:30 a.m. to 2:30 p.m.; and for dinner Sunday to Thursday from 5:30 to 10 p.m., on Friday and Saturday till 10:30 p.m. Reservations suggested.

Suzanne's, 1735 Connecticut Ave. NW, between R and S

Streets (tel. 483-4633), offers the kind of innovative and sophisticated cuisine your basic bicoastal being requires.

Downstairs, in a first-rate charcuterie, Suzanne's features delicacies from New York gourmet emporia like Dean & DeLuca and Silver Palate, along with items like homemade pâtés, endive leaves with herbed chèvre, scallop ceviche in lemon cups, baked clams with pesto, smoked chicken breast, fish mousses, imported cheeses, endive and fennel salad, Norwegian smoked salmon, crudités with hazelnut curry dip, and an array of exquisite home-baked breads and desserts.

Upstairs, you can enjoy such fare in a homey, lace-curtained dining room with a Victorian-era fireplace (not working), an ornate oak sideboard (used for floral and dessert displays), and wonderful French art nouveau posters on cream- and plum-colored walls. There's even good background music—usually jazz or classical. The menu changes daily. At a recent dinner appetizers ($3 to $5) included celeriac salad with apples, radishes, and poppy seeds, and a garlicky trout mousse with morels, asparagus, and green peppercorns. Among the entrees (mostly in the $9 to $12 range) were chicken in phyllo dough with apricots, walnuts, and scallions; quail with raspberry vinegar/garlic sauce; and bay scallops with pesto cream sauce. For dessert—a must here—a sinfully rich chocolate chestnut gâteau or chocolate espresso cheesecake are likely choices. A typical lunch menu (entrees $6 to $9) might offer a sandwich of smoked chicken breast with Boursin poivre on rye or a torta rustica —double-crusted Italian pie filled with sausage, tomatoes, peppers, onions, and cheese. Suzanne's features a wine bar that allows you to sample superb premium wines by the glass.

Open for lunch weekdays from 11:30 a.m. to 2:30 p.m., till 3 p.m. on Saturday; and for dinner Monday through Thursday from 6 to 10:30 p.m., till 11:30 p.m. on Friday and Saturday nights. After dinner (till 11 p.m. Monday to Thursday and till 1 a.m. on Friday and Saturday) and between lunch and dinner, drinks, wine bar offerings, and light fare are available.

INDIAN: Bombay Palace, 1835 K St. NW (tel. 331-0111), offering the Mughlai cookery of northern India, is the most upscale of Washington's Indian restaurants. No humble curry house this, it's the creation of restaurant "Moghul" Sant Chatwal, whose empire of elegant eateries includes Bombay Palaces in New York, London, New Delhi, Beverly Hills, and elsewhere. Chatwal is the kind of restaurateur who regularly hosts wine tastings and celebrity bashes. Everyone from Princess Elizabeth of Yugoslavia to Catherine Oxenberg (former Princess of Moldavia) has sampled his sublime samosas. Chatwal even catered meals for Indian Prime Minister Rajiv Gandhi and his wife when they visited the capital. The Palace's unique decor is strikingly attractive. Numerous arched shell-pink niches, used to display Indian religious and mythological sculptures, punctuate satin-smooth aqua walls and columns. Lit from behind, these niches create soft diffused lighting for the restaurant. Pink-linened tables and burgundy carpeting harmonize beautifully with this delicate color scheme, as do mauve banquettes and art deco chairs. Ragas played softly in the background further the mood. Service is notably polished and deft.

Throughout the day, your choice of appetizers ($3.75 to $4.75) includes vegetable samosas (crisp pastries stuffed with mildly spiced potatoes and peas), pakora (vegetable fritters), chooza pakora (chicken pieces marinated in yogurt, ginger, and garlic, and batter fried), and shammi kebab (subtly spiced minced lamb patties blended with egg, lentils, onions, nutmeg, and garlic). An assorted hors d'oeuvre platter ($7.25) obviates the decision-making process. There are also delicious soups like murgh shorba, made with chicken, garlic, ginger, cinnamon, cardamom, and other spices.

Tandoori specialties are featured (the restaurant has two clay ovens in operation at all times). Be sure to order one of the tandoor-baked breads, either a simple chewy and delicious nan ($1.75) or a more complex affair such as nan stuffed with chicken, nuts, and almonds ($2.75). With soup and an appetizer or salad, the latter could in itself comprise a meal. Our recommended entrees (most, but not all, under $10) include plumply juicy prawns or tangy chicken tandoori, gosht patiala (mildly spiced boneless beef or lamb cooked with potatoes, onions, ginger, and garlic), butter chicken (a sumptuous dish of chicken marinated in garlic, ginger, yogurt, vinegar, and other spices, and tandoor-baked with fresh tomatoes, butter, and cream), and the Palace nawabi biryani (long-grain rice flavored with saffron and 21 exotic spices, cooked with pieces of lamb, nuts, and egg). There are vegetable entrees as well; we like the tandoor-roasted eggplant, mashed and seasoned with herbs and roasted with sautéed onions. An order of raita—cool whipped yogurt with cucumber, tomatoes, potatoes, and mint—is a refreshing side dish. For dessert try the homemade mango ice cream.

During the week there are full lunches priced from $10.50: for example, a meal of lamb kebab; bread stuffed with onion, dry mango, and spices; salad; mixed vegetables cooked with nuts, mild spices, and cream; and rice pullao. On Saturday and Sunday lunch is an all-you-can-eat buffet ($9.50 per person), an excellent opportunity to sample a wide variety of dishes.

Open daily for lunch from noon to 2:45 p.m., for dinner Sunday through Thursday from 5:30 to 10 p.m., till 10:30 p.m. on Friday and Saturday nights. Reservations suggested.

INTERNATIONAL: Housed in a century-old former five-and-dime store, **Cities,** 2424 18th St. NW (tel. 328-7194), is a restaurant-cum-travelogue. Every six months, following a comprehensive research expedition by a chef/photographer/artist/owner/film-crew team, the restaurant is revamped to reflect the cuisine, character, and culture of a different city. The permanent features of the place are mottled gold columns, crumbling walls, black-lacquer chairs, white-linened tables, and a marbleized carpet. It's high-funk, war-torn chic, a New York import. On our last visit, when the featured city was Bangkok, vases were filled with large bird of paradise and bamboo arrangements; corrugated steel sheets overhead suggested Thai roofing; Greg Johnson's beautiful photographs of rickshaws and rice paddies lined the walls; Byron Peck's murals offered an artist's conception of Thailand; and sculptures, paper umbrellas, tapestries, fans, and other artifacts provided further evocation. The music always reflects the city under consideration, and waiters are attired in native dress or some facsimile thereof.

There's nothing funky, however, about the food. The kitchen, under the direction of Washington's premier chef, Le Pavillon's Yannick Cam (see first listing in this chapter), turns out thrilling interpretations of each city's cuisine (Istanbul and Rio preceded Bangkok). Turkish owner Sahir Erozan is a former Le Pavillon wine concierge. The city specialties are only a section of the menu; a less-frequently changing base of appetizers, entrees, and desserts (the latter from Le Pavillon) remain constant. This fare includes a wide-ranging selection: gourmet pizzas; pastas such as cold mustard tagliatelle with diced chicken and straw mushrooms; blinis topped with Sevruga caviar and crème fraîche; a salad of foie gras with artichoke; grilled salmon with garlic cream sauce; purée of turnip with prosciutto; even a New York strip steak. They're all exquisitely presented on white Limoges china. Thai selections include fried shrimp in a rich red curry made of tomatoes, coconut milk, coriander root, lemon grass, red chili, garlic, cumin, and Thai lime zest; chunky chicken sate in a delicate sauce of finely chopped peanuts, chili, lemon grass, coconut milk, and shallots on a marinated cucumber bed; and steamed perch with cucumber and curry. There's a small but expertly conceived wine and champagne list always enhanced by alcoholic beverages representing the city cuisine; premium wines are offered by the glass.

The menu offers grazing options, which means you can order many small portions, thus sampling a wide variety of dishes. Most full entrees range from about $12 to $18.50, but you can dine rather inexpensively on the mini portions. Don't pass up those Le Pavillon desserts like white chocolate mousse with hazelnut praline and banana bavarois with raspberry. After dinner, you might want to hang out at the open-air bar and check out the Adams Morgan scene. Or head upstairs to the dance club (details in Chapter VII).

Cities is open for dinner only, from 6 to 11:30 p.m. Monday through Thursday, till midnight on Friday and Saturday, and from 5 to 11 p.m. Sunday. The bar stays open till 2 a.m. weekdays, 3 a.m. weekends. Reservations essential.

ITALIAN: **Petitto's**, 2653 Connecticut Ave. NW, just across the street from the Woodley Park–Zoo Metro Station (tel. 667-5350), quotes Christopher Morley on the menu to the effect that "no man is lonely while eating spaghetti—it requires too much attention . . ." If you ask us, Morley misses the point. You won't be lonely, because you'll be blissed out eating fare as delicious as Petitto's (mostly the northern-style cuisine of Rome and Abruzzi, plus a few southern specialties). And your enjoyment will be further enhanced by lovely surroundings. There are three dining rooms in this converted turn-of-the-century town house, one (our favorite, upstairs) with its own working fireplace. Throughout, chocolate-brown walls (set off by neat white moldings and window frames) are hung with whimsical pasta-themed pen-and-ink drawings (for example, lovers at a romantic picnic in the woods; he's fantasizing about pasta). Seating in bentwood chairs at white linen-clothed tables sets a traditionally elegant tone, and soft, suffused lighting is provided by hanging lamps wrapped in creamy silk scarves. Operatic arias make for very appropriate background music. In good weather you can dine al fresco at umbrella tables on the street.

Petitto's is indeed simpático, but even if it was a hole in the wall, we'd eat here regularly. Seldom have we been disappointed. It's a great place to dine with a group in order to experience, via sharing, a more comprehensive variety of divine dishes. A shared pasta entree ($9 to $11; half portions also available) makes a marvelous appetizer course, perhaps falasche alla Pettito (homemade spinach and egg noodles tossed with mushrooms, prosciutto, and peas in a cream sauce) or penne all' Amatriciana (a ziti-like pasta with chunks of thickly sliced bacon and hot peppers in a lusty red sauce flavored with freshly grated Romano cheese). Then again there's a garlicky herbed linguine with a sufficiency of tender crabmeat, fabulous imported Italian olives, and mushrooms lightly flavored with lemon and fresh oregano; each of its subtle flavors comes through clearly, enhancing rather than obscuring the others. Spaghetti mixed with chunks of sautéed chicken breast, exotic mushrooms, and prosciutto in a sage/marjoram/rosemary-flavored butter wine sauce is also a winner. And the restaurant's fettuccine primavera tutto giardino —with seasoned vegetables and a lemon cream sauce—is so good the recipe has appeared in *Bon Appétit*. A salad course here is also a must. Light and refreshing is a harmonious arrangement of tomatoes (always bright red and delicious here; off-season they're imported from Holland or Mexico) and homemade mozzarella in an olive oil/basil dressing. But our favorite Petitto's salad is an exquisite affair of marinated squid and seafood with red peppers, onions, and black olives vinaigrette.

Nonpasta entrees ($12 to $16) change weekly, but always include excellent veal and fresh seafood dishes. On a recent visit we enjoyed plump jumbo shrimp grilled in garlic, oil, and fresh oregano; cacciucco—an array of shellfish (lobster, scallops, mussels, clams, and squid) served with linguine in a sauce of olive oil, garlic, and fresh tomatoes; and a filet of veal sautéed with fresh asparagus, tomato, scallions, and fresh rosemary. Entrees are served with flavorful al dente fresh vegetables and new potatoes prepared in various ways. We realize we're talking a lot of food here, but Petitto's is no place for moderation; loosen your belt and persevere. Breads—pan-fried in olive oil, flavored with garlic and parmesan, or toasted with tomato, parmesan, and basil—are famed house specialties, but you might forgo them in a good cause: leaving room for dessert. Enthusiastically recommended choices include zuppa inglese, a sponge cake layered with custard, real whipped cream, and fresh raspberries, saturated with Chambord liqueur; a superb tira misu (marscapone custard flavored with espresso over sponge cake, the entirety topped with powdered cocoa); the creamiest-ever orange cheesecake topped with fresh fruit; and the lightest of tortonis spiked with toasted almond slivers. A moderately priced and well-chosen list of Italian wines is augmented by a more recherché insert of costlier vintages (including French and California selections), and a few premium wines are available by the glass each night. At lunch, pasta, veal, and seafood entrees are in the $7 to $10 range.

Petitto's is open for lunch weekdays from 11:30 a.m. to 2:30 p.m., for dinner Monday to Saturday from 6 to 10:30 p.m. Reservations essential. If you have a large party (10 to 14 people), request the cozy private dining room.

Under the same auspices as the deluxe River Club (details above) is one of Georgetown's hottest restaurants, **Paolo's,** 1305 Wisconsin Ave. NW (tel. 333-7352). Restaurateur Paul Cohn is an virtuoso when it comes to creating a scene that crackles with excitement. "It's the closest thing to show business," he says. "You're on every night."

We never tire of the show at Paolo's. For one thing, the setting is *molto simpatico.* À la New York's trendiest new places, tables spill out onto the street from an open-air patio. The front room, with a stunning peach-hued Italian marble floor and black marble bar, centers on the warm glow of the pizza-oven fire. Red peppers, dried herbs, and strings of garlic are suspended above the wood-burning brick oven, which is fronted by a colorful display of pizza toppings —creamy white bowls filled with pine nuts, peppers, sausage, basil, sun-dried tomatoes, Italian cheese, etc. Here diners can watch the white-toqued chef preparing his luscious golden-crusted pies. The back room, richly paneled in cherrywood and agleam with copper mirrors, also centers on an open exhibition kitchen. Black Italian marble tables are adorned with fresh flowers, and, at night, candle lamps with frosted shades complement the subdued track lighting. Young, friendly, well-trained waiters and waitresses in Jackson Pollock splatter-motif aprons keep the mood relaxed, never formal or haughty. Taped classical music is played in the background.

On the front of Paolo's menu is the quote "Potrebbe ottenere la salute e tutto che desidere" (May you obtain all that you desire). A meal here is a good start.

Young chef Adam Ogza's made-from-scratch pizzas and pastas, fresh seafood dishes, and veal creations are scrumptious. He applies subtle nouvelle principles to traditional Italian fare, but don't worry —he doesn't skimp on portion size. A delightful surprise arrives as soon as you're seated—a bowl of tapenade (a Mediterranean spread of puréed olives, chickpeas, and roasted red peppers) along with a wooden cylinder of oven-fresh sesame-studded, chewy breadsticks made from pizza dough. You can dine lightly on a pizza ($7 to $9), running the gamut from smoked salmon to goat's cheese. The crunchy/chewy crust derives a soupçon of smoky savoriness from that wood-burning oven. Pastas ($8 to $16) include such temptations as quill-shaped penne pasta with prosciutto, red peppers, and marscapone cheese, tossed in a vodka rose sauce, or fresh ribbon noodles tossed with smoked salmon in a light sauce of garlic cream, topped with a sprinkling of fresh salmon caviar. Veal and seafood entrees ($15 to $19, less for chicken dishes) include medallions of veal served with strega-scented spinach and toasted pine nuts in fresh rosemary beurre blanc sauce and juicy jumbo shrimp scampi dusted with seasoned bread crumbs and served over fresh saffron-scented linguine. Wines, many available by the glass, are de riqueur with this food. And do check out the dessert tray laden with rich chocolate cakes, lemon-raspberry mousse cake with vanilla custard icing, and fresh raspberries with whipped cream in season.

Open Monday to Thursday and on Sunday from 11:30 to 2:30 a.m., Friday and Saturday till 3:30 a.m.; the whole menu is served until midnight, pizzas till 1 a.m., and the bar is lively till closing time. At Sunday brunch a classical ensemble entertains and special items (waffles, omelets, and more) are added to the menu. Paolo's takes no reservations, so plan a pre-dinner drink in the bar.

MOROCCAN: As intoxicating as an opium dream is **Dar Es Salam**, 3056 M St. NW (tel. 342-1925), a totally authentic Moroccan restaurant. This is not the place to grab a quick bite or take the kids; it's a place for lingering over long and romantic dinners or convivial late-night feasts with a group of good friends. The setting is stunningly exotic—the result of a year's work by 20 highly skilled Moroccan craftsmen who carved the filigreed rose plaster ceilings, studded the walls with handmade enameled terracotta mosaics, and created an enigmatic weave of ancient designs and patterns throughout the three dining rooms. Berber, Fez, and Rabat rugs, Moroccan antiques, low marquetry tables inlaid with mother-of-pearl, brass samovars, straw bread baskets, ceramic tajines, and other imported artifacts further enhance the setting. The front room has an alcoved fountain, another has a working fireplace, the third a stained-glass dome overhead. All are softly lit by candles, lamps, and sconces, and offer seating on low cushioned jade or plum velvet divans.

French owner Michel Sellier did more than just create an exquisite environment; he also assembled a staff of Moroccan cuisiniers headed by Mohamed Ougnou, who cooks for the Moroccan ambassador here. Meals are prix fixe, beginning at $18.95 for an appetizer, main course, and dessert, but we suggest you splurge on the $27.95 *diffa* (banquet). Moroccan culinary expert Paula Wolfert describes a true Moroccan diffa as consisting of dish after piquant dish until one achieves a state of *shaban,* or total satisfaction.

The diffa begins with a hand-washing ceremony, since everything is eaten with one's hands or scooped up in hunks of delicious homemade bread. (You can get silverware on request, but it does interfere with the total experience.) The first course is an assortment of raw and cooked marinated vegetable salads—sweet roasted red peppers, eggplant purées, shredded carrots with parsley and lemon, sweet-pea hummus, raisin-onion chutney, and more. Next comes the heavenly b'stilla—a feathery light pastry stuffed with shredded squab in onion sauce, layers of crushed almonds, raisins, eggs, and parsley, the top dusted with powdered sugar and cinnamon. A tajine (or stew) follows—perhaps chicken with pickled lemon and olives in a thick gravy flavored with garlic, ginger, saffron, turmeric, onion, and coriander; or a sweet-sour tender steamed lamb with prunes and sesame seeds. Eat slowly—and a bit sparingly. We find lots of wine helps pace the courses. Sometime during your meal the lights will dim and a belly dancer will appear, an entrancing interlude. Then comes the fluffy couscous, steamed over aromatic broth and garnished with big chunks of vegetables; flavor it by mixing hot red pepper harissa sauce into the broth. The serving of mint tea (prepared from scratch) is another ceremony, the tea poured dramatically from a height of several feet. And yes, there is dessert, too, but before you even begin your meal request that it be a dessert b'stilla, a specialty here but one that is not automatically served. The paper-thin pastry is layered with ground almonds, whipped cream, and honey in an orange-blossom sauce, once again topped with powdered sugar and cinnamon. After this paradisiacal finale your hands are again washed with rosewater. Now adjourn downstairs to the nightclub where a belly dancer undulates to the wailing strains and drum rhythms of a North African trio.

Dar Es Salam is open nightly from 5:30 p.m. to whenever the

downstairs club closes. The show begins at 10 p.m.; consider dining late so you won't have to wait around for it to start. Reservations accepted.

SEAFOOD: We love the C & O Canal, so when we discovered **The Sea Catch,** 1054 31st St. NW, just below M St. (tel. 337-8855), a stunning restaurant with canalside seating, we were thrilled. Outside on the long awninged wooden deck, mulberry and ailanthus trees form a verdant archway over the canal. The marble-topped tables are romantically candlelit in the evening; by day, you can watch the ducks, punters, and mule-drawn barges glide by while you dine. But don't pass up Sea Catch on days that are less than ideal for al fresco meals; the restaurant, housed in a historic Georgetown stone-and-brick building, is as beautiful within as without. There's a white Carrara marble raw bar adorned with exquisite floral and food displays and backed by a rustic stone wall; a white tile floor enhances the pristine ambience. An actual liquor-dispensing bar, conceived as a deluxe brasserie, adjoins, with seating in comfortable leather-upholstered banquettes under a low inn-style beamed ceiling; large windows overlook the canal, and there's a working fireplace. The main dining room, like other areas, has rough-hewn walls made of fieldstone dug from Georgetown quarries. The ceiling overhead, of rift-sawn white oak, replicates the intricate ceiling of the old Commodore Hotel in New York City; the flooring, equally notable, is random-plank white oak. This room, too, has a working fireplace. Excellent taped musical selections, ranging from classical to jazz, from Beatles to Sinatra, provide a fine acoustical background.

Chef Jacques Blanc, a nationally acclaimed Washington-based restaurateur (Le Provençal), oversees the kitchen, along with the former head pastry chef of the Paris Inter-Continental Hotel, Dominique A. Leborgne. The results are *formidable*.

Dinner here might begin with appetizers such as mussels provencale (brushed with herbed breadcrumbs and baked in garlic butter), a smoked fish platter, or gravlax with dill sauce ($5 to $8). Cold buffet entrees allow light dining options—perhaps couscous salad with tomatoes, cucumbers, and shrimp, or cold poached salmon in a sauce verde. More substantial entrees range from monkfish steak au poivre to crab cakes with linguine and lobster sauce ($11 to $17). And you can always opt for live lobster from the tank prepared to your specifications. The menu changes daily to reflect market specialties. Lunch entrees are about $1 to $2 less across the board.

Open daily from noon to 3 p.m. for lunch, later for drinks and raw-bar offerings. It's a great place for late-night snacking. Reservations suggested.

STEAK AND SEAFOOD: Blackie's House of Beef, 1217 22nd St. NW, at M Street (tel. 333-1100), was started by Ulysses

"Blackie" Auger (he has black hair and his World War II army buddies couldn't pronounce Ulysses), who finessed a small café into one of Washington's most successful restaurants—and a real estate empire as well. If you're out drinking and dancing at night, Blackie probably owns the place. The House of Beef comprises a warren of five attractive rooms, warm and inviting with Tiffany-style lamps, fireplaces, lush greenery, and opulent Victoriana evoking turn-of-the-century New Orleans. Since it shares the premises with Déjà Vu, one of D.C.'s top discos, it's the perfect place for a dinner-and-dancing night on the town.

The food—like the aged U.S. prime rib served with a big baked potato, tossed salad, bleu cheese and crackers, and a basket of breads and butter for under $12—is tops for the money. Generous portions have made this restaurant a favorite for over three decades. Other entrees, served with the above-described accompaniments, include roasted baby spareribs with barbecue sauce ($12.75), broiled sirloin or filet mignon ($17.25), and, for non-beef eaters, broiled baby African rock lobster tails in drawn butter ($21.50) and golden-fried Atlantic deep-sea scallops with tartar sauce ($11.75). A child's platter with ground sirloin is just $6.50. For dessert there's homemade cheesecake or pecan pie, among other choices. At lunch Blackie's serves hearty sandwiches like hot roast beef with mashed potatoes and kosher pastrami on rye with savory sauce, lettuce, tomato, melted cheese, and pickle; salads; half-pound burgers on onion roll with french fries; and platters, such as a sirloin club steak with whipped potatoes and salad, for $12.75.

Open Monday to Saturday from 11 a.m. to 2:30 p.m. for lunch and 4 to 10:30 p.m. for dinner. Sunday for dinner only from 4 to 10:30 p.m. Reservations advised.

MEDIUM-PRICED RESTAURANTS

The following selections are the restaurants most of us prefer for everyday dining. They all offer excellent meals at reasonable prices, in many cases with a fair amount of ambience thrown in for good measure. Many ethnic eateries are included in this category.

AFGHAN: When an ambassador from Afghanistan returned to his homeland, his chef stayed behind to open **Bamiyan Afghan,** 3320 M St. NW (tel. 338-1896). That was over a decade ago, and today that chef's son, Kamal Morrad, has taken over the restaurant's kitchen. We'd say his father trained him well. The food here is both interesting—because it consists largely of dishes new to most Americans—and delicious. Bamiyan Afghan is also quite an attractive place, with its dining room upstairs and a bar/lounge on the street level. White walls are hung with Afghan rugs and a large oil painting depicting *booz keshi,* the wild national game played on horseback and utilizing a dead goat for the ball! Tablecloths of cheerful Afghanistani geometric prints, hanging plants, curtained windows, and candles in glass holders combine to create a cozy atmosphere, which is enhanced by taped Afghan music.

The food is spicy but not hot unless you request it that way. A multicourse dinner for two, priced at $35, includes a demi-carafe of wine; noodle and vegetable soup with yogurt and ground beef; deep-fried pastries stuffed with ground beef, chick peas, and parsley; chicken pieces marinated in herbs and spices on a skewer; scallion-filled dumplings topped with yogurt and meat sauce; rice; salad; Afghan bread; desserts of baklava and another fried pastry dusted with sugar, cardamom, and pistachio nuts; and coffee or Afghan tea. You can also order à la carte; most entrees are in the $10 to $14 range.

Open Monday to Saturday for dinner only from 5:30 to 11 p.m. Reservations suggested.

AMERICAN: The **American Café,** 1211 Wisconsin Ave., between M and N Streets NW (tel. 944-9464), offers chic fare (croissant sandwiches, pesto, pasta, Häagen-Dazs, etc.) in a trendy '80s setting. The interior is modernistic with mirrors and wooden dividers in odd geometric shapes, gallery lighting, brass railings, and pink neon tubing and stars. Two back rooms have terracotta tile floors and glossy red enamel hanging lamps. It's a casual hangout offering light, reasonably priced fare, all of it prepared fresh daily on the premises.

Huge sandwiches ($5 to $6) include a croissant stuffed with chicken, crunchy water chestnuts, toasted almonds, and tarragon mayonnaise served with dilled cucumber salad, and the New York Club, a triple-decker of smoked turkey, ham, tomato, and bacon on whole-wheat with rémoulade dressing and a side order of caraway-studded coleslaw. Should you prefer hot fare, there's a bowl of rich beef chili topped with sour cream for $5. Or order the daily specials ($7.50 to $11) which might include mesquite-grilled chicken breast with basil butter, rice, vegetables, and Cajun cornbread, or a mushroom-and-pesto lasagne with herbed cheeses layered between fresh spinach noodles. There are also "desserts of the day," like chocolate cake with peanut butter filling and rich fudge frosting, not to mention an always-available hot fudge sundae made with Häagen-Dazs and topped with real whipped cream and a chocolate chip cookie. Delicious specialty drinks are available from the bar—everything from frozen daiquiris to hot buttered rum.

Open Monday to Thursday from 11 a.m. to 3 a.m., on Friday and Saturday to 4 a.m., on Sunday from 10:30 a.m. to 1 a.m. A carry-out operation is located upstairs, and there's another American Cafe at 227 Massachusetts Ave. NE (tel. 547-8500), plus a third at National Place, 1331 Pennsylvania Ave. NW (tel. 626-0770).

Arrive pre- or post-peak lunch and dinner hours to avoid long lines (they don't take reservations) at the very popular **Houston's,**

1065 Wisconsin Ave. NW, just below M Street (tel. 338-7760), where the barbecued ribs are tender and juicy enough to eat with a knife and fork, the large and delicious burgers are made from fresh-ground chuck, and the soups, salads, and desserts are prepared from scratch. A very simpático ambience further enhances this restaurant's appeal. Exposed brick walls are hung with framed mirrors, an old American flag, and flickering gaslight sconces. Overhead are rough-hewn wood rafters. Most seating is in roomy red leather booths at oak tables, lighting—from dark-green enamel lamps with amber bulbs—is subdued, and the background music is mellow rock and country. An area in the back has many large plants growing under a skylight ceiling.

The same menu is offered throughout the day. A hickory-grilled cheeseburger ($6.75) is served with a choice of iron skillet beans, potato salad, fresh-cut thick fries, or coleslaw. Choose two of these side dishes with an order of barbecued chicken breast ($7.95) or barbecued ribs ($13.75). If you're in the mood for something heartier, prime rib with a baked potato and house salad is also $13.75; something lighter might be a club salad—chopped lightly fried chicken on greens with diced avocado, crumbled bacon, tomatoes, croutons, and chopped egg in a vinaigrette dressing, served with cheese toast ($7.25). There's a full bar serving up drinks made with premium liquor brands only (Dewar's scotch, Bacardi rum, etc.) and fresh-squeezed juices. And for dessert an immense chewy brownie topped with vanilla ice cream and Kahlúa is hard to surpass.

Open Sunday to Wednesday from 11:30 a.m. to 11 p.m., on Thursday to midnight, on Friday and Saturday to 1 a.m.

Stevan's, on Capitol Hill at 231 Pennsylvania Ave. SE (tel. 543-8337), is a casual and friendly operation serving up inexpensive, fresh-cooked fare in simpático surroundings. Its attractions include a lively bar—above which sports events are aired, via satellite dish, on a big-screen TV—and good music. Stevan's decor is pleasantly rustic, with halophane lamps suspended from a yellow-pine ceiling, plank oak floors, exposed brick and mirrored walls, and planters of philodendrons. An additional dining room downstairs, a bistro-like setting, is used at lunch and other times when there's an overflow crowd.

You'll get some of the best burgers in town here, perhaps topped with bleu cheese and bacon ($5.95); they're served with delicious homemade onion rings or thick fresh-cut french fries. There's a wide selection of overstuffed deli sandwiches ($5 to $7)—everything from pastrami on rye to a hefty Reuben, club, or french dip. You might opt for a crabcake platter ($8.75) or a fried oyster platter ($8.25), both served with fries and slaw. Salads and chili are listed too, and the menu is always augmented by daily specials, like grilled salmon with lemon butter, rice, and vegetables ($11.95). For dessert, Stevan's serves up generous slabs of apple or chocolate mousse pie; the carrot cake is also notable. A special menu is offered at Saturday and Sunday brunch (11 a.m. to 3:30 p.m.), adding eggs Benedict, steak and eggs, fresh-squeezed orange juice, and fresh fruit-filled pancakes to your burger/sandwich/salad choices.

Hours are Monday to Thursday from 11:30 a.m. to midnight, on Friday to 2 a.m., on Saturday from 11 a.m. to 2 a.m., and on Sunday from 11 a.m. to midnight. The kitchen closes an hour before the bar.

Kramerbooks & Afterwords, a café, 1517 Connecticut Ave. NW, between Q Street and Dupont Circle (tel. 387-1462), is a schmoozy bookstore-cum-café of the San Francisco Beat-era genre. Well, it's not really that Bohemian, but for Washington. . . . There's cozy seating indoors at butcher-block tables behind the bookstore, at the bar, upstairs on a balcony, and also out on 19th Street under a two-story glassed-in solarium or at outdoor tables. Come by alone to while away a few hours with a good book; the well-read employees feature their favorite literature at the counter and will be happy to discuss their choices. This is also a popular post-movie haunt and a great place to discuss your love life with a friend over espresso and carrot cake on a sunny Sunday afternoon.

Of course al fresco breakfasts are also very nice. The café opens early, serving toasted bagels and cream cheese with Nova, tomato, and onion ($6.50), quiche Lorraine with a croissant ($6.25), or a fresh fruit and cheese platter served with bread and butter ($7.25), any of the above served with fresh-squeezed orange juice and coffee or tea. At Sunday brunch—served all day—you also get a complimentary Bloody Mary or glass of champagne. Entrees—same at lunch and dinner—are mostly in the $8 to $10 range and include fettuccine with tasso ham, sweet peppers, scallops, and shrimp sautéed with cream and Cajun-spiced butter; boneless breast of chicken stuffed with prosciutto and mozzarella, and tomato; and pan-seared prime tenderloin of beef finished with shallot butter and served with oven-roasted potatoes, seasonal greens, and a vegetable. Additionally, you might opt for a roast beef sandwich with horseradish mousse on French bread, served with a charcuterie salad ($5.75); a platter for two of fresh fruit and cheeses—triple-cream brie, English Stilton, gourmandise with walnuts, and white cheddar—served with bread and butter ($7.75); margaritas, served with nachos ($15 for a large pitcherful); luscious chocolate coconut sour-cream blackout cake; or an I'll-jog-tomorrow ice cream drink like the Rumrunner—two scoops of Sedutto vanilla, dark rum, and 151 rum ($4.25). The Afterwords accommodates every food mood. Meats are roasted fresh on the premises, fish are also fresh, and a selection of premium wines is offered by the glass.

Open Sunday to Thursday from 8 a.m. to 1 a.m. and around the clock from Friday at 8 a.m. through Sunday at 1 a.m. On Friday and Saturday nights there's live entertainment—piano, folk, jazz, or blues.

CONTINENTAL: The **Café Splendide,** in the heart of Dupont Circle at 1521 Connecticut Ave. NW (tel. 328-1503), is the homey domain of Austrian brothers Max and Walter Evangelisti. Kitschy paintings by Hans Rudolf Richter (Austria's answer to Norman Rockwell) adorn walls also decorated with trompe l'oeil red-and-white-checked gingham-curtained windows. There are vases of colorful cloth flowers on every table and baskets of cloth ferns overhead, and sun streams into the front room through a plant-filled bay window. Out back (entrance on 19th Street) are tables under a red awning neatly bordered by planters of geraniums, petunias, and other window-box blooms. In good weather this street café is always mobbed.

These Austrian brothers serve up hearty portions of the kind of food their momma used to make—entrees ($7.50 to $8.50) like paprika schnitzel in a sauce of onions, green peppers, mushrooms, and pimientos; broiled lamb chops with thyme and garlic; beef Stroganoff; and sautéed calves' liver with bacon and onions. A bit fancier: a classic duck à l'orange. All of the above are served with a fresh vegetable and a choice of rice, buttered noodles, or hash browns. In the $5 to $6 range, you might also opt for an order of broiled knackwurst served with homemade potato salad; a sandwich on homemade bread stuffed with ham, salami, Swiss cheese, tomato, pepperoni, and sauerkraut; an omelet with your choice of three toppings; or delicious homemade chicken salad. A bowl of French onion or Hungarian goulash soup also merits consideration. And in season, the Splendide does a beautiful job with soft-shell crab amandine. You'll no doubt have noticed a glass display case in the back of the restaurant filled with scrumptious homemade pastries. Order the crème brûlée: it's ambrosial.

You can come by off-hours, in the afternoon-tea spirit, to enjoy a dessert and beverage. The Splendide is open for breakfast too—fresh-from-the-oven cheese, poppyseed, apple, cherry, blueberry, or hazelnut danish; apple or cheese strudel topped with powdered sugar; or croissants with your morning coffee and fresh-squeezed orange or grapefruit juice. Want something more substantial? Order the "Scotch woodcock"—scrambled eggs on a muffin with capers and anchovies ($2.95). Both French and California wines are offered at the Splendide, not to mention daiquiris, piña coladas, ice cream/liqueur drinks, lemonade, cappuccino and espresso, apéritifs and dessert wines, imported beers, and hot apple cider with rum.

Open Tuesday to Thursday from 9 a.m. to 11:30 p.m., on Friday to 1:30 a.m., on Saturday from 8 a.m. to 1:30 a.m., and on Sunday from 8 a.m. to 11:30 p.m. Reservations suggested. No credit cards.

ETHIOPIAN: A large Ethiopian clientele—close to 50%—attests to the authenticity of cuisine at the **Red Sea,** 2463 18th St. NW, near Columbia Road (tel. 483-5000). Ditto the African selections on the jukebox. The main floor is liveliest, with many folks commingling at the bar, and on most Friday and Saturday nights after 10 p.m., live entertainment (Ethiopian singers and musicians). It's a cozy and casual place, with red-clothed tables, travel posters adorning a mirrored wall, and red curtains in the window. Upstairs, away from the bar, things are a bit less hectic and the robin's-egg-green walls are covered with baskets, artifacts, Ethiopian paintings on goatskin, and more travel posters.

The menu blurb expresses the hope that "you will find this a truly different and stimulating dining experience," and unless items like *zilzil wat* are staples of your diet, we're sure you will. For one thing, this spicy fare is eaten *sans* utensils; a pancake-like bread called injera is used to scoop up the food. Items listed as *wat* come seasoned with berbere sauce and are especially hot and spicy; *alechas* are more delicately flavored. If it's your first experience with Ethiopian food, order one of the Red Sea samplers ($7.50), which might contain doro wat (a hot chicken dish); yebeg alecha (lamb cooked in herb butter, onions, and green peppers); the above-mentioned zilzil wat (beef strips simmered in hot berbere sauce); bulghur wheat blended with herbed butter and spices, ground roasted yellow split peas simmered in red pepper sauce and flavored with tangy spices, spicy chopped greens cooked in herbed butter with onions and peppers, and cabbage sautéed with onions, peppers, and turmeric. The sampler is, in itself, almost an ample meal for two, but you might supplement it with a scrumptious injera sandwich filled with spiced greens, onions, peppers, and puréed yellow split peas ($2.75) or a small salad of black olives, onions, peppers, tomatoes, chicken, and egg on lettuce ($2.75). Wine and a wide selection of international beers are available, as are all drinks, including tej, an Ethiopian honey-mead wine.

Open daily from 11:30 a.m. to 2 a.m., till 3 a.m. on Friday and Saturday nights. Reservations suggested, especially on weekends.

FRENCH: La Ruche, 1039 31st St. NW, a block below M Street (tel. 965-2684), is a pretty little plant-filled restaurant with cushioned wicker-seated chairs, flower-bedecked tables (candlelit at night), and white walls adorned with framed art posters and baskets. The French countryside ambience is furthered by an outdoor courtyard café with Perrier umbrella tables amid lots of plants.

Inside, your eye is likely to be caught by the pastry case filled with exquisite fresh-baked desserts ($2.85 to $3.75)—banana tart with layers of custard and bittersweet chocolate, gâteau amande chocolat with layers of meringue and whipped cream, a classic tarte aux pommes, etc. Many people take an afternoon break from Georgetown rambles just for dessert and coffee here. Throughout the day menu offerings include a hearty potage parisien, fresh chopped leeks, potatoes, and cream ($2.95); salade niçoise ($6.25); a wedge of brie with apple and French bread ($4.50); croque monsieur, toasted French bread with ham and cheese ($5.50); quiche with a vegetable ($5.95); and escargots aux champignons ($5.95) —all the traditional specialties of a Paris brasserie. In addition, there are daily "spéciaux de chef Jean-Claude," which might include chicken breast in cream sauce and mussels in tomato and garlic sauce at lunch (prices are $5 to $8), rainbow trout amandine and filet mignon with green peppercorn sauce at dinner ($10.50 to $13.50). A carafe of house wine with your meal is $5.95 (domestic) or $6.95 (imported).

Open Monday to Thursday from 11:30 a.m. to midnight, on Friday and Saturday to 2 a.m., on Sunday to 11 p.m. Reservations suggested. A fabulous $8.95 prix fixe brunch—a mimosa, eggs Benedict, coffee, and pastry—is served weekends from 10 a.m. to 3 p.m.

One of our favorite Georgetown restaurants is the charming **Bistro Français,** 3124–28 M St. NW (tel. 338-3830), the interior of which does indeed capture the air of excitement we associate with Parisian bistros. Wainscotted walls are hung with mahogany-framed mirrors and French period posters from World Wars I and II. Floors are terracotta tile or bare oak, seating areas (of brown-leather banquettes) are defined by wrought-iron and brass railings, ceilings are ornate pressed copper, and etched- and stained-glass panels add to the cozy clutter. White-linened tables, adorned with fresh flowers and lit by candles in cut-glass holders, strike an elegant note.

The Bistro is actually a two-part affair, half of it a casual café, the other half a more serious dining room.

Depending where you sit, you have different menus to deal with, though the offerings are very similar. In either section, a good bet on weekdays from 5 to 7 p.m. is the Early Bird Special, offered once again from 10:30 p.m. to midnight. For $13.95 it includes a glass of house wine, soup du jour (perhaps cream of vegetable) or an appetizer like mussels niçoise, an entree (such as fresh softshell crab amandine or Moroccan couscous with lamb, chicken, sausage, meatballs, and vegetables), and a selection from the pastry cart. A similar menu is offered weekdays at lunch for $9.95. A la carte listings, also on both sides, include a selection of traditional French appetizers ($4.50 to $6.50) such as a plate of crudités, a seafood terrine with horseradish sauce, escargots with vegetables and garlic butter, and sherried chicken liver pâté. There are delicious salads, a classic French onion soup, and entrees ($11.50 to $15) such as poulet rôti with tarragon, fresh duck breast with apples and honey, veal chop with fresh mushrooms in cream sauce, and coquilles St.-Jacques with ginger and red-pepper sauce. Desserts also are the Paris café standbys—chocolate mousse, crème caramel, and pâtisseries maison—unless you want to get fancy and order a pêche Melba. Numerous daily specials supplement the menu, as does an extensive, mostly French, wine list. Several selections from the latter are offered by the glass each day. Liqueurs, fancy drinks made with them, brandies, cognacs, and dessert wines are additionally featured. At lunch I love the tropical salad of avocado, artichoke, and hearts of palm ($4.95), a satisfying meal in itself with French bread, a glass of white wine, a raspberry tarte, and espresso. At lunch throughout, and at any time in the café, you can also opt for a sandwich on French bread, like turkey, bacon, tomato, and mayonnaise. Everything is just delicious; it's hard to believe that prices are not considerably loftier.

Open Sunday to Thursday from 11 a.m. to 3 a.m., on Friday and Saturday till 4 a.m. Reservations suggested.

Au Pied de Cochon, 1335 Wisconsin Ave. NW, just below O Street (tel. 333-5440), like an actual Paris café/brasserie, is comfortable and unpretentious. The high-ceilinged interior is dimly lit, the walls aclutter with pottery, World War II photos, and copper pots. A whimsical Gallic mural of a pig being led to slaughter by chefs graces the back wall and is reproduced on the menus. Adjoining the main room is a yellow-brick-walled glass-enclosed café under an awning with bentwood chairs at marble-topped tables—a setting conducive to long Paris-style afternoons over pâtisseries and espresso.

Joggers and Georgetown students drift in for early breakfast—fresh-baked croissants ($1.25) or heartier fare such as scrambled eggs and bacon with delicious pommes frites ($4.25). Later in the day you might order an omelet fines herbes with pommes frites and ratatouille ($5.50), a salade niçoise ($6.25), onion soup au gratin ($3.95), a classic quiche Lorraine or chicken- and mushroom-filled crêpe served with ratatouille and pommes frites ($6.50), steamed lobster (a great bargain at just $10.95), or roast duck à l'orange ($8.95). Traditional café desserts include crème caramel and chocolate mousse. A glass of wine with your meal is $2.25.

Open 24 hours a day, Au Pied de Cochon is the perfect post-movie or post-party destination.

ITALIAN: Roger and Byron Petitto, original owners of the highly acclaimed and more upscale Petitto's (details above), launched an exciting new venture in 1985, the moderately priced **Café Petitto,** 1724 Connecticut Ave. NW (tel. 462-8771). It lures diners inside with an exquisite antipasto display in the front window—about 50 items including stringbean and fava bean salads, rice salads, marinated eggplant, artichokes, marinated mushrooms, snow peas with oil-cured olives, creamy egg salad, stuffed grape leaves, cold fried eggplant, pasta salads, escarole and pancetta (Italian bacon), homemade potato salad, tuna/tomato/onion salad vinaigrette, rice/peas/pepper salad, and much more. It's always changing, always fabulous, and you can sample as much as you can stack on a plate for $6.25. We do wish those plates were a trifle bigger. Still, it's a great buy. Then there are the scrumptious Calabrian pizzas, on flavorful bready dough that is lightly fried in olive oil before toppings are added and the entirety grilled. For $6.75 you'll get a pizza ample for two with Italian plum tomatoes, mozzarella, and fresh basil (fresh herbs, also oregano, sage, mint, rosemary, parsley, and dill, are used in all dishes here). Optional additions, priced from $1.35 to $2.75, include over 30 choices, among them hot sausage, pancetta, artichoke hearts, whole black olives, capers, sun-dried tomatoes, eggplant, roasted peppers, mussels, baby clams, and smoked mozzarella. All the more usual toppings are also available. A third menu category is hoagies—sandwiches on hard rolls with fillings like grilled chicken breast, fresh marinated tomatoes, basil, and olive oil ($5.25 to $6.95). Hoagies are served with roasted potatoes and greenbean salad. An order of "slats"—toasted garlic bread, baked with fresh marinated tomatoes, basil, and olive oil ($2.75)—is most recommendable. Ditto the chocolate amaretto cheesecake for dessert. Daily specials always include great pasta dishes. Italian wines are reasonably priced and available by the glass.

The setting is pleasant but unpretentious. Café Petitto has a black-and-white checkerboard floor, bare wood tables, and pine wainscotted cream stucco walls hung with a veritable Petitto family photo album—mom, dad, brother Tony at nine months, among others.

Open daily from 11:30 a.m. to midnight. No reservations. Arrive off-hours to avoid lines.

MIDDLE EASTERN: Winner year after year of *Washingtonian* magazine's "most romantic restaurant" award, the **Iron Gate Inn,** 1734 N St. NW (tel. 466-7029), is housed in the converted stable of Spanish and Indian War General Nelson A. Miles. The old horse stalls make for marvelous secluded booths. In winter it's the coziest place in town: a big fire always blazes in the immense brick fireplace, and the smell of burning wood is as alluring as the aromas of spicy dishes emerging from the kitchen. Framed equestrian prints line rustic dark-wood walls, and low lighting from amber lamps and flickering candles is flattering to all. There's additional seating up in the old hayloft. When the weather gets warm, however, you can dine beneath a grape arbor and a magnolia tree in a brick-walled gar-

den or at tables set along the cobbled carriage entranceway. This
outdoor eating area is the loveliest in Washington.

The Saah family, owners and chefs, boast a distinguished culinary background. They supervised kitchens for former King Saud of
Arabia, once catered a dinner consisting of an entire roast lamb
stuffed with rice and nuts for King Hussein, and are often sum-
moned to the White House to cook for visiting Arab dignitaries.

Begin your dinner with a few shared appetizers ($3.25 to
$4.25), perhaps baba ghanouj (puréed eggplant), hummus (puréed
chick peas), and stuffed grape leaves, all served with hot pita bread.
Pita also accompanies entrees ($8.50 to $13.95, but mostly $10 or
under) such as roast leg of lamb with pine nuts and rice, roast chick-
en sautéed with tomatoes and onions, and baked eggplant stuffed
with ground lamb and toasted pine nuts in tomato sauce. Mrs. Saah
makes exquisite homemade baklava and bread pudding for dessert,
either of which, ideally, should be enjoyed with rich Turkish coffee.
At lunch, weekday specials such as lamb curry made with fresh fruits
and vegetables are $7.50, and a $7.95 combination platter lets you
sample stuffed grape leaves, lamb meatballs in tomato sauce, baked
stuffed eggplant, stuffed squash, and stuffed cabbage.

Open daily from 11:30 a.m. to 10 p.m. Reservations advised.

Mama Ayesha "sits in her corner booth holding court," said
the *Washington Star*, "every bit as haughty as the Queen of Sheba."
On hand nightly to supervise the proceedings at her **Calvert Restaurant**, 1967 Calvert St. NW, just off 20th Street (tel. 232-5431),
this venerable Mama won't tell her age, but nephew Abdallah, the
Calvert's manager, swears she's in her 90s. Born in Palestine, Mama
emigrated to the U.S. in 1950 and started out as a cook in the Syrian
embassy. In 1958 she opened the Calvert and, by the force of her
personality and the high quality of her Middle Eastern cuisine, attracted and kept a loyal clientele. You'll see senators and
congresspeople here, people like reporter Helen Thomas, *Washington Post* reporters, Adams Morgan hippies, college kids, Arabs, and
maybe even the Israeli ambassador. The ambience is neighborhood
tavern with Arab music. Cheap wood paneling and flocked gold
wallpaper bear such adornments as made-for-the-tourist-market
Arab carpets. The front room has burgundy-leather booths with
jukeboxes at every table, diner style. The tacky atmosphere is part of
the Calvert's cachet. It's a "find" that everyone knows about. You
come because of Mama and the yummy homemade dishes her extended family (a host of nephews and cousins work in the place)
whip up in the kitchen. In summer, family members also grow produce (okra, parsley, tomatoes, squash, peppers, eggplant, etc.) for
the restaurant at Mama's 227-acre farm in Leesburg, Virginia.

Lunch or dinner (the same menu is offered all day) might begin
with an order of baba ghanouj ($2.25), hummus ($2.25), or Syrian

cheese and olives ($3.50). For an entree, try couscous with lamb, onions, carrots, and chick peas served with salad ($6.50); stuffed with vine leaves cooked with tomatoes and lemon juice, served with yogurt ($6.25); or perhaps half a fried eggplant topped with ground meat and pine nuts, cooked in tomato sauce, and served with special rice and salad ($6.75). If you can't decide, and Allah only knows, it's difficult, a combination dinner is $9.50. Leave room for home-made baklava and rich Turkish coffee for dessert.

Open Sunday to Thursday from 11:30 a.m. to 11 p.m., on Friday and Saturday till midnight.

BUDGET RESTAURANTS

Washington is filled with low-level government workers and impecunious students, and there are plenty of restaurants catering to their limited budgets. Actually, we often patronize those listed below for reasons other than monetary—the food is great or they're comfortable places to hang out. Most of the listings in the upcoming category, "Restaurants at Sightseeing Attractions," are also low priced.

Le Souperb/la Salade, 1221 Connecticut Ave. NW (tel. 347-7600), specializes in hearty homemade soups and stews (though that's not the half of it). It offers fresh, homemade fare at low prices and in a cheerful setting. White enamel lamps are suspended from a high ceiling that is obscured by large pipes festively painted in glossy red, white, and yellow. And the exposed brick walls are hung with framed art posters and David Levine caricatures of everyone from Proust to LBJ. Fresh flowers adorn every table.

Come by for breakfast and sample homemade bagels with eggs and bacon ($1.35) or go continental with fresh-from-the-oven sour cream coffee cake and coffee ($2). A glass of fresh-squeezed orange juice is $1.35. At lunch chef Dominique Jean Philip prepares onion soup and chili plus several additional soups (perhaps cream of broccoli with cheddar cheese, chicken noodle à la yenta, a matzoh ball, and navy bean à la Congress) and stews (pot au feu made with chicken, beef, carrots, potatoes); and a matzoh ball; chicken cacciatore; or fettuccine seafood. His repertoire is vast. A bowl of soup is $2.30 small, $3.50 large; stews are $2.85 and $4.05. With either soup or stew you get unlimited fresh-baked breads and butter—bagels, cornbread, rye, sourdough, and pumpernickel. Still hungry? Help yourself to salad bar offerings ($3 per pound). Other specialties include Le Souperb's subs in a baked potato ($2.29), and hefty sandwiches (roast beef or turkey cooked on the premises, $3.95). A glass of wine with your meal is $2.25.

Open weekdays from 7 a.m. to 4 p.m. Service is cafeteria-style. No credit cards.

Reeves, 1209 F St. NW (tel. 347-3781), is a century-old Washington landmark where the motherly waitresses have been on hand for decades and the high-quality, low-priced food is always excellent. Though inexpensive, Reeves has a certain cachet; it was a frequent lunchtime haunt of Lady Bird Johnson during her many years in Washington, and Helen Hayes calls it her favorite D.C. restaurant. Sad to say, a devastating fire ravaged the 1880s interior in 1984. However, owners George and Henry Abraham have lovingly restored it, retaining as much of the vintage ambience as possible. Comfortable brown-leather booths are lit by turn-of-the-century-style globe lamps, the original long central cherrywood counter/bar with stools has been replaced by an oak facsimile, the exposed brick walls have new oak wainscotting, and the big glass bakery counter up front is still stocked with delectable fresh-baked pies and cakes.

Mornings, you can't beat Reeves's breakfast bar buffet ($4.85 weekdays, $5.85 on Saturdays and holidays; children under 8 are charged $3.40 and $3.95, respectively). You can help yourself to unlimited portions of scrambled eggs, sausage, cream gravy, grits, bacon, home-fries, pancakes, creamed chipped beef, french toast, buttermilk biscuits, fresh fruit, compote, and irresistible homemade blueberry doughnuts. Or order à la carte—for instance, two eggs with hash browns, homemade cheese toast, and coffee for $3.70. Later in the day there are excellent sandwiches ($3 to $4), like chicken salad, ham salad, and all-white-meat turkey, with a side order of potato salad ($2.15). Maryland crabcakes with tartar sauce, served with french fries and coleslaw, are $6.95; a bowl of chili with beans, $2.90; lasagne with garlic bread and grated cheese, $5.50. There are also burgers, subs, and fried-chicken dinners, the latter available in adult or children's portions. Everything is homemade with the best available ingredients—the meats are cooked on the premises; potato salad, coleslaw, and even mayonnaise are prepared from scratch; and all breads and desserts are fresh from the oven. The desserts, by the way, are renowned, especially the scrumptious strawberry pie ($1.95) which, a waitress tells us, people come from California to sample. The pecan pie is also one of the best of its genre.

Open Monday to Friday 7 a.m. to 4 p.m., Saturday from 7 a.m. to 6 p.m. No credit cards.

We basically enjoy the **Trio,** 1537 17th St. NW, at Q Street (tel. 232-6305), because it's like a New York coffeeshop, and since it's so centrally located, it's a great spot for the morning bagel and cream cheese. Actually, this local hangout is more attractive than its New York counterparts, with brass chandeliers overhead, roomy burgundy-leather booths, a high ceiling, and hanging plants in the multipaned window. There are even fresh flowers on the Formica tables. Best of all, there's a large sidewalk café area under an awning that lures one back to the Trio for lunch, afternoon coffee or wine, and an occasional early dinner.

At breakfast fried eggs with bacon, toast, home fries, orange juice, and coffee comes to about $3.70. The same menu is offered all day, but there are very low-priced lunch specials ($4.25 to $6.50) like crabmeat cakes with tartar sauce, grilled pork chops with applesauce, and fried oysters—all served with two vegetables (perhaps baked macaroni au gratin and buttered fresh carrots) and a beverage. The same kind of specials are featured at dinner ($5.25 to $7.50), including not only vegetables and beverage but dessert. In addition, an extensive menu features such typical coffeeshop food as a chef's salad, chili con carne, a bacon, lettuce, and tomato sandwich, and a burger with fries and coleslaw. A hot fudge sundae for desset is $1.95. Drinks are available from the bar, and you can even pay with plastic here.

Open daily from 7:30 a.m. to midnight.

In March 1928, Pennsylvania Dutchman Evan A. Sholl opened his first Washington cafeteria. He offered fresh, wholesome inexpensive fare, prayers, and patriotism. Though Mr. Sholl died a few years ago, his newphews, who now run **Sholl's Cafeteria,** 1990 K St. NW, in the Esplanade Mall (tel. 296-3065), uphold all their uncle's traditions. On every table is a sheet announcing the weekly special (for example, oven-baked ham with peach half for $3.35), along with a biblical quote or prayer, the slogan "We pray together . . . We stay together," the Sholl's motto ("Live well for less money with quality food at more reasonable prices"), and perhaps an inspirational poem as well. Sholl's is a homey environment, its soft lighting and carpeted floors a pleasant change from the fluorescent/linoleum decor that characterizes so many cafeterias. Photographs of the president and Pope John Paul II are prominently displayed on the cream-colored walls, along with framed awards and testimonials to Evan Sholl from the Lion's Club and the National Restaurant Association.

Everything served here is prepared on the premises. All vegetables are fresh, pies and cakes are homemade, and chopped meat is ground daily. And the prices are not to be believed. At breakfast, load up your tray with scrambled eggs, bacon, biscuits, coffee, orange juuice, and home-fries for under $3. Lunch or dinner entrees (also all under $3) might include braised beef and rice, roast turkey and dressing, breaded veal cutlet, roast beef, or beef stew with potatoes, carrots, celery, and onions. Add corn or broccoli and a scoop of mashed potatoes for another $1.15, a piece of homemade peach or pumpkin pie for 75¢. It's cheaper than cooking yourself. Or, to quote a Sholl's flyer, "if you have problems with breakfast or dinner, just a meal at Sholl's and you'll be a winner."

Hours are Monday to Saturday from 7 to 10:30 a.m. for breakfast, 11 a.m. to 2:30 p.m. for lunch, and 4 to 8 p.m. for dinner.

For a good quick meal near the Capitol, it's hard to beat the **Chesapeake Bagel Bakery,** 215 Pennsylvania Ave. SE (tel. 546-0994), a pleasant plant-filled mini-cafeteria with a changing art and photography exhibit on its gallery-white walls. The bagels—good enough to pass muster with a New Yorker—are baked from scratch on the premises, and the aroma is divine. There are nine varieties (plain, cinnamon raisin, pumpernickel, whole-wheat, poppy, sesame, onion, garlic, and salt). You can get one spread with butter for 65¢; cream cheese ($1.15); cream cheese, walnuts, raisins, and carrots ($1.60); cream cheese and Nova ($3.60); or filled with chicken salad ($2.85), chopped liver ($2.75), or hummus and sprouts ($2.55). A cup of coffee is 60¢ (you can't have a bagel without coffee), and for dessert there are brownies, blondies, carrot cake, and such—all under $1.50.

Open weekdays from 7 a.m. to 8 p.m., on Saturday and Sunday to 7 p.m. No credit cards.

There's another location at 1636 Connecticut Ave. NW, between Q and R Streets (tel. 328-7985), in the Dupont Circle area, and a third at 818 18th St. NW (tel. 775-4690). The menu's the same.

RESTAURANTS AT SIGHTSEEING ATTRACTIONS

Given the hectic round of Washington sightseeing, you'll sometimes want to save time by eating at or near sightseeing attractions. Herewith a rundown of restaurants right in the Smithsonian, the Capitol, the Supreme Court, Library of Congress, and the Kennedy Center. Check out other sections of this chapter to locate additional restaurants close to sights you'll be visiting.

ON THE MALL: Since so much touring time is spent on the Mall, one would hope for a really good restaurant in the vicinity—but one would hope in vain. We like to leave the area for a while and linger over lunch (take the Metro to Farragut West or Dupont Circle where restaurants abound), then come back with renewed vigor for afternoon sightseeing. If your schedule is too tight for that, most of the Smithsonian museums do have cafeterias and/or restaurants, though none is very exciting from a culinary point of view. If the weather is good, consider purchasing food inside and eating it out on the Mall (there are café tables on the west side of the Air and Space Museum, or you can just plop down on the grass); it helps to get away from the hectic throng for a while, and picnicking beats sitting in a cafeteria amid hundreds of exuberant kids.

Though offering a limited menu, your best bet is the delightful **Full Circle at the Hirshhorn,** a plaza café just outside the museum, accessible from Independence Avenue. Its glass-topped white enamel tables—each adorned by a pot of gardenias—nestle in a cool, shaded area overlooking the Arts and Industries Building on one side, sculptures around the fountain on the other. Tables are additionally shaded by charming Oriental white-canvas umbrellas supported by bamboo sticks. It's a tranquil setting, a respite from the hustle and bustle of Mall activity, and service is deft and friendly. Only four items (all under $7) are offered: a pasta salad of rotini tossed with spinach, tomatoes, cauliflower, green peppers, carrots, broccoli, and zucchini in Italian dressing; a plate of cheeses with fresh fruit and crackers; a sandwich of thinly sliced turkey breast topped with Gouda cheese on a fresh whole wheat roll with cranberry mayonnaise, potato salad, and dill pickle; and a chicken-and-grape salad topped with walnuts and served with pineapple wedges and a large croissant. For the kids there's a peanut butter and jelly sandwich served with an apple and milk. There are yummy desserts like cheesecake with Mandarin oranges, peanut butter chocolate pie, or fresh strawberries with whipped cream. And wine and beer are among the available beverages.

Note: This Hirshhorn restaurant has a way of revising its decor and menu, so the summer you visit things may have changed a bit. Its good food and delightful ambience remain constant.

Open daily, Memorial Day to Labor Day only, from 11 a.m. to 4 p.m.

The **Concourse Buffet** in the concourse connecting the two wings of the National Gallery, is a cheerful cafeteria with many planters and potted palms; good acoustics keep the noise level bearable, and efficient operation keeps the lines moving quickly. A good choice here is the create-your-own-salad bar—$1.80 for greens, 50¢ to 80¢ for additional items like grated cheese, cucumbers, chopped egg, peas, pepperoni, cherry tomatoes, bacon, and mushrooms. Other choices are croissant sandwiches, frozen yogurts with varied toppings, burgers and hot dogs, a carvery for deli sandwiches, even a few hot entrees each day. There are fresh-baked desserts, and wine and beer are available. Prices are low to moderate. It's open from 10 a.m. to 4 p.m. Monday to Saturday, from noon to 6 p.m. on Sunday, with extended hours (till 6 p.m. Monday to Saturday) in summer.

In addition there are three rather charming restaurants in the National Gallery, all of which provide restful settings and good food. And an attractive lunch spot with waiter service is nothing to scorn when you've been trudging around museums all day. The **Cascade Café** is the least secluded, since it adjoins the above-described cafeteria, though it does overlook a waterfall. It's open Monday to Saturday from 11:30 a.m. to 4:30 p.m., noon to 4:30 p.m. on Sunday. The **Terrace Café**, in the East Building, overlooks the Mall, and the **Garden Café**, in the West Building, is under a skylight with tables around a fountain. The latter two are open Monday through Saturday from 11 a.m. to 4:30 p.m., from noon to 6 p.m. on Sunday.

All three have similar menus listing about five items each in the $5 to $7 range. They change from time to time, but might typically include a plate of chilled poached salmon served on a bed of spinach pasta with a basket of bread; a salmagundi salad (greens with cheddar cheese, eggs, black olives, anchovies, and Virginia ham); a six-ounce burger on a toasted roll with your choice of toppings (cheese, fresh mushrooms, bacon, guacamole, and/or horseradish sauce) served with potato chips; or a selection of cheeses and fresh fruit with country pâté, fresh-baked bread and butter, and a glass of wine. Fresh-baked pastries and delicious hot fudge sundaes are among your dessert options at all three eateries, as are wine, beer, and cappuccino/espresso.

NATIONAL PORTRAIT GALLERY:
Just off the courtyard that connects the Museum of American Art and the National Portrait Gallery is a tiny eatery called **Patent Pending** (tel. 357-1571). It's pristinely charming inside, with white marble floors and white walls hung with art posters, but the main lure of Patent Pending is its courtyard tables under the elms amid sculptures and fountains. At breakfast a croissant and coffee costs about $1.50; two eggs with bacon, juice, and coffee, $2.75. Lunchtime sandwiches are $2.60 to $4.50, and you can create a sandwich to order from an assemblage of breads (rye, pumpernickel, rolls, croissants, whole-wheat, white), meats (roast beef, ham, salami, and real sliced turkey breast), cheeses, and other fillings such as egg, chicken, turkey, and tuna salad. A salad bar and homemade soups are additional options. Add a carafe of chablis ($3.60) and you've got a lovely picnic.

Open weekdays for breakfast from 10 to 10:30 a.m. and for lunch daily from 11 a.m. to 3:30 p.m. No credit cards.

THE CAPITOL:
You can rub elbows with senators and congresspeople if you dine in the Capitol—a good choice when you're touring the building. Best bet of the several Capitol eateries is the rather elegant and very low-priced **House of Representatives Restaurant,** Room H118 at the south end (tel. 225-6300), where a large 19th-century fresco of George Washington receiving Cornwallis's letter of surrender at Yorktown is among the adornments. At breakfast, served 8 to 11 a.m. weekdays, two eggs, a buttered bagel, sausage patty, fresh-squeezed orange juice, and coffee runs $3.85; fresh melon and french toast are additional options. Lunch is served to the public from 1:15 to 2:30 p.m. weekdays. Bean soup—for which the recipe is generously given—is the featured item and has been since the day in 1904 when Speaker of the House Joseph G. Cannon ordered it and was informed the weather was too hot for soups. "Thunderation," roared Cannon, "I had my mouth set for bean soup. . . . From now on, hot or cold, rain, snow, or shine, I want it on the menu every day!" Try it; it's only $1. Other items include a quarter baked chicken with sage dressing and cranberry sauce ($6.25), broiled filet of sole with lemon butter ($5.45),

and an eight-ounce broiled New York strip steak with mushroom caps ($10.05). There are also sandwiches such as sliced turkey or hot beef with mashed potatoes and gravy, plus daily specials like baked lasagne and barbecued ribs. One low-cholestorol/low-salt item (for example, pan-broiled brook trout with lemon sauce, boiled parsley potato, and string beans for $7.65) is offered each day. For dessert a butterscotch sundae is a treat. If Congress is in session, dinner is also served here from 5 to 9 p.m.

A marvelous lunchtime option is the **Dirksen Senate Office Building South Buffet Room** (tel. 224-4249), wherein lavish all-you-can-eat meals are served weekdays between 11:30 a.m. and 2:30 p.m. To get here, you have to take a free subway that runs through the underbelly of the Capitol, a fun trip; ask Capitol police for directions. The marble-colonnaded setting for these buffets is most attractive, with seating in comfortable red leather chairs at white-linened, flower-bedecked tables. You can help yourself to unlimited viands from the carvery station (perhaps roast beef or leg of lamb), about eight additional hot entrees, vegetables, potatoes, rice, pasta, a full salad and fruit bar, a wide choice of desserts, soft drinks, and tea, coffee, or milk. The price: just $6.50 for adults, $4.50 for children under 12.

Another good choice for Capitol meals is the **Refectory,** a rather charming little public dining room with wainscotted walls and vaulted ceilings. Light fare—burgers, sandwiches, pecan pie—is offered here weekdays from 8 a.m. to 4 p.m. The Refectory (Room S112) is adjacent to the Senate Dining Room.

THE SUPREME COURT: Like the Capitol, the Supreme Court operates under the theory that lawmakers have to eat too, and can't always get out to do so. It's very likely you'll see a Justice or two in the ground-floor **cafeteria** here (tel. 479-3246), an attractive dining facility with red-and-gold carpeting, red-leather chairs, and brass chandeliers overhead. The food is good and low priced, with daily soup-and-entree specials for under $4 such as New England clam chowder with fish and chips, buttered spaghetti, and zucchini or navy bean soup followed by baked stuffed green pepper with whipped potatoes and broccoli. A sandwich of fresh-baked croissant stuffed with chicken salad or roast beef, lettuce, and tomato is $3.75. There's a salad bar as well, and homemade pies and cakes are just 75¢ to $1.25. Open for breakfast (there are fresh-baked muffins) from 7:30 to 10:30 a.m., for lunch to the public from 11:30 a.m. to 2 p.m. (except between noon and 12:15 p.m. and 1 and 1:15 p.m.). No credit cards.

THE LIBRARY OF CONGRESS: The James Madison Memorial Building of the Library of Congress, 101 Independence Ave. SE (tel. 287-8300), has a classy sixth-floor **cafeteria** that is open to the public. The decor is tasteful (rust wall-to-wall carpeting, Breuer chairs, and brown-leather booths lining a wall of windows for panoramic city views), the food fresh and homemade. Hot entrees like old-fashioned beef stew, salmon steak, and crabcakes with tartar sauce are in the $2 to $3.50 range; selections from the salad bar begin at $1.15 for a plate of greens, 25¢ for each additional topping (like tomato, egg salad, onion, mushrooms, chick peas, beans, and sprouts). Vegetables might include broccoli, noodles with mushrooms, mashed and au gratin potatoes, sautéed dilled tomatoes, spinach soufflé, and tempura. There are also sandwiches and fresh-baked pies and cakes.

Open weekdays from 8:30 to 10:30 a.m. for breakfast, 11 a.m. to 2 p.m. for lunch, till 3:30 p.m. for light fare. A no-smoking section is a plus.

Adjoining is the **Montpelier Room,** a more elegant setting with fresh flowers on linened tables, oak-paneled walls, lovely views from large windows on two sides, and a table at the entrance used to display sumptuous desserts and a large flower arrangement. The $7.25 prix-fixe lunch served here weekdays between 11:30 a.m. and 2 p.m. is one of the best deals in town. On a recent visit it included seafood chowder, roast leg of lamb with mint jelly, lyonnaise potatoes, honeyed carrots, bread and butter, and salad; desserts were $1.35 extra, wine or beer the same. Friday is the Montpelier's prime rib day. Reservations are requested for parties of four or more in this room.

KENNEDY CENTER: A meal at the ornate **Roof Terrace Restaurant** of the Kennedy Center adds a glamorous note to an evening at the theater. It's extremely plush, with red velvet Louis XV–style chairs, flocked silk wallpaper, crystal chandeliers, and big flower arrangements. The menu features regional American cuisine specialties. A dinner here, for intance, could begin with appetizers ($2.95 to $6.95) such as shrimp with papaya and prosciutto or herbed crabcakes on wilted spinach. And dinner entrees ($14 to $20) run the gamut from grilled salmon filet in beurre blanc sauce, to New York sirloin with chervil/garlic sauce, to Long Island duck with pecan crust in plum sauce. All entrees come with accompaniments like fresh baby vegetables and scalloped potatoes.

You might also dine in these posh precincts at lunch if you're touring the building or catching a matinee. Prices aren't nearly as lofty. Sandwiches like an open-faced Reuben or an oversized croissant filled with grilled pepper tenderloin and fontina cheese are in the $6 to $7.50 range. There are also delicious salads (like fettuccine with gravlax and caviar in sour cream/dill dressing), half-pound burgers, and hot entrees in the $7.50 to $11.25 range.

After-theater, light fare, and cocktails are served in the **Hors d'Oeuvrerie,** the adjoining, equally plush lounge. We love to stop here after the show for a glass of wine and a late supper. Items in the $5 to $6.50 range include petit Maryland crabcakes and grilled spring lamb chops. It's gourmet snack fare. Dessert and coffee are also options.

The Roof Terrace is open daily for lunch from 11:30 a.m. to 3 p.m. and for dinner from 5:30 to 9:30 p.m. (till half an hour after last curtain Tuesday to Saturday nights). Reservations advised. The Hors d'Oeuvrerie is open from 5 p.m. until a half hour after the last show.

You can also dine in less exalted but still very charming surroundings at the **Curtain Call Café,** an elegant coffeeshop with red-leather booths and banquettes and walls lined with framed photos of artists who've performed here. Dinner entrees are in the $9 to $13.95 range. It's open Tuesday to Saturday from 5 to 8 p.m.

And adjoining the Curtain Call is the **Encore Cafeteria,** another attractive eatery with windows all around providing gorgeous city views. Typical entrees—turkey tetrazzini, lasagne, fried chicken, rigatoni in meat sauce—plus sandwiches and salads, are all under $5, a glass of wine is $2.25, and there are fresh-baked pastries for dessert. Open daily from 11 a.m. to 8 p.m.

CHAPTER V

SIGHTSEEING IN WASHINGTON

□ □ □

People often come to Washington for a weekend expecting to see all the sights. Talk about life in the fast lane! The Smithsonian Institution alone consists of 14 Washington museums plus the National Zoo. Then there are the monuments and memorials (Washington, Lincoln, Jefferson, and Vietnam), the White House, the Capitol, the Supreme Court, the Library of Congress, the FBI, the Kennedy Center, the National Archives, and the National Cathedral—major sights one and all. About a dozen other very interesting attractions vie for your sightseeing time, and it is nice to get over to Georgetown, take a stroll on the canal, or visit nearby Mount Vernon, Arlington, Alexandria, and places of interest a little farther afield.

There's so much to see that you should consider spending at least a week. Even then, remember you can't see everything, and it's more rewarding to see a few attractions thoroughly than to race through dozens. To make the most of your time, read the following listings and plan a reasonably relaxed sightseeing itinerary focusing on the attractions that interest you most. As you plan, keep in mind: geographic proximity (don't waste energy zigzagging back and forth across town); days and hours attractions are open; and applicable warnings about arriving early to avoid long lines or secure necessary tickets. "Advance Planning" suggestions in Chapter II tell you how to obtain tickets in advance for VIP tours to some attractions.

Since even friends we've personally counseled to take it easy have exhausted themselves sightseeing in Washington, our advice to program a nice slice of leisure into every touring day will no doubt go unheeded. For the record, we do suggest a long, leisurely lunch and occasional relaxing outdoor attractions like a stroll through the beautiful gardens at Dumbarton Oaks, a river cruise, or a picnic at the Arboretum—anything that gets you off your museum-weary feet for a while. Speaking of those feet, you'll be on them a lot in Washington. Comfortable shoes are essential to bearing up under the rigors of sightseeing, and during sweltering summer days running shoes, shorts, and a T-shirt (or whatever little attire the shape you're in will tolerate) is the ideal costume.

Most museums offer highlight tours (call in advance for exact hours), a good way to get a meaningful overview in a limited time. The good news: Almost everything is free.

WASHINGTON WITH CHILDREN

Visiting the Capital with parents or classmates is as intrinsic a part of American childhood as baseball, hot dogs, and apple pie. Washington is a great place for family vacations, but how much fun you have depends on your approach and planning. Let the kids help in working out daily itineraries, a project that allows everyone to become acquainted with the sights and build up excitement over what you'll be seeing. The more you know about each place, the easier it is to communicate and create enthusiasm; it's also very helpful when taking tours if you can complement the guide's patter with child-oriented explanations. Kids tend to stay alert and interested when you discuss with them what you're seeing; leave them to their own devices and boredom—quickly followed by whining—sets in. This might mean doing a wee bit of homework (reading up a bit on the various attractions), but your efforts will enhance everyone's trip.

Once in town, be flexible. If the kids are exhausted, skip an item on the itinerary and spend a few hours at the hotel swimming pool. Choosing a hotel with a pool, by the way, allows everyone to get refreshed at the end of a tiring day, and unless kids are toddlers, gives parents a child-free hour or two.

FAVORITE CHILDREN'S SIGHTS: All listings in this chapter include details about special programs for youngsters. Kids, of course, like the **National Zoological Park.** Of the Smithsonian museums, **National Air and Space** is the great favorite, followed by the **National Museums of Natural History** and **American History** and the **Arts and Industries** 1876 Centennial Exposition. The **Capital Children's Museum** is especially for them with hands-on exhibits and educational computer games. Every child knows about Lincoln and enjoys visiting **Ford's Theatre** and the **House Where Lincoln Died.** On the same principle kids tend to enjoy the **Lincoln Memorial.** The **Washington Monument** attracts with its great views of the city. And the **FBI,** complete with gangster memorabilia and a sharp-shooting demonstration, is sure to enthrall.

A special treat is visiting any memorial or monument after dark. **National Geographic's Explorers Hall** with its moon rock, egg of an extinct elephant bird, etc., is like having the magazine come to life. Interestingly, the **DAR Museum** is a good choice, with a special area focusing on a child's life in colonial times and many period rooms that are fun to see. Riding the **Metro** is a kick, especially if there's no subway where you live; let the kids purchase and insert their own fare cards. The **White House,** the **Capitol,** the **Supreme Court,** and the **National Archives** (where the original Declaration of Independence, Constitution, and Bill of Rights are on display) all provide good opportunities for educational enhancement. At the **Old Stone House** in Georgetown, park rangers in colonial garb demonstrate 18th-century home-making skills. People of all ages like to see the piles of money on display at the **Bureau of Engraving and Printing.** Finally, check out the *"Weekend"* section in the Friday edition of the *Washington Post* for listings of child-oriented (mostly free) activities, museum events, theater, storytelling programs, puppet shows, and more.

THE MAJOR SIGHTS

These may or may not be major to you, and nowhere is it written that you have to see them all. Give equal consideration to "Additional Attractions" and Chapter VI, "Outdoor Washington and the Sporting Life," when planning your itinerary. These are, however, the sights most tourists choose to visit on trips to Washington.

THE SMITHSONIAN INSTITUTION: No longer referred to as "the nation's attic," which seemed somewhat musty, the Smithsonian Institution has been redubbed "the nation's showcase." That doesn't totally explain it either, for its collection of over 100 million specimens deals with the entire world and its history, and the peoples and animals (past and present) that have inhabited the earth. The sprawling institution employs in the neighborhood of 6,000 people, and they are assisted by almost an equal number of volunteers. Nine immense Smithsonian buildings are located between the Washington Monument and the Capitol on the Mall. Other buildings devoted to specialized exhibits are within walking distance of the Mall. And farther out, the National Zoological Park (the zoo) is a Smithsonian responsibility.

There's more beyond the District of Columbia too. The Astrophysical Observatory in Cambridge, Massachusetts, is a Smithsonian installation operating field stations at other U.S. sites and in several foreign countries. There's a Smithsonian Tropical Research Institute in Panama. And the Cooper-Hewitt Museum in New York is the Smithsonian Institution's National Museum of Design. Thousands of scientific expeditions sponsored by the Smithsonian have pushed into remote frontiers in deserts, mountains, polar regions, and jungles. Traveling exhibits are sent to other museums, schools, and libraries. And all this is a mere hint of the Smithsonian's scope and involvement.

The Smithsonian Institute began with a $500,000 bequest from James Smithson, an English scientist who had never visited this country. When he died in 1829, he willed his entire fortune to the United States "to found at Washington an establishment for the increase and diffusion of knowledge among men." In 1846 Congress created a corporate entity to carry out Smithson's will, and the federal government agreed to pay 6% interest on the bequest funds in perpetuity.

Since then, other munificent private donations have swelled Smithson's original legacy many times over. Major gallery and museum construction through the years and currently in progress stand as testament to thoughtful donors. The most recent major addition: the very exciting new $75-million Quadrangle complex on the Mall, detailed later in this chapter.

Information, Please

If you need to know what's happening at any of the Smithsonian museums, just get on the phone. A call to **Dial-a-Museum** at 357-2020 brings you news of all special events. **Dial-a-Phenomenon** can be reached by phoning 357-2000; this is recorded information about space and earth events in considerable detail (exact time of sunrise and sunset, of solar equinox, motion of the planets, etc.). A call to 357-2700 puts you in touch with the **Visitor Information and Associates Reception Center.** Here you get a real voice, even on Saturday (between 9 a.m. and 5 p.m.), to answer questions about all Smithsonian museums and their events.

Lunch Breaks

On the Mall, you'll find cafeterias in the National Museum of American History, the National Museum of Natural History, the National Air and Space Museum, the Hirshhorn (summer only), and the National Gallery of Art. If you walk north along nearby F Street, you'll find more restaurants and coffeeshops in all price ranges, where you usually won't have to stand in line on crowded days. Behind the castle to the south, several more restaurants are located in the modern L'Enfant Plaza Hotel. And there are plentiful hot dog and ice cream stands for picnic snacks.

The Castle on the Mall

The Castle on the Mall, 1000 Jefferson Dr. SW (tel. 357-2700), built in 1849, originally housed the entire Smithsonian Institution. The red sandstone edifice looks like a Norman castle with Victorian overtones, and it's become the Smithsonian's symbol. At the Great Hall on the ground floor, information and maps covering the museums and galleries in Washington are available. Helpful volunteers are on hand to answer your questions. Recent refurbishing has reemphasized the period when the castle was built, the Victorian era.

Note: The Castle will be closed through July 1989 for the installation of the Smithsonian Information Center, which will be the primary information point for the museum complex.

The National Museum of American History

On the north side of the Mall between 12th and 14th Streets NW, with entrances on Constitution Avenue and Madison Drive (tel. 357-2700). Open daily from 10 a.m. to 5:30 p.m. Closed Christmas Day. Metro: Smithsonian or Federal Triangle.

The National Museum of American History deals with "everyday life in the American past" and the external forces that have helped to shape our national character. The museum occupies three floors, with exhibits running the gamut from a Revolutionary War general's tent, to Dizzy Gillespie's trumpet, to Archie and Edith Bunker's chairs.

On the first floor (entered on Constitution Avenue), exhibits explore the development of farm machines, power machinery, transportation (including a 280-ton Pacific-type steam locomotive and over 100 ship models), electricity, timekeeping, phonographs, and typewriters. The Palm Court on this level is a turn-of-the-century re-creation—a carefully researched one—with etched mirrors flanked by Victorian rosettes, a stained-glass-paneled backbar, an ornate pressed-tin ceiling, period stenciling on the walls, and a baby grand "reproducing" piano (like a player piano). It includes the interior of Georgetown's Stohlman's Confectionary Shop as it appeared around 1900 and part of an actual 1902 Horn & Hardart Automat. Light fare is served at round marble-topped tables. You can have your mail stamped Smithsonian Station at a post office that was located in Headsville, West Virginia, from 1861 to 1971, when it was brought lock, stock, and barrel to the museum; it doubles as a country store. There's also a beautiful textiles display here. An important new first-floor exhibit is "Changing Lifestyles: A Material World," exploring the changing composition of artifacts—from predominantly natural materials such as wood and stone, to manufactured materials such as steel, finally to the vast range of synthetics that exist today. The exhibit, enhanced by interactive video displays, demonstrates how the material composition of items in our everyday life serve as indicators of our shifting cultural values.

If you enter from the Mall, you'll find yourself on the second floor facing the original Star-Spangled Banner, 30 by 42 feet, that inspired Francis Scott Key to write our national anthem in 1814. Its tattered fabric must be protected by a curtain, but every hour on the half hour the curtain parts and a patriotic sound-and-light show takes place. The most fascinating exhibit on the second floor—and perhaps in the entire museum—is the Foucault Pendulum. It's a copy of the original model exhibited in Paris in 1851 with the accompanying teaser, "You are invited to witness the earth revolve." The heavy pendulum, suspended from the roof, swings monotonously from one side to the other, never varying in its arc, yet knocking over, one by one, a series of red pointers which form a circle around it. How? Because although the pendulum has an unvarying arc, the earth revolves beneath it. To make a complete "circuit" and to knock over all the pointers takes 38 hours in Washington; at the North Pole it would take 24 hours. Currently on the second floor as well is a small part of the First Ladies' gowns display (including Rosalynn Carter's and Nancy's white satin sheath); the full exhibit, which begins with Martha Washington's hand-painted silk gown, will reopen in 1991.

"After the Revolution" is a major exhibition about the everyday activities of ordinary 18th-century Americans—their work, family life, and communities. Its components include an 18th-century log house, rooms from Virginia and Massachusetts, a hands-on history room, and a performance area for 18th-century concerts, puppet shows, and other amusements. The lives of both urban and rural families are examined, with focus on the lifestyles of African-Americans, American Indians, southern planters, and Yankee merchants. And "A Nation of Nations," explores the experiences that have united diverse cultures to form the American way of life. These include schools, military service, common enthusiasm for sports and entertainment, and the labor community.

A vast collection of ship models, uniforms, weapons, and other things military is found on the third floor. Other selections include Money and Medals, News Reporting (from teletype to space satellite), Printing and Graphic Arts, Ceramics and Glass, Stamps (over 75,000 rare specimens on display), and Photography. Here, too, is the first American flag to be called Old Glory (1824) and Lingering Shadows—an area where you can create shadow art (kids adore it). "A More Perfect Union: Japanese Americans and the U.S. Constitution," examines the constitutional process, focusing on the internment of thousands of Japanese Americans during World War II.

Inquire at the information desks (at the Madison Drive and Constitution Avenue entrances) about highlight tours, Demonstration Center hands-on activities for children and adults, films, lectures, and concerts. Holidays are especially event-filled times. There are two museum shops. The larger, on the lower level near the cafeteria, contains the Smithsonian Bookstore and stocks books and objects relating to all aspects of Americana, as well as toys, crafts, gift items, models of vehicles and ships, and jewelry. It's great fun;

don't miss it. A no-smoking section is a plus in the museum's cheerful cafeteria.

The National Museum of Natural History

On the north side of the Mall between 9th and 12th Streets NW, with entrances on Madison Drive and Constitution Avenue (tel. 357-2700). Open daily from 10 a.m. to 5:30 p.m. Closed Christmas Day. Metro: Smithsonian or Federal Triangle.

The National Museum of Natural History contains over 118 million artifacts and specimens—everything from one of the largest African elephants ever bagged by a hunter in our time (it dominates the Rotunda on the Mall-entrance level) to the legendary Hope Diamond, the single most popular display in the museum (it rests on white brocade in its own glass-faced vault in the Hall of Gems on the second floor).

Free highlight tours are given daily at 10:30 a.m. and 1:30 p.m., but if you have the time, the self-guided audio tour (available at the Rotunda information desk; adults pay $3, seniors and students $2.50, children under 12, $1.25) provides the most comprehensive commentary on exhibits. A Discovery Room, filled with creative hands-on exhibits and games for children, is on the first floor; it's open Monday to Thursday from noon to 2:30 p.m., on Friday, Saturday, and Sunday from 10:30 a.m. to 3:30 p.m. One adult must accompany every three children, and tickets, obtained at the Rotunda information desk, are required on weekends and holidays. If you have kids, this is a must.

On the Mall level, off the Rotunda, evolution is traced back billions of years in Fossils, comprising such exhibits as a 3.5-billion-year-old fossil of a single-celled organism from Australia and a 70-million-year-old dinosaur egg from France. An animated film shows how the earliest forms of life on earth originated. And the latest addition to this section is the jaw of a carcharodon megalodon, the biggest shark that ever lived! The jaws of one of these creatures were big enough to consume a Volkswagen bug in one gulp; some of its 48 front teeth are five or six inches long. You'll encounter Ice Age mammoths and Neanderthals and explore African, Asian, Pacific, Indian, and Eskimo cultures (included are displays with taped Chinese opera and African music). A revolting but riveting tableau in the Dynamics of Evolution section demonstrates the necessity for the weeding-out process known as survival of the fittest; it's a kitchen in which every roach born for three generations has survived. If every roach survived through eight generations, by the way, there would be 15,969,850,417,242 of them. Yecch! Also on this floor: the World of Mammals and Life in the Sea, the latter including a spectacular living coral reef in a 3,000-gallon tank. A second 3,000-gallon tank houses a subarctic sea environment typical of the Maine coast. Also on this level is Hydrolab, the stationary underwater lab that revolutionized oceanographic research by allowing scientists to live and work in the depths of the sea for long periods.

On the second floor, along with the Hope Diamond, you'll see such dazzling gems as the 182-carat Star of Bombay Sapphire that belonged to Mary Pickford, a rare red diamond (one of five in the world), and Marie Antoinette's diamond earrings. Nearby are geological specimens ranging from meteorites to moon rocks. Kids will enjoy the Insect Zoo's Plexiglas cages housing tarantulas, centipedes, and the like. Numerous skeletons—from the gigantic extinct Stellar sea cow to the tiny pocket mouse—are displayed in Bones. Additional exhibits include "South America: Continent and Culture," with objects from the Inca civilization, among others; "Human Origin and Variation" (including the remains of an 18th-century man who turned to soap, a phenomenon that occurs sometimes when groundwater comes into contact with buried bodies); and "Western Civilization: Origins and Traditions"—from about 10,000 years ago to A.D. 500.

There's a plant-filled cafeteria off the Rotunda and an adjoining shop featuring books on natural history and anthropology for adults and children, jewelry, crafts, fossil reproduction kits, shells, minerals, etc.

The National Air and Space Museum

On the south side of the Mall between 4th and 7th Streets SW, with entrances at 6th Street on Jefferson Drive or Independence Avenue (tel. 357-2700). Open daily from 10 a.m. to 5:30 p.m. Closed Christmas Day. Metro: L'Enfant Plaza (7th and Maryland exit).

One of the "world's most popular museums" (attendance is over nine million annually), the National Air and Space Museum chronicles the story of man's mastery of flight—from Kitty Hawk to outer space. And it does so superbly in 23 galleries filled with exciting exhibitions. Plan to devote at least three or four hours exploring them; and especially during the tourist season and on holidays, arrive just before 10 a.m. to make a rush for the film ticket line when the doors open. The not-to-be-missed IMAX films shown in the Samuel P. Langley Theater here, on a screen five stories high and seven stories wide, are immensely popular; tickets tend to sell out quickly. These films include *To Fly,* an aerial tour of America from a balloon ascension in the 1800s to a space venture (it's magnificent); *On the Wing,* dramatizing the relationship between natural flight (bugs, birds, and bats) and human flight, including the flight of a replica of a 65-million-year-old pterodactyl; and *The Dream Is Alive,* the first film ever to be shot in outer space with an IMAX camera. See as many as you have time for. Tickets cost $2 for adults, $1 for children, students, and senior citizens.

You'll also want to catch (same prices) a show at the Albert

Einstein Planetarium, so after you've purchased IMAX tickets make the planetarium ticket booth on the second floor your next stop.

In between shows, you can view the exhibits; free 1½-hour highlight tours are given daily at 10:15 a.m. and 1 p.m. Recorded tours, narrated by astronauts, are also available for rental. Computer games and slide and video shows enhance the exhibits throughout.

Highlights of the first floor include famous airplanes (such as *Spirit of St. Louis*) and spacecraft (the *Apollo II* Command Module); the world's only touchable moon rock; numerous exhibits on the history of aviation and air transportation; galleries in which you learn how a helicopter works, design your own jet plane, and study astronomy; rockets, lunar exploration vehicles, manned spacecraft, guided missiles, even the U.S.S. *Enterprise*. Here, too, is a fabulous museum shop of flight-related items, including freeze-dried ice cream and strawberries. All the aircraft, by the way, are original.

Kids love the "walk-through" Skylab orbital workshop on the second floor. Other galleries here highlight balloons and airships, the solar system, U.S. manned space flights, air-sea operations, aviation during the World Wars, and artists' perceptions of flight.

A new exhibit that will open shortly after this book goes to press is "Beyond the Limits: Flight Enters the Computer Age." Occupying seven exhibit areas, it will illustrate the primary applications of computer technology to aerospace—application in design, aerodynamics, manufacturing, flight testing, air and space operations, and flight simulation. Visitors will be able to utilize hands-on interactive computers. Displays will include one of the first production-model supercomputers, CRAY-1, which can perform billions of calculations in seconds and generate graphics that can model aerodynamic forces as well as the most sophisticated wind tunnels; with CRAY-1, engineers were able to "flight-test" engines and wing design before building costly prototypes. Other highlights: a full-scale model of the X-29 aircraft, a radically innovative product of supercomputer design; HIMAT, an unmanned, radio-controlled aircraft used to test the effects of high acceleration forces; and items tracing the evolution of computers, from the large vacuum tubes of the 1940s to the tiny but powerful microchips of the future.

A brand-new cafeteria and restaurant are featured at this museum. Built on the museum's east terrace, this 39,000-square-foot enclosure is all glass, providing diners with views of the Mall and the Capitol. Its surrounding terraces are attractively landscaped with seasonal flowers, trees, and plants.

The Paul E. Garber Facility: Under the auspices of the National Air and Space Museum, located in Suitland, Maryland (tel. 202/357-1400), this facility houses the museum's reserve collection of historically significant air- and spacecraft. Here you'll see over 140 aircraft and spacecraft exhibits, albeit in a no-frills environment without such enhancements as video shows. You can also get a behind-the-scenes look at the restoration workshop where skilled craftspeople repair and preserve air/spacecraft and other objects. If NASM whets rather than sates your appetite for this kind of thing, this one's for you. Free tours are given, by appointment only, weekdays at 10 a.m., weekends at 10 a.m. and 1 p.m. For reservations and information, call between 9 a.m. and 3:15 p.m. Monday to Friday. Or write ahead to Tour Scheduler, National Air and Space Museum, Smithsonian Institution, Washington, D.C. 20560.

The National Museum of American Art

On 8th and G Streets NW (tel. 357-2700). Open daily except Christmas Day from 10 a.m. to 5:30 p.m. Metro: Gallery Place.

Over two centuries of American art history are represented in the National Museum of American Art's 34,000-plus works, about 1,000 of which are on display on its three gallery floors at any given time. The museum—along with the adjoining National Portrait Gallery—is housed in the Old Patent Office Building, partially designed by Robert Mills (who designed the Washington Monument) and Thomas U. Walter (architect of the Capitol dome). This mid-19th-century Greek Revival building, with columned portico patterned after a classic Parthenon façade, is worth a look-see in itself.

Exhibits are arranged chronologically, ascending toward the 20th century on the third floor. An exception (on the first floor) is James Hampton's *The Throne of the Third Heaven of the Nations' Millennium General Assembly,* an impressive piece of visionary religious folk art done in the 1950s by a black South Carolina–born short-order cook and janitor who believed he saw God. The piece contains 177 glittering objects sheathed in aluminum and gold foil. Otherwise, this floor contains Early American art (works of Benjamin West, George Henry Durrie, Thomas Hart Benton, Charles Willson Peale, Samuel F. B. Morse, Gilbert Stuart, Thomas Sully, Ralph Earl) and an Art of the West gallery in which you'll see works of John Mix Stanley and Charles Bird King documenting the American West and George Catlin's Indian portraits (the museum owns 445 of them).

On the second floor are works of such mid- to late-19th-century artists as Thomas Cole, Albert Pinkham Ryder, Winslow Homer, Thomas Eakins, John Singer Sargent, Albert Bierstadt, Childe Hassam, and Thomas Moran. A permanent exhibit here is the Hiram Powers Gallery wherein are the contents of the 19th-century classic sculptor's studio in Florence.

On view in two galleries on the third floor—the Patricia and Phillip Frost Gallery and the Irene and Herbert F. Johnson Gallery—are works by Edward Hopper, Leon Kroll, Stuart Davis, Lee

Krasner, and Morris Kantor, as well as paintings commissioned during the New Deal era. Works by post–World War II artists (Joseph Cornell, de Kooning, Kline, Warhol, Noguchi, Rauschenberg, and many others, along with a collection of 20th-century folk art), are shown in the beautiful third-floor Lincoln Gallery, where 4,000 revelers celebrated Lincoln's second inaugural in 1865; it's a magnificent room with marble columns and high vaulted ceilings.

Pick up a map and calendar of events at the information desk when you enter. Free walk-in tours are given at noon weekdays and at 1:45 p.m. on Sunday. American art books, slides, prints, posters, and gift items are sold at the first-floor gift shop, and there's a lovely courtyard restaurant, Patent Pending, about which you'll find details in Chapter IV.

The National Portrait Gallery

On 8th and F Streets NW (tel. 357-2700). Open daily except Christmas Day from 10 a.m. to 5:30 p.m. Metro: Gallery Place.

The concept of a national portrait gallery first evolved in the mid-19th century when Congress commissioned G. P. A. Healy to paint a series of presidential portraits for the White House. However, it was not until 1962 that the museum was actually established by an Act of Congress, and another six years elapsed before it opened to the public.

Sharing the palatial quarters of the Old Patent Office Building with the Museum of American Art, the National Portrait Gallery houses a collection of "likenesses of the heroes and villains, thinkers and doers, conservatives and radicals, represented in various media and gathered together by historical theme and period." They range from Revolutionary-era portraits of great men and women by Gilbert Stuart and Charles Willson Peale to *Time* magazine cover portraits of moderns like Woody Allen.

With the exception of presidents—and special exhibitions—portraits are not permitted into the permanent collection until ten years after the subject's death. Exhibits include 19th-century silhouettes of notables by French-born artist August Edouart; miniature copper-plate engravings of prominent people by C. B. J. Févret de Saint-Mémin, an artist who fled France after the Revolution and settled in New York; Gilbert Stuart's famed "Lansdowne" portrait of Washington and "Edgehill" portrait of Jefferson (they alternate as the dramatic centerpiece of the second-floor rotunda); Jo Davidson's sculpture portraits; the classic photographs of the J. Frederick Hill Meserve Collection documenting Civil War and post–Civil War America; and the Hall of Presidents on the second floor. In addition to the rotating permanent collection, there are interesting temporary exhibits. Some recent shows have included "The Artist's Mother: Portraits and Homages" (highlighting works by Bellows, Hockney, and Marisol); "Davy Crockett: the Gentleman from the Cane"; "American Colonial Portraits: 1700– 1776"; and "Masterpieces from Gripsholm Castle: The Swedish National Portrait Collection."

Pick up a calendar of events at the information desk when you come in to find out about the museum's comprehensive schedule of lunchtime lectures, concerts, and dramatic presentations. Walk-in tours are given at varying hours—usually between 10 a.m. and 3 p.m. (call 357–2920 for details).

The Renwick Gallery of the National Museum of American Art

On Pennsylvania Avenue at 17th Street NW (tel. 357-2700). Open daily except Christmas Day from 10 a.m. to 5:30 p.m. Metro: Farragut West (Farragut Square exit).

A curatorial department of the National Museum of American Art, the Renwick is housed in a historic mid-1800s landmark building of the French Second Empire style. The original home of the Corcoran Gallery, it was saved from demolition by President Kennedy in 1963 when he recommended that it be renovated as part of the Lafayette Square restoration. In 1965 it became part of the Smithsonian and was renamed for its architect, James W. Renwick (he also designed the Smithsonian "castle"). Although the setting —especially the magnificent Victorian Grand Salon with its wainscotted plum walls and 38-foot skylight ceiling and the lavish Octagon Room—evokes another era, the museum's contents are mostly contemporary. The Renwick is a national showcase for American creativity in crafts. A rich and diverse display of objects here includes both changing exhibitions of contemporary works and pieces dating from 1900 to the present that are part of the museum's permanent collection.

The two above-mentioned Victorian galleries on the second floor are furnished in opulent 19th-century style, their walls hung with gilt-framed paintings by 18th- and 19th-century artists. Over the years, exhibits here have focused on American art deco, traditional and innovative pottery, the ceramic sculpture of Stephen De Staebler, Dan Dailey glass, contemporary North American Indian objects, and Cynthia Schira's fiber works.

An additional part of the American Art Museum complex is the **Barney Studio House,** 2306 Massachusetts Ave. NW (tel. 357-3111). Here, in the early 1900s, painter and prominent society leader Alice Pike Barney provided Washington with an art center-cum-salon. Barney studied in Paris with Whistler before returning to the capital for a one-woman show at the Corcoran. Studio House, said a *Washington Society* magazine of her day, was the "meeting place for wit and wisdom, genius and talent, which fine material is leavened by fashionable folk, who would like to be a bit Bohemian if they only knew how." Donated to the Smithsonian in 1931 by Barney's daughters, the Studio House, with many of its original furnishings, family records, and photographs, is open to the public for tours October through May by appointment only. Call ahead for reservations.

Hirshhorn Museum and Sculpture Garden

On the south side of the Mall at Independence Avenue and 8th Street SW (tel. 357-2700). Open daily from 10 a.m. to 5:30 p.m. Closed Christmas Day. Metro: L'Enfant Plaza (7th Street and Maryland Avenue exit).

The Hirshhorn Museum and Sculpture Garden opened in 1974 as the first major museum of contemporary art in Washington, a much-needed addition to the cultural scene. It houses the magnificent collection of more than 6,000 paintings and sculptures (now more than doubled by additional Hirshhorn bequests, acquisitions, and gifts from other donors) given to the nation by the late Joseph Hirshhorn (1899–1981)—the Latvian immigrant who made a fortune in uranium mining and amassed the most extensive private collection of 20th-century art ever assembled. The museum's dramatically contemporary cylindrical concrete-and-granite building, 231 feet in diameter, was designed by architect Gordon Bunshaft. Fourteen feet above the ground on sculptured supports, the building shelters a plaza courtyard where sculpture is displayed. The light and airy interior, like New York's Guggenheim, follows a simple circular route that makes it easy to see every exhibit without getting lost in a maze of galleries. Natural light from floor-to-ceiling windows makes the inner galleries the perfect venue for viewing sculpture, second only, perhaps, to the magnificently beautiful tree-shaded sunken sculpture garden (don't miss it). Paintings and drawings are installed in the outer galleries, artificially lit to prevent light damage.

A rotating show of about 600 pieces is on view at all times on the second and third floors. It features just about every well-known 20th-century artist and provides a comprehensive overview of major trends in Western art from the turn of the century to the present. Among the artists represented are Picasso, Brancusi, Arp, Rodin, de Kooning, Dali, Mondrian, Sargent, Eakins, Tobey, Homer, Rothko, Warhol, Pollock, Nevelson, Noguchi, Giacometti, Dubuffet, Golub, Wiley, Lewitt, and Calder—and that's not the half of it. Among the best-known pieces are Rodin's *The Burghers of Calais,* four bas-reliefs by Matisse known as *The Backs,* and an important collection of the works of Henry Moore. Recent temporary exhibits have included "Expressiv: Central European Art Since 1960," "Different Drummers" (a group show of idiosyncratic American artists), and "Alberto Giacometti 1901–1966." One-gallery

"Directions" shows and the site-specific WORKS series highlight more experimental forms of contemporary art on an ongoing basis.

Pick up a free calendar when you come in to find out about free films (everything from Werner Herzog documentaries to *The Cabinet of Dr. Caligari* to *Looney Toons* starring Porky Pig and Daffy Duck), lectures, and concerts. Free docent tours are given Monday to Saturday at 10:30 a.m., noon, and 1:30 p.m., on Sunday at 12:30, 1:30, and 2:30 p.m. Art books, posters, and prints are sold at the museum shop, and in summer, the museum's outdoor plaza café is a good choice for lunch (details in Chapter IV).

The Freer Gallery of Art

On the south side of the Mall at Jefferson Drive and 12th Street SW (tel. 357-2700). Open daily except Christmas Day from 10 a.m. to 5:30 p.m. Metro: Smithsonian (Mall exit).

A gift to the nation from Charles Lang Freer, a collector of Asian art and American works from the late 19th and early 20th centuries, the Freer Gallery opened in 1923. Freer's original interest was, in fact, American art, but his good friend James McNeill Whistler encouraged him to collect Asian works as well. Eventually the latter become predominant. Freer's gift included funds to construct a museum (the building is modeled after a Florentine Renaissance palace), and an endowment to add objects of the highest quality to the Asian collection only, which has been generally augmented over the years. It includes Chinese and Japanese sculpture, painting, lacquer, metalwork, and ceramics; early Christian illuminated manuscripts; Japanese screens and woodblock prints; Korean and Chinese jades and bronzes; Persian manuscripts, metalwork, and miniatures; and Indian sculpture, manuscripts, and paintings.

Among the American works, not surprisingly, are over 1,200 pieces by Whistler, including the famous Peacock Room permanently installed in Gallery XII. Originally a dining room designed by an architect named Jeckyll for the London mansion of F. R. Leyland, the Peacock Room contained a Whistler painting called *Rose and Silver; The Princess from the Land of Porcelain.* But after his painting was installed, Whistler was dissatisfied with the room as a setting for his work. When Leyland was away from home, he painted peacocks all over Jeckyll's meticulously planned interior of Spanish gilded leather and walnut paneling, and in so doing pleased no one but himself. A permanent rift developed between Whistler and Leyland, and Jeckyll was, understandably, enraged. After Leyland's death, Freer purchased the painting and eventually shipped the entire room here from London. Other American painters represented in the collections are Childe Hassam, Winslow Homer, Thomas Wilmer Dewing, Albert Pinkham Ryder, Dwight William Tryon, Abbott Henderson Thayer, and John Singer Sargent.

A museum shop on the first floor features books relating to the collection and reproductions from it. Tours are given daily at noon.

Note: Throughout most of the lifetime of this edition, the Freer will be closed for a construction project. Readers interested in Asian art should visit the nearby Arthur M. Sackler Gallery, described later in this chapter.

Arts and Industries Building

On the south side of the Mall, 900 Jefferson Dr. SW (tel. 357-2700). Open daily from 10 a.m. to 5:30 p.m. Closed Christmas Day. Metro: Smithsonian.

Built in 1881 as the first National Museum, this red-brick-and-sandstone structure was the scene of President Garfield's Inaugural Ball. Later it housed exhibits from the 1876 United States International Exposition in Philadelphia—a celebration of America's 100th birthday that featured the latest advances in technology. The Exposition was re-created in 1976 for the Bicentennial and has remained here ever since. Thousands of objects from the original fair are complemented by additional displays related to the period. It's lots of fun walking through this turn-of-the-century melange of furnishings, printing presses, corn mills, carriages, weaponry, clocks, musical instruments, and such Victorian whimsey as French lace and flowers. Some of the exhibits are rather large, such as a steam locomotive and a 42-foot model of the naval cruiser *Antietam*, a steam sloop-of-war. There are also state exhibits, e.g., on California wines or Tennessee lumber.

Singers, dancers, puppeteers, and mimes perform in the Discovery Theater Tuesday to Saturday, October to June (call 357-1500 for show times and ticket information; admission is charged). Don't miss the charming store on the first floor—everything from glassware to potpourri. In summer, there's a carousel across the street.

The National Zoological Park

Located in Rock Creek Park, main entrance in the 3000 block of Connecticut Avenue NW (tel. 673-4800 or 673-4717). Open daily, weather permitting, May 1 to September 15: grounds from 8 a.m. to 8 p.m., animal buildings from 9 a.m. to 6 p.m.; rest of the year: grounds from 8 a.m. to 6 p.m., animals buildings from 9 a.m. to 4:30 p.m. Closed Christmas Day. Metro: Cleveland Park or Woodley Park.

Established in 1889, the National Zoo is home to over 3,000 animals of some 500 species, many of them rare and/or endangered. A leader in the care, breeding, and exhibition of animals, it occupies 163 beautifully landscaped acres and is one of the country's most delightful zoos. Star residents are Hsing-Hsing and Ling-Ling, the giant pandas given by the People's Republic of China during President Nixon's 1972 visit. Best time to catch the pandas is at feeding time, 11 a.m. and 3 p.m. The Panda Café has umbrella tables overlooking their habitat, so you can sit comfortably nibbling on pizza or drinking soda while you wait for an appearance.

It's best to enter the zoo at the Connecticut Avenue entrance, which puts you right by the Education Building. Here you can pick up a map and see films (shown daily at regular intervals in summer, weekends only the rest of the year) about giant pandas and activities at the zoo's Conservation and Research Center. You can also get tickets for ZOOlab (available on a first-come, first-served basis), a learning lab where visitors can handle and examine such objects as hummingbird eggs, read zoology texts, and peer at specimens through a microscope. It's open Tuesday to Sunday noon to 3 p.m. Similar in concept is HERPlab, a center for the study of reptiles and amphibians, open Wednesday to Sunday from noon to 3 p.m. (tickets are free at the lab). There's also a BIRDlab for which no tickets are required. All three feature educational hands-on exhibits that kids love.

Of course, the main reason to come to the zoo is to see the animals. They live in large open enclosures simulating their natural habitats on six easy-to-follow color-coded trails. All begin and end at Olmsted Walk, the zoo's main pathway. You can't get lost, and you won't unintentionally miss anything. In total, there are 3½ miles of trails. Signs indicate the presence of baby animals born in captivity.

Lions, tigers, panthers, leopards, monkeys, apes, reptiles, and small animals live along the Orange Trail. The Brown Trail contains the four largest land mammals—hippos, rhinos, giraffes, and elephants. Kangaroos, zebras, antelopes, and the famed pandas are on the Black Trail. Deer and guanaco (wild lamas) coexist with abundant birdlife on the Green Trail. Smokey the Bear of forest-fire fame shares the Yellow Trail with big cats and North American mammals. And additional bears can be seen on the Blue Trail along with otters, wolves, seals, and sea lions.

Zoo facilities include stroller-rental stations ($3 plus a $25 deposit or a driver's license), a number of gift shops, a bookstore, and several parking lots. These fill up quickly, especially on weekends, so arrive early or take the Metro. There is a fast-food eatery, the Mane Restaurant/Cafeteria near the Beach Drive entrance, but we'd suggest a picnic lunch.

The Complex on the Quadrangle

Bordered by Independence Avenue, the Freer Gallery, the "castle," and the Arts and Industries Building, this $75-million addition to existing Smithsonian facilities, first conceived in 1965 and opened in 1987, houses two major museums—the Arthur M. Sackler Gallery (of Asian and Near Eastern art) at 1050 Independence Ave. SW, and the relocated National Museum of African Art at 950 Independence Ave. SW. Also part of the project are the International Center (a forum for international exhibits) at 1100 Jefferson Dr. SW, and the Victorian-style 4.2-acre Enid A. Haupt Garden. Closest Metro stop: Smithsonian.

The original plan for the pair-of-pavilions complex was the inspiration of Japanese architect Junzo Yoshimura, later revised by American architect Jean Paul Carlhian. Though 96% of the exhibition space is subterranean, there are two above-ground pavilions, one with a pyramidal motif, the other utilizing a circular theme of rounded arches. Both were designed with a classical sense of proportion and appropriate architectural detail to harmonize with neighboring landmark buildings. The African pavilion's domed roofs reflect the arch motif of the Freer, while the pyramidal silhouette of the Sackler is related to the Victorian Arts and Industries Building. And the subterranean areas are enlivened by dramatic descents, vast north-facing skylights, a spacious concourse, lush plantings, and indoor fountains. The exterior of the Sackler Gallery is faced with dark-beige Rockville granite, the African art pavilion with a light-pink granite. Floor paving throughout is pink Columbia granite, and limestone is used extensively inside both pavilions, for walls, the kiosk, and on the monumental entrance staircases. Roofing material is copper treated to oxidize green continuously as it ages. And ceilings consist of a series of beams disposed in layers as filigrees to be contrasted against brilliantly painted backgrounds, pyramidal in the Sackler, shell-shaped in the NMAA. Though the pavilions are relatively small in size, their scale is monumental. The three-story skylit concourse borders the northern edge of the underground Quadrangle. Descending in a sequential series of spaces from the kiosk, it contains a mural by Richard Haas of surrounding Smithsonian buildings.

Among the many donors who made this project possible are the governments of Japan and Korea, Sackler, and Haupt.

The Arthur M. Sackler Gallery: This thrilling new addition to the Smithsonian museum complex, opened in September of 1987, has 18,000 square feet of exhibition space used to display its vast collection spanning 5,000 years of Asian art. Its nucleus is the nearly 1,000 rare and valuable objects donated by New York psychiatrist and medical publisher Arthur M. Sackler (he also provided $4 million toward construction). His Chinese collection includes significant numbers of bronzes from the Shang (1700–1028 B.C.) through the Han (206 B.C.–A.D. 220) Dynasties; Chinese jades spanning the millennia from 3,000 B.C. to the 20th century; paintings from the 10th through the 20th centuries; and lacquerware. Large groups of metalwork, including Sasanian silver, sculpture from the Near East, and stone and bronze sculpture from South and Southeast Asia, are also represented. And a 1986 acquisition added a comprehensive survey of Persian manuscripts, miniatures, calligraphies, illuminations, bookbindings, and textiles. The gallery's holdings will continue to grow in coming years through the purchase and donation of significant works of art. Museum holdings are supplemented by loan exhibitions and major international shows. Past exhibits here have included: "Nomads and Nobility: Art of the Ancient Near East," "Monsters, Myths, and Minerals" (exploring the ancient Chinese tradition of depicting animals, real and mythic, in art, literature, and folk tales), "Pavilions and Immortal Mountains: Chinese Decorative Art and Painting," and "A Jeweler's Eye: Islamic Arts of the Book from the Vever Collection." A 2,000-square-foot gallery shop on the premises offers a broad range of books on Asian art, history, and culture, as well as jewelry, textiles, metalwork, and other items related to the exhibitions here. The Sackler shares curatorial and conservation staffs and research facilities with its Oriental-oriented neighbor, the Freer. Eventually an underground passageway will connect the two museums.

For information about museum programs, inquire at the information desk. There are fascinating lectures, films, docent-led tours, and children's programs, among other events. The museum is open daily 10 a.m. to 5:30 p.m. For further details, call 357-2700.

The National Museum of African Art: Previously housed in the first Washington home of famed black orator, abolitionist, journalist, and statesman Frederick Douglass, this very fine institution is the only museum in the United States devoted solely to the collection, study, and exhibition of African art. Though the Douglass home was itself a point of interest, we're happy to see the NMAA in a more easily accessible location. Its fascinating permanent collection of over 6,000 objects, shown in rotating exhibits, highlights the traditional arts of the vast sub-Saharan region while also encompassing the ancient and contemporary arts of the entire continent, including North Africa. The majority of the collection dates from the 19th and 20th centuries. Works from the western part of the Sudan and the Guinea Coast regions are particularly well represented. NMAA's holdings are sometimes supplemented by loans from other museums and collections. Exhibitions here have included a show of African textiles; 100 works from the permanent collection in wood, ivory, and metal; and "African Art and the Cycle of Life," reflecting African attitudes about fertility, birth, death, ancestors, etc.

Inquire at the desk about workshops (including children's programs), lectures, docent-led tours, films, and demonstrations. The museum is open daily from 10 a.m. to 5:30 p.m. For further information, call 357-1300.

The International Center: Sponsoring exhibits and public symposia focusing on all the world's cultures, especially the ancient and evolving cultures of the non-Western world, this facility is entered through an elegant bronze-domed circular kiosk at 1100 Jefferson Dr. SW. From the kiosk, you proceed along a skylighted Grand Concourse to the 8,700-square-foot International Gallery. The aptly chosen opening exhibition here, "Generations: The Roots of Becoming," explored the mythology and rituals surrounding the universal theme of birth, touching on anthropological, ethnographic, and folkloric aspects. It was followed in 1988 by an exhibition on the world's rapidly disappearing rain forests. In an effort to help visitors gain perspective on their own cultures, exhibits here will contrast Western beliefs and attitudes with non-Western concepts and traditions. Long-term plans call for programs relating to Latin America and the upcoming Columbus quincentenary (1492–1992).

Inquire at the kiosk about lectures, films, performances, and demonstrations. For further details, call 357-2700.

The Enid A. Haupt Garden: With its central Victorian parterre and 1870s cast-iron furnishings, elaborate flower beds and borders, plant-filled turn-of-the-century urns, and lush baskets hung from 19th-century-style lampposts, this tranquilly beautiful oasis on the Mall is named for its donor, a noted supporter of horticultural projects. Though on ground level, it's really a rooftop garden above the subterranean museum complex. The magnolia-lined parterre, following 19th-century fashion, has multicolored swags and ribbon beds adapted from the 1876 Philadelphia Centennial Exposition's horticultural hall. The swags are comprised of 30,000 green and yellow Alternanthera, supplemented by seasonal displays of spring pansies, summer annuals, and autumn kale. A winter Oriental garden near the Sackler Gallery, entered via a nine-foot moongate, has benches backed by English boxwoods under the shade of weeping willows and cherry trees; half-round pieces of granite in its still pool are meant to suggest ripples. A summer Islamic garden outside the African art museum provides granite seating walls shaded by hawthorn trees, with tiny water channels fed by fountains and a waterfall or "chadar" inspired by the gardens of Shalimar. Three small terraces, shaded by black sour gum trees, are located near the Arts and Industries Building, as is a majestic century-old European linden tree. And a small courtyard sheltering a cutleaf Japanese maple surrounded by yew hedges is on the east side of the NMAA. Additional features include wisteria-covered dome-shaped trellises, clusters of trees (Sargent crabapples and little-leaf lindens) separating the pavilions from Independence Avenue, ginkgo trees, American hollies, a weeping European beech, and rose gardens. Elaborate cast-iron carriage gates made according to a 19th-century design by James

Renwick, flanked by four pillars made from the same red Seneca sandstone used to construct the "castle," have been installed at the Independence Avenue entrance to the garden.

Open from 7 a.m. to 9:15 p.m. Memorial Day through Labor Day, till 5:45 p.m. the rest of the year.

The Anacostia Neighborhood Museum

Located across Washington's other river, the Anacostia, at 1901 Fort Place SE in Fort Stanton Park (tel. 357-2700). Open from 10 a.m. to 5 p.m. daily. Closed Christmas Day. No Metro here; take a B-4 bus from Pennsylvania Avenue.

Not exactly one of Washington's major sights, but bracketed here with the rest of the Smithsonian complex for consistency's sake, this facility was created in 1967 as a neighborhood museum, with major focus on the history and cultural interests of the predominantly black Anacostia community. It has expanded its horizons over the years to include every aspect of black history, art, and culture, both American and worldwide. There's no permanent collection; the Anacostia produces a varying number of shows each year and offers a comprehensive schedule of free educational programs and activities in conjunction with exhibit themes. For instance, to complement an exhibition called "Climbing Jacob's Ladder: The Rise of Black Churches in Eastern American Cities, 1740–1877," the museum offered films, gospel music programs, and lectures by black ministers. And an earlier show, "Black Wings: The American Black in Aviation," was enhanced by panel discussions with black airmen, lectures by black NASA scientists, children's story hours about the events and personalities shown in the exhibits, and a lunchbox forum with Col. C. D. "Lucky" Lester, USAF, whose military career spanned 28 years.

Call for an events calendar (which always includes children's activities) or pick one up when you visit.

THE NATIONAL GALLERY OF ART:
On the north side of the Mall between 3rd and 7th Streets NW, with entrances at 6th Street and Constitution Avenue or Madison Drive, also at 4th and 7th Streets between Madison Drive and Constitution Avenue (tel. 737-4215). Open Monday to Saturday from 10 a.m. to 5 p.m., on Sunday from noon to 9 p.m., with extended hours (Monday to Saturday till 9 p.m.) Memorial Day through Labor Day. Closed Christmas and New Year's Days. Metro: Archives or Judiciary Square.

Note: Most people don't realize it, but the National Gallery of Art is not really part of the Smithsonian complex (though it is, in some arcane way, related to it). Hence its listing here apart from the other Mall museums.

The National Gallery of Art, housing one of the world's foremost collections of Western painting, sculpture, and graphic arts from the Middle Ages through the 20th century, has a dual personality. The original West Building, designed by John Russell Pope (he was also the architect of the Jefferson Memorial and the National Archives), is a neoclassic marble masterpiece with a domed rotunda over a colonnaded pool and fountain and high-ceilinged corridors leading to spacious garden courts. Dedicated by President Franklin D. Roosevelt in 1941, it was a gift to the nation from Andrew W. Mellon, who also contributed the nucleus of the collection. It included 21 masterpieces from the Hermitage—two Raphaels among them—which the post-Revolutionary Russian government, in need of cash, sold to Mellon in the late 1920s.

The East Building, opened in 1978, is an asymmetrical trapezoid with glass walls and lofty tetrahedron skylights designed by noted modern architect I. M. Pei. It is built of pink Tennessee marble, as is the West Building, and the marble was taken from the same quarry for both constructions, forming a link between the old architecture and the new. Its construction funded by the Andrew W. Mellon Foundation (and other Mellon family bequests), the East Building houses changing exhibits. In recent years these have included "Impressionist to Early Modern Paintings from the USSR: Works from the Hermitage and the Pushkin Museum of Fine Arts"; "Henri Matisse, the Early Years in Nice, 1916–1930"; "The Art of Paul Gauguin"; and "Japan: The Shaping of Daimyo Culture, 1200–1800." A massive aluminum Calder mobile suspended from the skylight, an immense bronze sculpture by Henry Moore, and a delightful Miró tapestry are among the works on permanent display. All three were specifically commissioned for the museum.

Between the East and West Buildings is an outdoor cobblestone courtyard called the Plaza, a visual link between the new and traditional architectural styles. Defined by glass pyramids which serve as skylights on the Concourse below, the Plaza is graced by a fountain and waterfall.

On the main floor of the West Building, about 800 paintings are shown at all times. Galleries to the right of the Rotunda feature 17th- to 19th-century French paintings, works of late 19th-century Americans like Homer and Sargent, and of slightly earlier British artists like Constable, Turner, and Gainsborough. To the left are the Italians (Renaissance, 17th, and 18th centuries), including the only da Vinci outside of Europe, *Ginerva De' Benci.* Paintings by El Greco, Goya, and Velázquez highlight the Spanish galleries; Grunewald, Dürer, Holbein, and Cranach can be seen in the German; Van Eyck, Rubens, and Bosch in the Flemish; and an excellent collection of Rembrandts in the Dutch. The interior of each of these main-floor galleries is decorated to reflect the period and country of the paintings exhibited; for example, the walls of the Italian galleries are covered in silk brocade, the Dutch galleries are paneled in dark oak, and the French rooms have ornate plaster detail.

Down a flight are 17th- and 18th-century prints, 19th- and 20th-century sculpture (with many pieces by Daumier, Degas, and Renoir), American Naïve 18th- and 19th-century paintings, Chinese porcelains, small Renaissance bronzes, 16th-century Flemish tapestries, decorative 18th-century arts, and an immense shop offering art books and prints. Special exhibitions also take place on this level, such as "Michelangelo: Draftsman/Architect"; "The Pastoral Landscape: the Legacy of Venice"; and "English Drawings and Watercolors: 1630–1850," the latter including works by Constable, Blake, and Turner. While you're in the West Building, seek out the lovely colonnaded Garden Courts. Under arched skylights, with comfortable upholstered chairs overlooking putti fountains, these courts are sublime settings in which to contemplate art and life while resting museum-weary feet.

Another museum shop is located in the concourse connecting the two wings; here, too, are the Concourse Buffet and the Cascade Café (details on National Gallery restaurants in Chapter IV).

Pick up a floor plan and calendar of events at an information desk (there's one at every entrance) to find out about exhibits, films, tours, lectures, and concerts. You might catch anything from a Cocteau film to a string quartet. Highly recommended are the free highlight tours of the West Building (Monday to Saturday at 3 p.m. and Sunday at 5 p.m.) and the East Building (Monday to Saturday at 11 a.m., Sunday at 1 p.m.).

THE TRIUMVIRATE OF PRESIDENTIAL MEMORIALS:

Only three American presidents have been singled out for recognition with great monuments in Washington, D.C. They are George Washington, Abraham Lincoln, and Thomas Jefferson.

The first monument to be built (to Washington) was begun in 1848, the last (to Jefferson) was dedicated in 1943 during Cherry Blossom time. There are wreath-laying ceremonies on Lincoln's and Jefferson's birthdays at their respective monuments.

The Washington Monument

On 15th Street and Constitution Avenue NW (tel. 426-6839). Open daily from the first Sunday in April through Labor Day from 8 a.m. to midnight, from 9 a.m. to 5 p.m. the rest of the year. Closed July 4th and Christmas Day. Metro: Smithsonian.

It's the world's tallest masonry structure—555 feet 5⅛ inches high, with marble walls 15 feet thick at the base and 18 inches at the top. Though a monument to George Washington was first conceived in 1783—16 years before his death—it was, in fact, built close to a century later, between 1848 and 1884. Most of the funds came from public subscription, but they were slow in coming, and construction bogged down on several occasions.

You can enjoy one of the finest views of Washington from the top of the monument—the Capitol Building to the east, Jefferson Memorial to the south, Lincoln Memorial to the west, and the White House to the north. There's a lot to see when you're up that high. It's especially lovely at night.

If you had a map based on the original L'Enfant plan of Washington, you'd note that the Washington Monument isn't exactly where the French designer had positioned it, at the axis where the White House would face the direct east-west line along the Mall at a 90° angle. The reason: The Mall was a marsh, too soggy at the position designated by L'Enfant to support the huge monument. So the position was shifted slightly eastward.

The Washington Monument was designed by Robert Mills, who was also the architect of the Old Patent Office Building and the Treasury Building. He had specified a circular colonnaded Greek temple base, but, due to lack of funds, that part of his plan, quite fortunately we think, was never added. The monument, in its present pure simplicity, is impressive, contemporary, timeless.

Looking upward from the base of the monument, you'll notice that the color of the marble stones is darker past a point about 150 feet up. The change of hue marks a time gap that occurred when work stopped after funds petered out for two reasons: the escalation of problems that led to the Civil War and an incident of religious significance. Pope Pius IX had sent a block of marble from Rome to be included in the monument. When the block was stolen in 1854, the robbery caused considerable discontent, on religious and political grounds, and contributions sank to an all-time low. Eventually the government took over the project in the mid-1870s and work was resumed. After that date, marble came from another strata of quarry, and it was darker than the earlier stones.

The Washington Monument was opened to the public in 1888, four years after construction was completed. Total cost: $1,187,710.

In tourist season, arrive before 8 a.m. to avoid long lines. Climbing the 897 steps is verboten, but a large elevator whisks visitors to the top in just 70 seconds. If, however, you're avid to see more of the interior, **"Down the Steps" tours** are given, subject to staff availability, at 10 a.m. and 3 p.m. daily. For details, call before you go or ask a ranger on duty. On this tour you'll learn more about the building of the monument and get to see the 190 carved stones inserted into the interior walls. They range from a piece of stone from the Parthenon to plaques presented by city fire departments.

Light snack fare—a bagel and cream cheese, burritos, lemonade, ice cream, etc.—is sold at a snackbar on the grounds; consider buying, or bringing, the makings for a picnic on the grassy expanse surrounding the monument.

The Lincoln Memorial

Directly west of the Mall in Potomac Park, at 23rd Street NW, between Constitution and Independence Avenues (tel. 426-6895). Open 24 hours daily, year round, except Christmas Day. Park staff on duty 8 a.m. to midnight. Metro: Foggy Bottom.

Though planned as early as 1867, this famous landmark was not completed until 1922, a little over half a century after President Abraham Lincoln was assassinated in Ford's Theatre by John Wilkes Booth.

The inspiration for the Lincoln Memorial is classic—a rectangular Doric temple with 36 marble columns similar in design to the Parthenon in Greece. Its tapered columns, and their placement in a slightly convex arrangement, follow the ancient Greek theory of temple construction. The columns represent the 36 states that belonged to the Union when Lincoln died; their names appear on the frieze above the row of columns. Names of the 48 states in the Union, as of 1922, are inscribed toward the top of the monument. The memorial faces the Capitol from the west end of the Mall, in perfect alignment with it and with the Washington Monument. Architect for the structure was Henry Bacon.

Inside the 100-foot (or approximately nine-story) structure is the 19- by19-foot statue of the seated Lincoln in deep contemplation, which many consider one of the great sculptures of the world. Twenty-eight blocks of pure-white marble were required for the statue, which took four years to complete; it is flanked by two rows of Ionic columns. The sculptor was Daniel Chester French, whose other works include the bronze doors of the Boston Public Library, the famous *Minuteman,* the colossal *State of the Republic* for the World's Columbian Exposition in Chicago, *John Hancock,* and some statuary in the Capitol. The statue's awe-inspiring effect is well described in these words by Walt Whitman: "He was a mountain in grandeur of the soul, he was a sea in deep undervoice of mystic loneliness, he was a star in steadfast purity of purpose and service, and he abides."

Lincoln's Second Inaugural Address and his Gettysburg Address are engraved on the interior limestone walls of the memorial. And two 60-foot murals by Jules Guerin allegorically depict the freeing of the slaves and the unity of North and South, Lincoln's major achievements.

In the foreground of the memorial is the reflecting pool, which mirrors the Washington Monument and the Capitol at night when they're illuminated. It's Washington's most spectacular vista. We also like to come at night because the crowds are thinner and minus the rambunctious classroomfuls of children. In relative silence, one can more fully experience this moving testament to the spirit of a great American and to the best of what America represents.

However, you haven't seen the entirety of the Lincoln Memorial until you've taken a free 40-minute **Under the Lincoln tour,** given year round except in July and August. Led by a park ranger, you'll visit a cavern forming under the monument's foundation and view stalagmites and stalactites. You have to book months in advance (these tours are popular) by calling 426-6841 or writing to the National Parks Service, Mall Operations, 900 Ohio Dr. SW, Washington, D.C. 20242.

There are picnic tables under the trees across the street by the Reflecting Pool—a lovely spot for an outdoor lunch if you bring picnic fare.

The Jefferson Memorial

At the bottom of Tidal Basin Drive on the south shore of the Tidal Basin (tel. 426-6821). Open daily from 8 a.m. to midnight. Best transportation is via Tourmobile.

This was the third great presidential monument to be erected in Washington. It's a late arrival, authorized by Act of Congress only in 1934, and dedicated nine years later on April 13, 1943, Jefferson's birthday. The subject was the author of our Declaration of Independence, third president of the United States, and father of the University of Virginia. He was an intellectual who thrived on the body of world knowledge, a thinker whose vision included the abolition of slavery, religious freedom, and laws and constitutions that "go hand in hand with the progress of the human mind."

At a White House reception for Nobel Prize winners in 1962, President John F. Kennedy nodded toward the Jefferson Memorial directly south of the White House, then to his guests, and said, "I think this is the most extraordinary collection of talent, of human knowledge, that has ever been gathered together at the White House—with the possible exception of when Thomas Jefferson dined alone."

The site for the Jefferson Memorial, in relation to the Washington and Lincoln Memorials, was of extraordinary importance. The Capitol, the White House, and the Mall already were located in accordance with L'Enfant's plan, and there was no spot for such a project if the symmetry that guided L'Enfant was to be maintained. So the memorial was built on land reclaimed from the Potomac River, now known as the Tidal Basin. Yet in relation to the other monuments the choice of the spot for the Jefferson memorial is perfect.

It's a beautiful memorial, a columned rotunda in the style of the Pantheon in Rome which Jefferson so admired.

On the Tidal Basin side, the sculptural group above the entrance depicts Jefferson with Benjamin Franklin, John Adams, Roger Sherman, and Robert Livingston, who worked on drafting the Declaration of Independence. The domed interior of the memorial contains the 19-foot bronze statue of Jefferson standing on a six-foot pedestal of black Minnesota granite. The sculpture is the work of Rudulph Evans, who was chosen from more than 100 artists in a nationwide competition. Jefferson is depicted wearing a fur-collared coat given to him by his close friend, the Polish general, Thaddeus Kosciuszko.

Inscriptions from Jefferson's writing engraved on the interior walls expand on Jefferson's philosophy best expressed in the circular frieze quotation: "I have sworn upon the altar of God eternal hostility to any form of tyranny over the mind of man."

THE WHITE HOUSE: 1600 Pennsylvania Ave. NW (tel. 456-7041). Entrance at the East Gate on East Executive Avenue. Open to visitors Tuesday to Saturday from 10 a.m. to noon. Metro: McPherson Square.

It's the oldest public building in Washington, home to every president of the United States except George Washington. The interior is a repository of art and furnishings that dynamically showcases the tastes of our chief executives and First Ladies from the beginning of the American Republic.

You will be taken through five rooms in the White House—the East Room, Green Room, Blue Room, Red Room, and State Dining Room—and be given glimpses of several of the other rooms, like the Library (at the beginning of the tour), as well as the Jacqueline Kennedy garden.

The **East Room** has seen great and gala receptions, dances, marriages of presidents' daughters, and other dazzling events. Heads of state have been entertained here, Presidents McKinley and Kennedy lay in state here, and funeral and memorial services for Presidents Harrison, Taylor, Lincoln, Harding, and Franklin D. Roosevelt were conducted here. On the east wall, you'll see a Gilbert Stuart portrait of George Washington.

The **Green Room** was Thomas Jefferson's dining room. He designed a revolving tray, really a revolving door with trays on one side, so servants could leave dishes on the kitchen side. Then he would twirl the door, take the food from the shelves, and serve his own guests. Thus his privacy was uninvaded. (Bugging in those days was strictly ear-to-door.) Walls here are covered in green watered-silk fabric, and some of the early-19th-century furnishings are attributed to the famous cabinetmaker Duncan Phyfe. There are notable paintings by Gilbert Stuart and John Singer Sargent.

The **Blue Room** has not always been blue. Mrs. John F. Kennedy learned that the room may have been white during the Madison administration, and she changed the blue walls to white silk. It was beautiful and simple. Then Mrs. Richard M. Nixon tried her hand at redecorating the Blue Room—she gave it its current blue-bordered beige wallpaper, a reproduction of a 19th-century design. The

French Empire furnishings still include many of those here during the administration of President James Monroe (1817–1825). It is in this room that the president and First Lady often receive visitors, that President Cleveland was married, and that Reagan greeted the returning Iranian hostages.

Several portraits of past presidents—plus Albert Bierstadt's *View of the Rocky Mountains* and a Gilbert Stuart portrait of Dolley Madison—hang in the **Red Room.** This is where the First Lady occasionally receives her guests. It's also used as a reception room, usually for small dinners. The satin-covered walls and most of the Empire furnishings are red, set off by white wainscoting and moldings.

The white-walled, gold-accented **State Dining Room** is a superb setting for state dinners and luncheons. The white marble mantel is a reproduction; the original mantel was presented to President Harry Truman when he was having the White House renovated in 1948; it may now be seen in the Truman Library in Independence, Missouri.

Since its cornerstone was laid in 1792, the White House has gone through numerous changes. It was designed by Irishman James Hoban, so it isn't surprising that it's a lot like the house of the Duke of Leinster of Dublin. In 1824 the South Portico was added. Benjamin Henry Latrobe executed the design, as he did for the North Portico extending out over the front door and driveway (added in 1829). Electricity was first installed during President Benjamin Harrison's residence in 1891.

In 1902, repairs and refurnishings of the White House cost almost $500,000. No other great change came about until Harry Truman added his controversial "Balcony" inside the columns of the South Portico. Also in 1948, when Harry Truman was worried that his bathtub might sink through the floor during a state reception, nearly $6 million was allotted for reconstruction of the building. The Trumans moved to Blair House across the street for four years while the White House interior was taken apart and put back together again, piece by piece. Steel girders and concrete shored up the place. It's as solid as Gibraltar now.

In 1961 Mrs. John F. Kennedy formed a Fine Arts Committee, and she and her group set about restoring the famous rooms to their original grandeur. Her artistic touch will be in evidence for generations to come. Another Kennedy legacy is the superb Monet landscape donated by the Kennedy family in memory of President John F. Kennedy.

Seeing the White House

Over a million people line up annually to see the Executive Mansion. Best bet is to get tickets in advance from your congressperson or senator for the VIP tours at 8:15, 8:30, and 8:45

a.m. (details in Chapter II). This ensures your entrance, even in tourist season when over 6,000 people try to squeeze in during the two hours each day the White House is open. It also entitles you to a more extensive—and guided—tour; on later visits there are guides on hand to answer questions, but no actual tour is given. A good idea, before you take any tour, is to pick up a book called *The White House, An Historic Guide,* available in bookstores here and at many other District sights. Then you'll know what to look for in each room, and your experience will be greatly enhanced.

Most of the year, if you don't have VIP tour tickets, you just get in line at the East Gate before 10 a.m. (visitors enter in groups between 10 a.m. and noon). Arrive early to be sure you get in. Between Memorial Day and Labor Day tickets are required. They are available (only one to a customer) at one of the kiosks on the Ellipse (at 15th Street and Constitution Avenue NW) from 8 a.m. on the day of your visit only; lines begin forming even earlier. There's no charge. Once you've obtained your ticket (the tour time is stamped on it), you can go to a nearby hotel for breakfast, like the Washington at 15th Street and Pennsylvania Avenue, or the classier, and pricier, Hay-Adams at 1200 16th St. Or you can sit and wait in the bleachers while glee clubs and bands entertain. Spring and summer there are occasional garden tours from 2 to 5 p.m. on weekends; no tickets are required, but call for details. Some days the White House is closed for official functions, so check before leaving your hotel; you can call the above number 24 hours a day.

THE CAPITOL: Capitol Hill at the east end of the Mall, with an entrance on East Capitol Street and 1st Street NW (tel. 225-6827). Open from 9 a.m. to 4:30 p.m. (tours till 3:45 p.m.) daily except Thanksgiving, Christmas, and New Year's Days. Metro: Capitol South.

As our most tangible national symbol since its first wing was completed in 1800, and the place where all our laws are enacted, the Capitol is perhaps the most important edifice in the United States. It's also one of the most beautiful. Historian Allan Nevins called it "the spirit of America in stone." For 134 years it sheltered not only both houses of Congress but the Library of Congress and the Supreme Court.

Seeing the Capitol

As at the White House, VIP tour tickets from your congressperson or senator for the morning tours are a definite advantage (details in Chapter II). Only on the longer VIP tours do you visit the House and Senate chambers. Write as far in advance as possible—allotments are limited—specifying the dates you can visit. Also request Visitor's Passes for each member of your party to view a session of the House and/or Senate. If you don't get advance tickets, free 35-minute guided tours leave from the Rotunda every 15 minutes between 9 a.m. and 3:45 p.m. And if you don't receive Visitor's Passes in the mail, they're obtainable at your senators' offices on the Constitution Avenue side of the building (for noncitizens it's even easier: you just have to present your passport at the House galleries or Senate door). You'll know when the House or Senate is meeting when you see flags flying over their respective sides of the Capitol. Or you can check the "Today in Congress" column weekdays in the *Washington Post* for details on times of House and Senate committee meetings. This column also tells you which sessions are open to the public and allows you to pick a subject that interests you rather than attending, say, a hearing on official mail costs. Certainly "political developments in El Salvador" or "technology lessons learned from Chernobyl" (all offered on a given day) would have been more intriguing. If you're interested in a particular bill, call the above-listed number for information.

The **Rotunda,** where the tours begin, had a dome of copper over wood until 1855. That's when the great cast-iron dome was begun. Completed during the Civil War, when soldiers of the Union Army used the room as a barracks, it weighs nine million pounds. In the eye of the 180-foot-high dome is an allegorical fresco by Constantino Brumidi portraying George Washington watching over the nation—one of the several noteworthy pieces of art here. Beneath the Rotunda is the **Crypt.** It was reserved for George Washington's remains, but his family refused to have him buried outside the family tomb in Mount Vernon. So the Crypt has remained empty ever since. Nine presidents have lain in state here for public viewing; for JFK the line of mourners stretched 40 blocks.

National Statuary Hall originally was the chamber of the House of Representatives, but it was abandoned for that purpose because of its poor acoustics. Your guide will demonstrate that a whisper can be heard clear across the room from a certain spot. In 1864 it became Statuary Hall, and the states were invited to send two statues each of native sons to the hall. As the room filled up, statues spilled over into the Hall of Columns, corridors, anywhere that might accommodate the bronze and marble artifacts. Many of the statues honor individuals who have had important roles in American history, such as Henry Clay, Ethan Allen, and Daniel Webster.

On Congressional VIP tours (or with Visitor's Passes) you'll also visit either the House or Senate chambers and relearn how our government works. Bills begin in the House, go to the Senate, and, when approved, to the president. A two-thirds vote of the House and Senate can override a presidential veto.

The **House of Representatives Chamber,** 139 feet by 52 feet, is the largest legislative chamber in the world. Representatives' seating is arranged in a crescent, one side for Democrats, the other for Republicans. The **Senate Chamber,** redecorated in the 1950s, is sedate, with marble, mahogany, and damask.

THE SUPREME COURT: 1st Street NE, between East Capitol Street and Maryland Avenue (tel. 479-3030). Open Monday to Friday from 9 a.m. to 4:30 p.m. Metro: Capitol South or Union Station.

Brought into being by Article III of the Constitution (just as the legislative and executive branches of our government were created by Articles I and II respectively), the Supreme Court is charged with deciding whether actions of Congress, the president, the states, and lower courts are in accord with the Constitution and with interpreting that document's enduring principles and applying them to new situations and changing conditions. It has the power of "judicial review"—authority to invalidate legislation or executive action that conflicts with the Constitution. Only about 150 cases are heard each year by the Supreme Court, many of them dealing with issues vital to the nation. Their rulings are final, reversible only by another Supreme Court decision, or, in some cases, an act of Congress or a Constitutional amendment.

Until 1935 the Supreme Court met in the Capitol. Architect Cass Gilbert designed the stately Corinthian marble palace that houses the Court today, its noble intention etched in a frieze over the colonnaded entrance, "Equal Justice Under Law." The building was considered rather grandiose by early residents: one Justice deemed it "wholly inappropriate for a quiet group of old boys such as the Supreme Court"; another remarked that the Justices ought to enter such pomp precincts on elephants.

If you're in town when the Court is in session, you should definitely see a case being argued. The Court meets Monday to Wednesday from 10 a.m. to 3 p.m. (with a lunch-hour recess from noon to 1 p.m.) from the first Monday in October through late April, alternating, in approximately two-week intervals, between "sittings" to hear cases and deliver opinions and "recesses" for consideration of business before the court. Mid-May to early July, you can attend brief half-hour sessions at 10 a.m. on Monday, during which time the Justices release orders and opinions. You can find out what cases are on the docket by checking the *Washington Post's* "Court Calendar." Arrive at least an hour early—even earlier for a highly publicized case—to line up for seats, about 150 of which are allotted to the general public.

At 10 a.m. the entrance of the Justices is announced by the Marshal, and all present rise and remain standing while the Justices are seated following the chant: "The Honorable, the Chief Justice and Associate Justices of the Supreme Court of the United States. Oyez! Oyez! [It's law French for 'Hear ye.'] All persons having business before the Honorable, the Supreme Court of the United States, are admonished to draw near and give their attention, for the Court is now sitting. God save the United States and this Honorable Court!" There are many rituals here. The Court has a record before it of prior proceedings and relevant briefs, so each side is allowed only a 30-minute argument. If the Court is not in session during your visit, you can attend a free lecture in the courtroom about Court procedure and the building's architecture. Lectures are given from 9:30 a.m. to 3:30 p.m. every hour on the half hour.

After the talk, explore the Great Hall and see the 30-minute film on the workings of the Court down a flight of steps. The ground floor is a good vantage point to view one of two grand spiral staircases here similar to those at the Vatican and the Paris Opera. There are also interesting exhibits and a gift shop on this level, and good meals are served at the adjoining cafeteria (details in Chapter IV).

THE LIBRARY OF CONGRESS: On 1st Street SE, between Independence Avenue and East Capitol Street, lower level (tel. 287-5000). Open weekdays from 8:30 a.m. to 9:30 p.m., on Saturday to 6 p.m. Closed Sundays and holidays. Metro: Capitol South.

This is the nation's library, designed in 1800 "for the purchase of such books as may be necessary for the use of Congress," but over the years expanded to serve all Americans—from the blind for whom books are recorded on cassette and/or translated into Braille, to research scholars and college students. Its first collection of books was destroyed when the British burned the Capitol (where the library was then housed) during the War of 1812. Thomas Jefferson then donated his personal library of 6,487 books as a replacement, and this legacy became the foundation of what would grow to be the world's largest library. Today the collection includes over 85 million items housed in three buildings, including not only some 22 million books in all languages but 4 million maps and atlases dating to the middle of the 14th century, Stradivari violins, letters of George Washington, the earliest motion picture print (made by Thomas Edison in 1893), Thomas Jefferson's rough draft of the Declaration of Independence, etc., etc., etc. All knowledge is the province of this treasury in which Americans can find "all the answers stored in a single place." The library also maintains the Dewey Decimal System; offers a year-round program of concerts, lectures, and poetry readings; and houses the Copyright Office.

Almost as awesome as the scope of the library's effects and activities is the ornate Italian Renaissance–style **Thomas Jefferson Building,** erected between 1888 and 1897 to contain the burgeoning collection and establish America as a cultured nation with magnificent institutions equal to anything in Europe. Fifty-two artists worked for eight years on its interior, utilizing over 1,500 fully developed architectural drawings. There are floor mosaics from Italy, allegorical paintings on the overhead vaults, over a hundred murals, and numerous ornamental cornucopias, ribbons, vines, and garlands within, as well as 42 granite sculptures and yards of bas-reliefs on the outside. Especially impressive are the exquisite marble Great Hall and the Main Reading Room, the latter under a 160-foot dome.

Tours leave every hour on the hour weekdays from 9 a.m. to 4 p.m. from the Visitor Services Center in the west entrance ground-floor lobby at the above address. A prelude to each tour is an 18-minute introductory slide-sound presentation called *America's Library,* shown hourly from 8:45 a.m. to 8:45 p.m. weekdays, till 5:45 p.m. on Saturday. The tour takes in the Great Hall, Main Reading Room (though it may be closed for renovation when you read this), and permanent exhibits such as the *Gutenberg Bible* (one of three perfect surviving examples) and the *Giant Bible of Mainz,* an illuminated manuscript executed by hand on vellum about the same time the *Gutenberg* was printed.

On the way out, pick up a Calendar of Events at the ground-floor exit. You might also want to check out the nearby **James Madison Memorial Building,** at 101 Independence Ave. SE (tel. 287-5000), which along with the **John Adams Building** provides additional storage space. The Madison Building offers interesting exhibits and features classic, rare, and unusual films in its Mary Pickford Theater. It also contains a noteworthy restaurant and cafeteria (details in Chapter IV), though picnic tables out front here and at the Thomas Jefferson Building provide a tempting alternative.

THE NATIONAL ARCHIVES: Constitution Avenue between 7th and 9th Streets NW (tel. 523-3000 for information on exhibits and films, 523-3220 for research information). Open daily from April 1 to Labor Day from 10 a.m. to 9 p.m.; from the day after Labor Day to March 31, 10 a.m. to 5:30 p.m. Metro: Archives.

Keeper of America's documentary heritage, the National Archives displays our most cherished treasures in appropriately awesome surroundings. Housed in the Rotunda of the Exhibition Hall are the nation's three charter documents—the Declaration of Independence, the Constitution of the United States, and its Bill of Rights—which are on view daily to the public. Every night these three "Charters of Freedom" are lowered 20 feet into a 50-ton vault for safekeeping, and every morning they are raised for exhibition. During the day, armed guards stand on duty in the hall.

High above and flanking the documents are two larger-than-life murals painted by Barry Faulkner. One, entitled *The Declaration of Independence,* represents Thomas Jefferson presenting a draft of the Declaration to John Hancock, the presiding officer of the Continental Congress; the other, entitled *The Constitution,* shows James

Madison submitting the Constitution to George Washington and the Constitutional Convention.

In the display cases on either side of the Declaration of Independence are exhibits, such as the recent "The American Experiment: Creating the Constitution," celebrating the 200th anniversary of that hallowed document. The 1297 version of the Magna Carta, one of the bases for fundamental English privileges and rights, is on display in the Rotunda indefinitely, and the soon-to-open "Securities for Liberty" exhibition, commemorating the Bill of Rights, will be open through 1991. It features over 30 documents—including an early version with changes in John Adams' hand—that weave together the ideas, events, and political struggles which culminated in the Bill of Rights.

But the Archives serves as much more than a museum of cherished documents. Charged with sifting through the accumulated papers of America's official life—millions of pieces each year—the Archives is a repository for two centuries' worth of census figures, military records, naturalization papers, passport applications, maps, charts, photographs, slave-ship manifests, and a good deal more. It's famous as a center of genealogical research. Alex Haley began his work on *Roots* here, and if you'd like to trace your own, consider doing the same. Stop first, though, in Room 400 (enter via Pennsylvania Avenue) where a staff member can tell you how to go about it and whether it's worth the effort. Archives' holdings are available for research purposes to anyone 16 or older with valid photo ID; call for details.

Like so many other important Washington institutions, the National Archives is housed in an impressive neoclassic building, designed in the 1930s by John Russell Pope, architect of the Jefferson Memorial and the National Gallery. Seventy-two Corinthian columns grace the four façades, great bronze doors herald the Constitution Avenue entrance, and allegorical sculpture adorns the pediment.

Free docent tours are given weekdays at 10:15 a.m. and 1:15 p.m. by appointment only; call 523-3183 for details. Pick up a schedule of events such as lectures, films, and genealogy workshops when you visit.

If you're visiting during 1989, be sure to see the "Petitions" exhibit in the Circular Gallery—a showcase of over 60 petitions written by private citizens to the Federal government. Ranging from 1775 to 1980, they include a 1789 antislavery petition signed by Benjamin Franklin, Thomas Edison's 1879 petition re a brutal lynching in Arkansas, and a 1945 petition from 70 scientists who worked on developing the atomic bomb urging President Truman to consider the moral implications of its use.

THE FEDERAL BUREAU OF INVESTIGATION: The J. Edgar Hoover FBI Building, E Street between 9th and 10th Streets

NW (tel. 324-3447), is open weekdays only, from 8:45 a.m. to 4:15
p.m.; closed weekends and holidays. Metro: Archives, Metro Center, or Federal Triangle.

Over half a million annual visitors thrill to the evil doings of the
criminal element while touring the headquarters of the FBI. The attraction is especially popular with kids. To beat the crowds, arrive
for the 1¼-hour tour before 8:45 a.m. or write to your senator or
congressperson for a scheduled reservation as far in advance as possible (details in Chapter II).

The tour begins with a short videotape presentation about the
priorities of the bureau—organized crime, white-collar crime, terrorism, and foreign counterintelligence. En route, you'll learn
about this organization's history (it was established in 1908) and its
activities over the years. You'll see photos of big-time gangsters like
Al Capone and Doc Barker and some of the weapons they used: an
actual counterintelligence surveillance videotape of a foreign agent
giving instructions to an American double agent; ingenious espionage devices that spies have used to transport microfilm; photos of
the ten most wanted fugitives (415 of them—only seven of them
women—have made the list since its inception in 1950; 388 have
been captured, and two were actually recognized at this exhibit by
people on the tour and apprehended).

The U.S. Crime Clock gives the grim statistics about the number of murders (one every 25 minutes), burglaries (one every 10 seconds), and rapes (one every six minutes) committed in this country.
Other exhibits deal with TV shows and movies about the FBI,
white-collar crime, illegal gambling, hijacking, use of fingerprints
for identification, and agent training. On display are over 4,000
weapons, many of which have been confiscated from criminals;
they're used for reference purposes. And a Drug Enforcement Administration exhibit includes drug paraphernalia and substances, a
world map showing routes via which illicit drugs enter the country,
and ways the FBI/DEA are attempting to combat illicit drugs—
educational as well as investigational.

You'll visit the serology lab; the Document Section (where
fraudulent checks and holdup notes are examined); the Firearms
Identification Unit (where it's determined if a bullet was fired
from a given weapon); the Instrumental Analysis Unit (where from
a tiny piece of paint the FBI can determine the approximate
make and model of a car); the unit where hairs and fibers are examined; and a Forfeiture and Seizure Exhibit—a display of jewelry,
furs, and other proceeds from illegal narcotics operations. The tour
ends with a firearms demonstration given by a sharp-shooting
agent.

THE JOHN F. KENNEDY CENTER FOR THE PERFORMING ARTS: At the southern end of New Hampshire Avenue NW

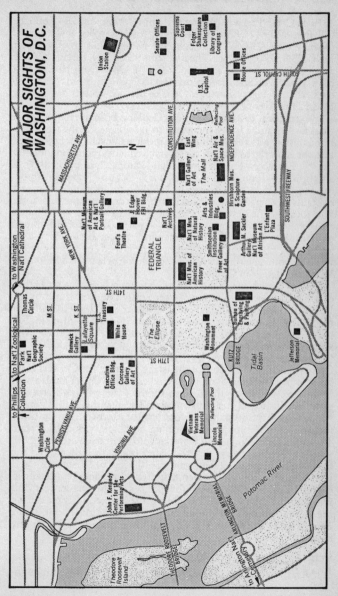

MAJOR SIGHTS OF WASHINGTON, D.C.

at Rock Creek Parkway (for general information, call 254-3600, or toll free 800/424-8504 nationwide; for box office information: Opera House, 254-3770; Eisenhower Theater, 254-3670; Concert Hall, 254-3776; Terrace Theater, 254-9895; the Instant Charge number for credit-card sales is 857-0900). Open from 10 a.m. to 9 p.m. Monday to Saturday, from noon to 9 p.m. on Sunday and holidays. Metro: Foggy Bottom. Or take the no. 46 bus down New Hampshire Avenue from Dupont Circle.

Opened in 1971, the Kennedy Center is both our national cultural facility and a living memorial to John F. Kennedy, whose administration was very enthusiastic about its development. Carved into the center's river façade are several Kennedy quotations, including ". . . the New Frontier for which I campaign in public life can also be a New Frontier for American art." Set on 17 acres overlooking the Potomac, the striking $73-million performing arts center contains an opera house, a concert hall, two dramatic theaters, and a film theater. The best way to see the Kennedy Center—including areas you can't visit on your own—is to take a free 50-minute guided tour; they're given Monday to Saturday between 10 a.m. and 1 p.m. Once again, you can beat the crowds by writing in advance to your senator or congressperson for tickets for a 9:30 a.m. VIP tour (details in Chapter II).

The tour begins in the Hall of Nations, where, in alphabetical order, all the flags of the countries recognized diplomatically by the U.S. are displayed. Throughout the center you'll see the gifts of many nations, including all the marble used in the building (3,700 tons), which was donated by Italy. First stop is the Grand Foyer—scene of many free concerts and programs and reception area for all three theaters on the main level; the 18 crystal chandeliers are a gift from Sweden. You'll also visit the Israeli Lounge; the Concert Hall, home of the National Symphony Orchestra; the Opera House with its Matisse tapestries; the African rooms (where African arts and crafts are displayed); the Eisenhower Theater; the Hall of States where flags of the 50 states and four territories are hung in the order they joined the Union; the Performing Arts Library; and the Terrace Theater, a Bicentennial gift from Japan. If rehearsals are going on, visits to the theaters are omitted. After the tour, walk around the building's terrace for a panoramic 360° view of Washington and plan a meal in one of the Kennedy Center restaurants (details in Chapter IV). See Chapter VII for specifics on theater, concert, and film offerings. There is parking below the Kennedy Center during the day at $2 for the first hour, $2 for each additional hour with a maximum of five hours and $6; nighttime parking is $4 for any length of time.

THE WASHINGTON NATIONAL CATHEDRAL: Mount
St. Alban, Massachusetts and Wisconsin Avenues NW, with its en-

trance on Wisconsin Avenue (tel. 537-6200). Open Monday to Saturday from 10 a.m. to 4:30 p.m. Metro: Tenleytown. Or take any N bus up Massachusetts Avenue from Dupont Circle.

The Cathedral Church of Saint Peter and Saint Paul, also known as the National Cathedral, seeks to serve the entire nation as a house of prayer for all people. It has been the setting for every kind of religious observance; even Jewish congregations have worshipped here while waiting for synagogue construction to be completed. The concept of such a cathedral dates back to 1791 when Pierre L'Enfant specified "a great church for national purposes" in his plan for the city. But the foundation was not laid until 1907 (by Theodore Roosevelt using the mallet with which George Washington set the Capitol cornerstone), and the principal—though not original—architect, Philip Hubert Frohman, watched over the construction from 1921 until his death in 1972. Construction work still goes on today on the world's sixth-largest cathedral. It's modeled on the 14th-century English Gothic style but, in addition to flying buttresses and gargoyles, it has some distinctly 20th-century American touches, such as a stained-glass window commemorating the Apollo XI flight and containing a piece of moon rock. Its setting —on 57 beautifully landscaped acres on the highest point in the city —is worthy of a great institution. On the premises are lovely gardens, four schools (including a College of Preachers), an herb garden, a greenhouse, a shop called the Herb Cottage, and a carver's shed where you can see stonecarvers at work.

The cathedral has seen much history. Services were held here to celebrate the end of World Wars I and II. The funerals of Presidents Wilson (he and his wife are buried on the grounds) and Eisenhower took place here. At her request Helen Keller and her two companions were buried here. Martin Luther King preached his last sermon at the cathedral, and during the Iranian crisis, a 24-hour prayer vigil was held in the Holy Spirit Chapel until the hostages were released; at a prayer service they attended soon after, Col. Thomas Schaefer greeted the nation with the words, "Good morning, my fellow Americans. You don't know how long I've been waiting to say those words." More recently, President Reagan's second-term inaugural was held here with the Rev. Billy Graham officiating.

You can explore the cathedral's art and architecture on a free one-hour tour Monday to Saturday from 10 a.m. to 3:15 p.m., Sunday 12:15 to 2:45 p.m. Tours depart continually during those hours. Allow time to see the grounds after the tour, to visit the Observation Gallery where 70 windows provide panoramic views, and to check out the offerings in the large museum shop (replicas of cathedral statuary, Christmas cards, religious art, etc.) whose proceeds go to the cathedral's upkeep and continued construction. Construction, by the way, is set to be completed in 1990, heralding an entire year of special events and celebrations.

Of course, you can also attend services (Monday to Saturday at 7:30 a.m., noon, and 4 p.m.; on Sunday at 8, 9, and 11 a.m. and 4 p.m.; September to June there's a folk guitar Mass on Sunday at 10 a.m.). In addition there are numerous concerts (Ravi Shankar played sitar at a memorial for Gandhi, and Leonard Bernstein conducted the National Symphony here at a Stravinsky Centennial), lectures, workshops in everything from brass rubbing to needlepoint, and other events. The 53-bell carillon is played on Saturday at 5 p.m. in spring and summer, at 12:30 p.m. in fall and winter; organ recitals are given on the great organ following Sunday evensong services at 5 p.m.; the superb men's and boy's choir can be heard Sunday mornings at 11, the boys alone Monday to Wednesday at 4 p.m.; and there are free concerts every Tuesday at 8 p.m. during summer.

THE BUREAU OF ENGRAVING AND PRINTING: 14th and C Streets SW, just a block south of the Mall (tel. 447-0193). Open from 9 a.m. to 2 p.m. weekdays only; closed legal holidays. Metro: Smithsonian.

This is where every last dollar of U.S. currency—$66 billion annually—is produced at the rate of 22.7 million notes a day by a staff of 2,300 working around the clock! In addition the bureau prints postage stamps (35 billion per year), Treasury bonds, and White House invitations. It's the only security printing plant in the world open to the public.

Some days as many as 5,000 people line up to get a peek at all that moolah; so arrive early, especially in tourist season. Twenty-five-minute self-guided tours depart continuously during the above hours.

Most printing here is done from engraved steel plates in a process known as "intaglio." It's hardest to counterfeit, because the slightest alteration will cause a noticeable facial change in the portrait in use. Incidentally, by law, no portrait of a living person can be used on stamps or currency. Each sheet is forced, under extremely heavy pressure, into the finely engraved lines of a plate to pick up the ink. The backs of the notes are printed with green ink on one day, and the faces are printed with black ink on the following day. Here's where the tourist invariably lingers, watching the completed sheets roll off the presses. You'll see the inking, stacking (each stack of dollar bills contains $320,000), cutting, and examination for defects. There are also exhibits of counterfeit money, of a $100,000 bill used in official transactions, of bills no longer in use, etc.

Upon completion of the tour, leave time to explore the Visitor Center, where the history of money is examined from "pieces of eight" to current currency. There are video displays money-related electronic games, a display of $1 million, a visitor-operated printing press (for a nominal charge you can produce a piece of paper embossed with the bureau seal), and interesting exhibits on subjects like the evolution of a stamp from the original artwork to finished product and the art of engraving. Here, too, you can buy unique gifts like bags of shredded money and uncut sheets of notes at inflationary prices (like a sheet of four $1 bills for $7.50).

ADDITIONAL ATTRACTIONS

FORD'S THEATRE AND LINCOLN MUSEUM: At 511 10th St. NW, between E and F Streets (tel. 347-4833 for box office information, 426-6927 for the museum). Open daily from 9 a.m. to 5 p.m. Closed Christmas Day. Metro: Metro Center.

Ford's Theatre was built in 1863, and undoubtedly would have been pulled down long ago but for an event on April 14, 1865: President Abraham Lincoln was shot there by John Wilkes Booth during a performance of a celebrated comedy called *Our American Cousin.* Doctors carried Lincoln to the house of William Petersen across the street, and the president died there the next morning.

After Lincoln's assassination, the theater was closed by order of Secretary of War Stanton. For many years afterward it was used by the War Department for clerical work. In 1893, 22 clerks were killed when three floors of the building collapsed. It remained in disuse until the 1960s when it was remodeled and restored to its appearance on the night of the tragedy (the seating copied from the original design has proved to be too uncomfortable for present-day theatergoers, so velvet cushions have been added). Except when rehearsals or matinees are in progress (call before you go), visitors can see the theater and trace Booth's movements on that fatal night. Free 15-minute talks on the history of the theater and the story of the assassination are given at 10 and 35 minutes after the hour between 9:10 a.m. and 4:35 p.m. Be sure to visit the Lincoln Museum in the basement, wherein are exhibits on Lincoln's life. In addition to Lincoln memorabilia, the museum displays the derringer pistol used by Booth and the killer's diary outlining his rationalization for the deed. The museum may, however, be closed for a complete revamping sometime during the lifetime of this book. For information on theatrical presentations here, see Chapter VII.

The House Where Lincoln Died

The House Where Lincoln Died, across the street at 516 10th St. NW (tel. 426-6830), has been restored to its appearance when the president succumbed at 7:22 a.m. on April 15, 1865. Shortly after being shot at 10:15 the night before, Lincoln was laid to rest on a bed in the rear room of the house. While Lincoln's wife remained in the front room, Secretary of War Stanton held a cabinet meeting in the adjoining bedroom.

Six years after Lincoln's death, the Petersen family sold the house to Louis Schade, who published a newspaper called the *Washington Sentinel* in its basement for many years. In 1896 the government bought the house for $30,000, and it is now maintained by the National Park Service. It is open for self-guided tours every day of the year except Christmas Day from 9 a.m. to 5 p.m. No charge for admission.

THE VIETNAM VETERANS MEMORIAL: Just across from the Lincoln Memorial, east of Henry Bacon Drive between 21st and 22nd Streets NW (tel. 634-1568). Open 8 a.m. to midnight. Metro: Foggy Bottom.

Honoring the men and women who served in the armed forces during the Vietnam War—the longest in our nation's history—the Vietnam Memorial consists of two long black-granite walls inscribed with the names of the 58,156 who died or remain missing as a result of that conflict. It is very moving in its simplicity. The two walls designed by Maya Ying Lin are 246¾ feet long and angled at 125° to point to the Washington Monument and the Lincoln Memorial; their mirror-like surface reflects the surrounding trees, lawns, and monuments. They're inscribed in chronological order, documenting the war as a series of individual sacrifices from the date of the first casualty in 1959 to the last in 1975. Many people are moved to tears during the slow walk past the names of so many who died. It's a powerful evocation of the tragedy of all wars that in no way glamorizes the military.

The memorial was conceived by Vietnam veteran Jan Scruggs and built by the Vietnam Veterans Memorial Fund, a nonprofit organization that raised $7 million for the project. The VVMF was granted a site of two acres in tranquil Constitution Gardens to erect a memorial that would make no political statement about the war and would harmonize with neighboring surroundings.

The wall was erected in 1982. In 1984 a life-size sculpture of three Vietnam soldiers by Frederick Hart was installed at the entrance plaza. He describes his work this way: "They wear the uniform and carry the equipment of war; they are young. The contrast between the innocence of their youth and the weapons of war underscores the poignancy of their sacrifice . . . Their strength and their vulnerability are both evident." Near the statue a flag flies from a 60-foot staff.

NATIONAL GEOGRAPHIC'S EXPLORERS HALL: At 17th and M Streets NW (tel. 857-7588). Open from 9 a.m. to 5 p.m. Monday to Saturday, from 10 a.m. to 5 p.m. on Sunday and holidays. Closed Christmas Day. Metro: Farragut North (Connecticut Avenue and L Street exit) or Farragut West.

Explorers Hall is the National Geographic Society's extensive exhibit space. Located in the lobby of the society's headquarters, it's within walking distance of the White House. It's a great place to take children.

The exciting history of our planet and man's attempt to explore his world are told in photographs, videos, and taped commentaries over individual earphones. Exhibits—all on one floor—explore the earth's jungles, deserts, and mountain peaks, the sea, moon, and stars; pick up an orientation map at the 17th Street entrance.

You'll see a video theater presentation on early man; an exhibit on Jacques Cousteau's pioneer explorations below the sea, including a scale model of the diving saucer in which he descended to 25,000 feet, his camera, and underwater photographs; the flag and dog sledge, among other equipment, of Adm. Robert E. Peary, first man to reach the North Pole (his 1909 expedition was funded by the National Geographic Society), along with a recording he made; a 3.9-billion-year-old moon rock; a specimen *Aepyornis maximus* egg from Madagascar's extinct, 1,000-pound flightless "elephant bird"; and the orrery, a working model of the solar system. An impressive exhibit is the world's largest free-standing globe (34 feet around the equator with a scale of one inch for every 60 miles). And, in a jungle setting, a brightly colored talking macaw named Henry stands guard over a full-size replica of a giant Olmec stone head dating to 32 B.C., from La Venta in Mexico.

In addition there is an ongoing program of temporary exhibits, a fascinating collection of holograms, the Kodak International Awards snapshots, and a display on the cenote sacrifice well of Chichén Itzá. Like the magazine, their subject matter is wide-ranging. The desk sells all National Geographic publications, plus maps, globes, games, and videos.

THE FOLGER SHAKESPEARE LIBRARY: Located at 201 East Capitol St. SE (tel. 544-7077). Open from 10 a.m. to 4 p.m. Monday to Saturday; closed on federal holidays. Metro: Capitol South.

Life as it was four centuries ago, in Shakespeare's time, is the special field of expertise at the marvelous Folger Shakespeare Library—an important research center for Shakespearean scholars and anyone studying any aspect of 16th- and 17th-century England. In a building adorned outside with nine bas-relief scenes from Shakespearean plays and a statue of Puck, it houses the massive collection of Shakespeareana amassed by Henry Clay Folger, including 93,000 books (a number almost tripled today), 50,000 prints and engravings, and thousands of relevant manuscripts. In 1930 Folger and his wife, Emily, also an enthusiast, made a gift of the collection to the American people.

But this is not merely an esoteric attraction to appeal to the scholarly few. The Great Hall exhibit gallery delights the general public with rotating displays, many of them from the collection—playbills, promptbooks, costumes, correspondence, Renaissance instruments, portraits and busts of Shakespeare, etc. And the hall itself, its intricate plaster ceiling decorated with Shakespeare's coat-of-arms and fleurs-de-lis and hung with heraldic flags of important personages and places in Elizabethan times, is lovely. Great Hall special exhibits have ranged from "The Compleat Gentleman: Books from English Country Houses," to "Time: The Great Innovator," treating the history of timekeeping and time consciousness in early modern Europe.

At the end of the Great Hall is a theater evocative of an Elizabethan inn yard. It's one of the few places in the world where you can see Shakespearean plays performed in a setting similar to that for which they were intended. If there's no rehearsal going on, you can take a look around; otherwise, you'll have to come back for a performance, a good idea in any case (details in Chapter VII). Free walk-in tours are given between 11 a.m. and 1 p.m.

THE PHILLIPS COLLECTION: In the Dupont Circle area at 1600–1612 21st St. NW, at the corner of Q Street (tel. 387-2151). Open from 10 a.m. to 5 p.m. Tuesday to Saturday, on Sunday from 2 to 7 p.m. Closed on Monday, July 4, Thanksgiving, Christmas, and New Year's Day. Metro: Dupont Circle.

Conceived as "a museum of modern art and its sources," this intimate gallery houses—in an elegant 1890s Georgian Revival mansion and a wing added in 1960—the exquisite collection of Duncan and Marjorie Phillips, avid collectors and proselytizers of modernism. The museum's carpeted rooms with plush furnishings, leaded-glass windows, and oak panelling are among the world's most delightful and comfortable settings for viewing art. The original building was once the Phillipses' elegant home, though always doubling as a museum. When their collection totaled 600 paintings, they moved out and had it renovated entirely as a museum. Today it contains over 2,500 works. Among the highlights are superb collections of Daumier, Dove, and Bonnard paintings; some splendid small Vuillards; three Van Goghs; Renoir's *Luncheon of the Boating Party;* five Cézannes, and five works by Georgia O'Keeffe. Ingres, Delacroix, Manet, El Greco, Goya, Corot, Constable, Courbet, Giorgione, and Chardin are among the "sources" or forerunners of modernism represented. Modern notables include Rothko, Hopper, Kandinsky, Kokoschka, Marin, Matisse, Avery, Ryder, Klee, Degas, Rouault, Picasso, and many others. It's a collection no art lover should miss. An ongoing series of temporary shows is presented, with works from the Phillips supplemented by loans from other museums and private collections.

In May 1989, the Phillips will complete the second phase of its renovation program, enabling the museum to exhibit 50% more of the permanent collection than was previously possible and to utilize a suite of galleries on the third floor as a permanent space for temporary exhibitions.

Free tours are given on Wednesday and Saturday at 2 p.m., and a full schedule of events includes gallery talks, lectures, and free concerts in the ornate music room (every Sunday at 5 p.m. September to May; early arrival is advised at these popular performances).

On the lower level, there's a charming little restaurant serving light gourmet fare—chilled cream of soup fine herbes, a pâté and cheese plate with cornichons, quiche and salad, and pastries from Suzanne's, a local fine food emporium/restaurant (details in Chapter IV).

THE CORCORAN GALLERY OF ART: On 17th Street between E Street and New York Avenue NW (tel. 638-3211). Open from 10 a.m. to 4:30 p.m. Tuesday to Sunday, with extended hours Thursday evenings until 9 p.m. Closed Christmas and New Year's Days. Metro: Farragut West or Farragut North.

Half a block from the White House is Washington's first art museum—and one of the first in the country—the Corcoran Gallery, specializing in American and European art and the education of young artists in its school on the premises. Founded in 1869 by philanthropist, collector, and prominent Washington banker William Wilson Corcoran, the collection was housed until 1896 in the red-brick and brownstone building that is now the Renwick. It was transferred to its current beaux arts building, the interior of which features a double atrium with two levels of fluted columns, in 1897.

The collection—shown in rotating exhibits—is rich in American art, spanning three centuries from 18th-century portraiture, to 19th-century works (Bierstadt, Remington, Thomas Cole, Fredrick Church, Asher Durand, Whistler, Sargent, Cassatt, Eakins, and Homer, plus the famous white-marble female nude, *Greek Slave,* by Hiram Powers), to 20th-century artists like Diebenkorn, Frankenthaler, Warhol, Rothko, and Noland.

On the first floor is the eclectic collection donated by Sen. William Andrews Clark; it includes Dutch and Flemish masters, French impressionists, Barbizon landscapes, a Louis XVI salon transported in toto from Paris, Delft porcelains, and more. Another collection housed here comprises Corot landscapes, medieval tapestries, and Daumier lithographs donated by Dr. Armand Hammer.

In addition to showing its own collections, the Corcoran features numerous special exhibitions supplemented by loans, such as "An American Vision: Three Generations of Wyeth Art," and the fabulous "Odyssey: The Art of Photography at National Geographic."

Free 30-minute tours are given Thursday to Sunday at 12:30 p.m. and Thursday evenings at 7 p.m. The museum shop has a terrific selection of art reproductions, books, jewelry, and art nouveau glassware, among other things. And do pick up a schedule of events —gallery talks, concerts, art auctions, etc.

THE NATIONAL MUSEUM OF WOMEN IN THE ARTS:

At 1250 New York Ave. NW (tel. 783-5000). Open Tuesday to Saturday 10 a.m. to 5 p.m., Sunday noon to 5 p.m. Metro: Metro Center.

Opened in 1987, this impressive museum celebrating "the contribution of women to the history of art" centers on a permanent collection of over 600 works by 230 women, its nucleus donated by founders Wilhelmina and Wallace Holladay. Their collection, which spans the 16th through the 20th centuries, germinated in the 1960s. While abroad, the Holladays became intrigued with the work of Clara Peeters, a 17th-century Flemish still-life painter exhibited at the Prado in Madrid. Upon returning home, the Holladays were shocked to find that not only was no mention made of Peeters's work in the standard art text, H.W. Janson's *History of Art,* but that no women were included. (This, by the way, did not change until a few years ago.) They began collecting women's art, and soon they conceived the idea of a women's art museum to correct the inequities of underrepresentation. Even today, though women comprise some 40% of working artists in the U.S., over 95% of the works hanging in American museums are by men.

Artists represented in the collection include Rosa Bonheur, Judy Chicago, Helen Frankenthaler, Barbara Hepworth, Georgia O'Keeffe, Lee Krasner, Nancy Graves, Mary Cassatt, Elaine de Kooning, and Käthe Kollwitz, along with many other lesser-known but notable artists from previous centuries. We were interested to discover here, for instance, that the famed Peale family of 19th-century portrait painters included a very talented sister, Sarah Miriam Peale.

Shows have included the "Sculptures of Camille Claudel, 1864–1943" (Rodin's mistress, Claudel worked with him on major pieces such as *The Burghers of Calais),* "Women Artists of the Thirties" (prints, drawings, and photographs from the WPA era), and "Significant Colorado Women Artists of the 20th Century," one of many state exhibitions that will take place here.

The museum is housed in a magnificent landmark building designed in 1907 as a Masonic temple by noted architect Waddy Wood (he also designed Woodrow Wilson's house). It's a lavish, Renaissance-revival, flatiron-shaped building; you enter via an opulent Great Hall with Turkish white-marble floors, silk-brocaded walls, gilded moldings, and Belgian crystal chandeliers suspended from an ornately detailed ceiling. The museum's library contains over 2,000 volumes.

THE CAPITAL CHILDREN'S MUSEUM: At 800 3rd St. NE, at H Street (tel. 543-8600). Open seven days a week from 10 a.m. to 5 p.m. Closed Thanksgiving, Christmas, New Year's Day, and Easter. Admission: $4 per person, $1 for senior citizens. Metro: Union Station.

Kids are, of necessity, rather restrained at most Washington sightseeing attractions; here's their chance to let loose on three floors of child-oriented hands-on exhibits. They can pet Rosie the goat, grind Mexican chocolate and prepare tortillas, send a message on a teletype, make slides and film shows, create shadow art on a wall (one of our favorite activities), and send messages—by a Greek torch system that dates to A.D. 300, by Morse code using naval lamps, and by African drums. A replica of a 30,000-year-old cave, complete with water dripping and the howling of distant beasts, illustrates the use of cave drawings and rituals as Ice Age means of communication. Kids will see a hologram (always a treat) and explore a giant camera from the inside in the photography section; play metric shopkeeper and measure each other's feet for shoes in Metricville; and test skills on numerous computer learning games. There's also a maze with optical illusions to wander through, a talking (in 22 languages) Tower of Babel staircase, and a telecommunications area with an old-fashioned operable switchboard and telephones of the future.

Inquire about ongoing workshops, demonstrations, and theater presentations for children.

THE U.S. BOTANIC GARDEN CONSERVATORY: At 1st Street and Maryland Avenue SW (tel. 225-8333). Open daily from 9 a.m. to 5 p.m., till 9 p.m. June through August. Metro: Federal Center.

Right at the foot of the Capitol, the Botanic Garden is a lovely oasis, a series of connected glass-and-stone buildings and greenhouses (they call it a "living museum under glass") filled with pots of brightly colored flowers, rock beds of ferns, Spanish moss, palms, and shrubs. Tropical, subtropical, and desert plants are the highlights of the collection. There's a section filled with cactus; another where you can wander along tiled paths over a bridge, past a waterfall, and under trees. Benches in shady corners create the illusion of a carefully tended woods. Poinsettias bloom at Christmas, chrysanthemums in fall; spring is heralded by lilies, tulips, hyacinths, and narcissi; and a large collection of orchids is on display year round. The Summer Terrace, with umbrella tables amid plants and flower beds overlooking the Capitol's reflecting pool, is a lovely spot for a picnic lunch. For information on special shows (perhaps a rose show or a Japanese flower arrangement display), tours, lectures on subjects like "Lawn Care" and "Perennials," and classes such as "Growing Begonias and African Violets," call the above number. You can also call 225-7099 for a recording of events and to find out what's in bloom.

DUMBARTON OAKS: At 1703 32nd St. NW; entrance to the collections on 32nd Street, between R and S Streets; garden entrance at 31st and R Streets (tel. 338-8278 or 342-3200). Collections open from 2 to 5 p.m. Tuesday to Sunday; the garden, from 2 to 5 p.m. daily, weather permitting (till 6 p.m. April 1 to October 31). Both are closed national holidays and the day before Christmas. Admission to the garden, April 1 to October 31 only, is $2 for adults, $1 for children under 12 and senior citizens; the latter are admitted free on Wednesday.

Most people associate Dumbarton Oaks, a 19th-century Georgetown mansion named for a Scottish castle, with the 1944 international conference which led to the formation of the United Nations. Now the 16-acre estate is the home of the Center for Byzantine Studies and programs in the history of landscape architecture and pre-Columbian art and archeology. Its gardens, which wind gently down to Rock Creek Ravine, are magical, modeled after European gardens but with many original touches. Half-hidden benches and shady nooks offer retreats from the heat of a Washington summer. The pre-Columbian museum, designed by Philip Johnson, is a small gem; the Byzantine collection is a rich one, dating back to the 6th century.

This unusual combination of offerings dates to the occupancy of Robert Woods Bliss and his wife, Mildred. The couple pursued three major interests: both were avid collectors of Byzantine art, plus he was equally fascinated by pre-Columbian, and she by landscape gardening. In 1940 they turned over the estate, the Byzantine collection, a library of works on Byzantine civilization, and 16 acres (including ten acres of exquisite formal gardens) to Mr. Bliss's alma mater, Harvard, and provided endowment funds for continuing research in Byzantine studies. In the early '60s they also donated their pre-Columbian collection and financed the building of two wings —one to house it, the other to contain Mrs. Bliss's collection of rare books on landscape gardening. The Byzantine collection is one of the world's finest; it includes illuminated manuscripts, a 13th-century icon of St. Peter, mosaics, ivory carvings, a 4th-century sarcophagus, jewelry, and more. The pre-Columbian works, displayed chronologically in eight marble- and oak-floored glass pavilions, features Olmec jade and serpentine figures, Mayan relief panels, textiles from 900 B.C. to the Spanish Conquest, funerary pottery, gold necklaces made by the lost-wax process, and sculptures of Aztec gods and goddesses.

The historic music room, furnished in French, Italian, and Spanish antiques, was the setting for the 1944 Dumbarton Oaks

Conversations. It has an 18th-century parquet floor, a beamed, painted 16th-century French-style ceiling, and an immense 16th-century stone fireplace. Among its notable artworks is El Greco's *The Visitation.*

Don't miss the formal gardens. They contain on Orangery, a Rose Garden (final rsting place of the Blisses amid 1,000 rose bushes), wisteria-covered arbors, herbaceous borders, groves of cherry trees, and magnolias. The gardens adjoin Dumbarton Oaks Park, 27 acres that once belonged to the estate—a lovely setting for a picnic lunch.

You can visit the house and tour its galleries on your own during the hours noted above. Guided tours—1½ hours in duration given at 10:30 a.m. on Tuesday, Wednesday, Thursday, and Saturday—are for groups only, but individuals are often permitted to join if space allows. Cost is $5. Call 342-3212 for reservations.

CHAPTER VI

OUTDOOR WASHINGTON AND THE SPORTING LIFE

□ □ □

Too much museum-going can do you in. A change of pace is the answer. Catch a Redskins game, go ice skating, take a stroll along the canal, play a few sets of tennis, or relax on a Potomac River cruise. All this, and more, is described below. In addition, check the Friday "Weekend" section of the *Washington Post* for information on all sports activities—fishing, boating, river rafting, cycling, hiking, golf, running, volleyball, etc.

SPECTATOR SPORTS: Home to the Washington Redskins (NFL) and the Washington Diplomats (soccer) is the 55,000-seat **Robert F. Kennedy Memorial Stadium,** East Capitol Street at 22nd Street NE (tel. 547-9077). The adjoining 10,000-seat **D.C. Armory,** 2001 East Capitol St. SE (tel. 547-9077), is used for ice shows, rodeos, the circus, horse shows, nationally televised boxing and wrestling, etc. The facility is easily reachable by Metro (Stadium Armory stop).

For the most part, those sporting events that don't take place at RFK happen at **Capital Centre,** Exit 15A or 17A off the Capital Beltway in Landover, Md. (tel. 350-3400, 432-0200 to charge tickets). Home of the Washington Bullets (NBA) and the Washington Capitals (NHL), this 20,000-seat arena is also used for Georgetown University basketball games, Harlem Globetrotter games, the Washington International Horse Show (every October), wrestling, the Ice Capades, World Professional Figure-Skating Championships, and big-name concerts.

ACTIVE SPORTS: Just about any sport that interests you is available in the Washington area.

Boating

Canoes and rowboats can be rented from **Fletcher's Boat House,** Reservoir and Canal Roads NW (tel. 244-0461), between 9 a.m. and dusk from late March to the end of November (hours may vary a bit seasonally, so call before you go). It's right on the canal. Fletcher's also sells bait and fishing tackle, and maintains a refreshment stand. If you're up for a few miles of hiking, you can walk from Georgetown.

Thompson's Boat Center, on the Georgetown Channel at Virginia Avenue at Rock Creek Parkway NW (tel. 333-4861 or 333-9543), rents canoes, rowboats, sailboats, Sunfish, and Alden rowing shells during the same season. Bait and fishing tackle is also obtainable here.

Cycling

Both **Fletcher's** and **Thompson's** (see "Boating," above) also rent bikes, as does **Big Wheel Bikes,** 1034 33rd St. NW, just below M Street (tel. 337-0254), open from 10 a.m. to 6 p.m. daily, till 7 p.m. May through August. Other Big Wheel stores are located at 1004 Vermont Ave. NW, off K Street (tel. 638-3301), and on Capitol Hill at 315 7th St. SE (tel. 543-1600). Both are open from 10 a.m. to 6 p.m. Vermont Avenue is closed on Sunday, Capitol Hill on Monday.

Fishing

There's good fishing from late February to November and great fishing from mid-March through June (spawning season) right on the Potomac, and the Washington Channel offers good bass and carp fishing year round. No license is required in the District at this writing, but the subject is under discussion. Check with a local fishing-equipment store for the latest information.

Golf

In the District, East Potomac Park and Rock Creek Park contain public courses (details below). Dozens of other public courses are within easy driving distance.

Hiking

Check the *Washington Post* "Weekend" section for listings of hiking clubs; almost all are open to the public for a small fee. Do inquire as to the difficulty of any hike you join and the speed with which the club proceeds; some do not stop to smell the flowers.

On your own, there are numerous hiking paths. The **C&O Canal** offers 184½ miles alone; it would be hard to find a more scenic setting than the **Arboretum's** 9½ miles of road (details later in this chapter); **Theodore Roosevelt Island** has 88 wilderness acres to explore including a 2½-mile nature trail (short but rugged); and in **Rock Creek Park** there are 15 miles of hiking trails for which maps are available at the Visitor Information Center or park headquarters.

The **Sierra Club** (tel. 547-2326) is a good source of additional information; they also organize guided hikes just about every weekend.

Ice Skating

Winter skating on the **C&O Canal,** its banks dotted with cozy fires, will make you feel like Hans Brinker. It's also lovely to glide along the **Reflecting Pool** from the Lincoln Memorial to the Washington Monument, especially by night when all is lit. Outside the Hirshhorn Museum, the **National Sculpture Garden Ice Rink** (tel. 347-9041) offers skate rentals, as do the **Pershing Park** rink, at 14th Street and Pennsylvania Avenue NW (tel. 737-6937), and the **Fort Dupont Ice Arena,** at 3779 Ely Pl. SE at Minnesota Avenue (tel. 581-0199). The last three are all run by Guest Services and charge about $3.50 for adults, $2.75 for children under 12. The Sculpture Garden and Pershing Park rinks are open from December 1 to February 28; Fort Dupont, from Labor Day to the end of April.

Riding

Rock Creek Park (tel. 362-0117) has 17 miles of wooded trails to explore and a stable renting horses for trail rides and instruction.

Swimming

Call the **D.C. Department of Recreation Aquatic Program** (tel. 576-6436) to find out which of their 43 swimming pools is convenient for you. Among the nicest are the outdoor pool in **East Potomac Park,** the indoor-outdoor **Capitol East Natatorium,** and the **Georgetown** outdoor pool at 34th Street and Volta Place NW. Most D.C. pools are open from Memorial Day to Labor Day.

Tennis

The District has 144 outdoor courts under the auspices of the Department of Recreation (60 of them lighted for night play) at 45 locations. You need a free permit to use them. To obtain it, send a stamped, self-addressed envelope with your request to the **D.C. Department of Recreation,** Permit Section, 3149 16th St. NW, Washington, D.C. 20010 (tel. 673-7646). They'll send it by return mail. Need it right away? Visit the office in person weekdays between 8:30 a.m. and 12:30 p.m. or 1:30 and 4:30 p.m. Court locations are listed on the permit. Most courts are open year round, weather permitting. There are also courts in **Rock Creek** and **East Potomac Parks** (details below).

ROCK CREEK PARK: One of the largest and most beautiful city parks in the country, Rock Creek is Washington's playground—a 1,754-acre valley extending 12 miles from the Potomac to the Maryland border where it becomes Rock Creek Regional Park (another 2,700 acres). It's offerings include the zoo (described earlier), the Carter Barron Amphitheater (about which more in Chapter VII), playgrounds, an extensive system of hiking trails, old forts to explore, and numerous sports facilities. For full information on the wide range of park programs and activities, visit the **Rock Creek Nature Center,** 5200 Glover Rd. NW (tel. 426-6829), Tuesday to Sunday from 9 a.m. to 5 p.m. Weekdays only from 7:45 a.m. to 4:15 p.m. try **Park Headquarters,** 5000 Glover Rd. (tel. 426-6832). The Nature Center itself is the scene of numerous activities—weekend planetarium shows for little kids (4 to 7) and adults, nature films, live animal demonstrations, and guided nature walks, plus a daily mix of lectures, films, musical events, puppet shows, etc. A calendar is available on request. Self-guided nature trails begin here. All activities are free, but sometimes you need to pick up tickets a half hour in advance. There are also nature exhibits on the premises.

You can see a water-powered early-19th-century gristmill grinding corn into wheat at Tilden Street and Beach Drive (tel. 426-6908). It's called **Pierce Mill** (a man named Isaac Pierce built it), and it's open to visitors from 8 a.m. to 4:30 p.m. Wednesday to Sunday. Pierce's old carriage house is today the **Art Barn** (tel. 426-6719), where works of local artists are exhibited; hours are Wednesday to Saturday from 10 a.m. to 5 p.m., on Sunday from noon to 5 p.m.

Call 673-7646 or 673-7647 for details, locations, and group reservations at the park's 30 **picnic areas,** some with fireplaces. A brochure available at Park Headquarters or the Nature Center also provides details on picnic locations.

There are 17 soft-surface and five hard-surface **tennis courts** at 16th and Kennedy Streets NW (tel. 722-5949). April through mid-November you must make a reservation in person at Guest Services on the premises to use them. The fee is about $7.50 for clay, $5.25 for hard courts on weekends, holidays, and after 4 p.m. weekdays, less during the week from 8 a.m. to 4 p.m. Six additional soft-surface courts are located off Park Road just east of Pierce Mill; they're open May to September for the same rates and with the same reservations policy. The rest of the year you can play on the hard courts free on a first-come, first-served basis.

Poetry readings and workshops are held frequently at the one-time residence of High Sierra poet **Joaquin Miller,** Beach Drive north of Military Road. Call 426-6832 for information.

The 18-hole **Rock Creek Golf Course** and clubhouse, 16th and Rittenhouse Streets NW (tel. 723-9832), are open daily year round from dawn to dusk. A fee is charged. Clubs, lockers, and carts can be rented.

The above-mentioned stables (see "Riding") are at the **Rock Creek Park Horse Center,** near the Nature Center on Glover Road NW (tel. 362-0117). Trail rides are offered Tuesday to Friday from 1:30 to 4:15 p.m., on weekends between noon and 5:30 p.m. Call for rates and information on riding instruction.

You have to rent bikes elsewhere, but there is an 11-mile **bike path** from the Lincoln Memorial through the park into Maryland, much of it paved, and on weekends and holidays it's mostly closed to vehicular traffic.

Finally, joggers will enjoy the 1.5-mile **Perrier Parcourse** with 18 calisthenic stations en route. It begins near the intersection of Cathedral Avenue and Rock Creek Parkway.

POTOMAC PARK: Its 720 riverside acres divided by the Tidal Basin, East and West Potomac Parks are most famous for their spring display of **cherry blossoms** and all the hoopla that goes with it.

West Potomac Park has 1,300 trees bordering the Tidal Basin, 10% of them Akebonos with delicate pink blossoms, the rest of the Yoshino variety with white cloud-like flower clusters. It's the focal point of many of the week-long celebrations, which include the lighting of the 300-year-old **Japanese Stone Lantern** near Kutz Bridge, presented to the city by the governor of Tokyo in 1954; a Cherry Blossom Parade with floats, bands, clowns, Clydesdale horses, and Cherry Blossom princesses; dancers, entertainers, a black-tie ball with celebrity guests; and much, much more. If you manage to be in town for Cherry Blossom Week, details on all events and activities are available from the **Washington, D.C., Convention and Visitors Association** (tel. 789-7000), the **National Park Service** (tel. 426-6700), and the **Washington Post.** The parade and ball require advance tickets. You can buy them via Ticketron or from the Downtown Jaycees (tel. 293-0480). Of course, unless you're planning a long vacation, arriving the right week is a matter of luck or flexibility. The trees bloom for a little less than two weeks beginning somewhere between March 20 and April 17; April 7 is the average date.

Though West Potomac Park gets more cherry blossom publicity, East Potomac Park has more trees (1,800 of them) and more varieties (11). Here, too, are picnic grounds with fire grills; 24 tennis courts, including five indoors (tel. 554-5962); one 18-hole and two 9-hole golf courses (tel. 554-7660); a large swimming pool (tel. 724-4369); and biking and hiking paths by the water.

West Potomac Park encompasses Constitution Gardens; the

Vietnam, Lincoln, and Jefferson Memorials; a small island where ducks live; and the Reflecting Pool.

THE CHESAPEAKE & OHIO CANAL NATIONAL HISTORICAL PARK: Paralleling the Potomac for 184½ miles from Georgetown to Cumberland, Md., the C&O Canal, with its adjacent towpath, is a prime D.C. recreation area. It was built in the 1800s when water routes were considered vital to transportation, but even before it was completed, the B&O Railroad (of Monopoly fame), which went up at about the same time and along the same route, had begun to render it obsolete. Today, perhaps, it serves an even more important purpose as an urban refuge for jogging, hiking, biking, and boating in a lush, natural setting.

Headquarters for canal activities is the **Office of the Superintendent,** C&O Canal National Historical Park, Box 4, Sharpsburg, MD 21782 (tel. 301/739-4200); also knowledgeable is the **National Park Service** office at Great Falls Tavern (tel. 301/299-3613). And in summer, Wednesday to Sunday, the **Georgetown Information Center,** 1055 Thomas Jefferson St. (tel. 202/472-4376), can also provide maps and information.

Hiking any section of the flat dirt towpath—or its more rugged side paths—is a pleasure. There are **picnic tables** (at **camping areas**), some with fire grills, about every five miles from Carderock (about ten miles out of Georgetown) to Cumberland. Use of campsites is on a first-come, first-served basis. Enter the towpath in Georgetown. To see **Great Falls** (14 miles from Georgetown), a point where the Potomac becomes a stunning waterfall plunging 76 feet, you'll have to drive. Take 495N to Rte. 193 (Old Georgetown Pike) west and make a right on Old Dominion Drive.

Fletcher's Boat House, mentioned above (see "Boating") is about 2½ miles along the towpath from Georgetown; stop here to rent bikes or boats or purchase bait and tackle for fishing. A snackbar and picnic area are on the premises. It's also accessible by car.

Much less strenuous is a **mule-drawn 19th-century canal boat trip** led by Park Service guides in period dress. They regale passengers with canal legend and lore and sing river songs. These boats depart Wednesday through Sunday from mid-April to mid-October; call 202/472-4376 or 301/299-2026 for departure times. Tickets are available at the Georgetown Information Center (address and phone above). Fare is $4 for adults, $2.50 for children under 12, and $3 for senior citizens.

Call any of the above information numbers for details on riding, rock climbing, fishing, birdwatching, concerts, ranger-guided tours, skating, camping, and other canal activities.

THEODORE ROOSEVELT ISLAND: This 88-acre wilderness preserve in the Potomac River was authorized by Congress in 1932

to memorialize President Theodore Roosevelt's contributions and dedication to nature and conservation. Under his administration, the U.S. Forest Service, five national parks, 150 national forests, 51 bird refuges, and four game refuges were created; nearly extinct bison herds were saved; in the West irrigation converted desert into fertile land; and conservation agencies were formed in 41 states.

Theodore Roosevelt Island was inhabited as far back as the 1600s by Indians. Over the years it passed through many owners before becoming what it is today—an island preserve of swamp, marsh, and upland forest; a haven for rabbits, chipmunks, great owls, red and gray fox, muskrat, turtles, and groundhogs; and a complex ecosystem in which cattails, arrowarum, and pickerelweed growing in the marshes create a hospitable habitat for abundant birdlife, and willow, ash, and maple trees rooted on the mudflats create the swamp environment favored by the raccoon in his search for crayfish. You can observe all this flora and fauna in their natural environs on 2½ miles of foot trails.

In the northern center of the island, overlooking an oval terrace encircled by a water-filled moat, stands a 17-foot bronze statue of our 26th president. From the terrace rise four 21-foot granite tablets inscribed with the tenets of Roosevelt's philosophy: "There are no words that can tell the hidden spirit of the wilderness, that can reveal its mystery, its melancholy, and its charm. The Nation behaves well if it treats the natural resources as assets which it must turn over to the next generation increased and not impaired in value."

In addition to hiking, there's fishing for bass, crappie, carp, and catfish. Picnicking is permitted on the grounds near the memorial.

To get to the island, take the George Washington Memorial Parkway exit north from the Theodore Roosevelt Bridge. The parking area is accessible only from the northbound lane; from there a pedestrian bridge connects the island with the Virginia shore. You can also rent a canoe at Thompson's Boat Center (see "Boating" above) and paddle over, or walk across the pedestrian bridge at Rosslyn Circle, two blocks from the Metro station.

For further information contact the Superintendent, Theodore Roosevelt Island, George Washington Memorial Parkway, c/o Turkey Run Park, McLean, VA 22101 (tel. 703/285-2598).

RIVER CRUISES: When the weather's fine, a river excursion is one of the most pleasant ways we know to spend a day. **Washington Boat Lines, Inc.,** Pier 4 at 6th and Water Streets SW (tel. 554-8000), offers a variety of such trips daily from late March through the end of December. All cruises include a 20-minute Broadway revue. Call for departure times and make reservations in advance. The following trips are offered at this writing; check when you arrive, because they tend to change with some frequency:

Afternoon Lunch Cruises aboard a 350-passenger luxury ship are two-hour-long sun-dappled cruises on the Washington Channel. The meal is a buffet of teriyaki chicken, Maryland crabcakes, seafood Alfredo, baked fish in mornay sauce, salads, vegetables, desserts, and beverages. The fare, including the meal, is $16.95. Departures Tuesday to Saturday.

Sunday Brunch Cruises, including a meal and live entertainment along with narrated sightseeing, cost $18.95.

And a very popular half-day excursion takes in D.C. sights en route to **Mount Vernon** plantation. The trip is 1½ hours each way. Adults pay $12.75 one way, $15.75 round trip; children 2 to 11 pay $7.50 one way, $8.50 round trip; those prices include entrance to Mount Vernon.

Finally there are 2½-hour late-night **Moonlight Dance Cruises** Friday and Saturday evenings featuring live bands, cash bars, and complimentary hors d'oeuvres. The music is 1940s to Top 40, geared to adults, not teens. The boats head in the direction of Alexandria. Cost is $13.50.

THE UNITED STATES NATIONAL ARBORETUM: A research and educational center focusing on trees and shrubs, the Arboretum, 3501 New York Ave. NE (tel. 475-4815), is one of the great joys of Washington. Its 9½ miles of paved roads meander through 444 hilly acres of rhododendrons, azaleas (the most extensive plantings in the nation), crabapples, magnolias, hollies, peonies, irises, dogwoods, day lilies, boxwoods, cherry trees, aquatic plants, and dwarf conifers. The highlight for us is the National Bonsai Collection—a $4.5-million Bicentennial gift from Japan of 53 beautiful miniature trees, some of them over three centuries old. Each one is an exquisite work of art. We agree with Bill and Phyllis Thomas, authors of a book called *Natural Washington:* "The collection alone is worth a trip to Washington." The Herbarium contains 500,000 dried plants for reference purposes. The Herb Garden, another highlight, includes a historic rose garden (100 old-fashioned fragrant varieties), a contemporary interpretation of a 16th-century English-style "knot" garden, and ten specialty gardens—a dye garden, a medicinal garden, a culinary garden, etc. The National Bird Garden features berrying shrubs which attract feathered friends. Along Fern Valley Trail is the Franklin tree—a species now extinct in the wild—discovered in 1765 by a botanist friend of Benjamin Franklin. And a magnificent sight is the Arboretum's acropolis—22 of the original U.S. Capitol columns designed by Benjamin Latrobe in a setting created by the noted late English landscape artist Russell Page. The columns, the sole remaining elements of Capitol architect Latrobe's original façade, were removed a few decades ago when they were deemed too fragile to support the building's new marble construction. They couldn't have found a more beautiful home.

Camellias, magnolias, and early bulbs bloom in late March or early April; rhododendrons, daffodils, and flowering cherry trees in mid-April; azaleas and peonies in May; lilies and hibiscus in summer. In autumn the Arboretum is ablaze in reds and oranges as the leaves change color.

The Arboretum is open daily except Christmas Day: weekdays from 8 a.m. to 5 p.m., on weekends and holidays from 10 a.m. to 5 p.m. Take bus B-2, B-4, or B-5 from the Stadium Armory Metro station to Bladensburg Road and R Street NE. Or hop in a taxi; it's only a few dollars. If you drive, parking is free, though you can drive through. Frequent tours, lectures, and workshops (including bonsai classes) are offered. *Note:* The Bonsai Collection can be seen between 10 a.m. and 2:30 p.m. only.

CHAPTER VII

WHEN THE SUN GOES DOWN IN WASHINGTON

□ □ □

Not so many years ago, Washington rolled up the sidewalks at an early hour. But today, just as D.C. has more sightseeing attractions than any other city, it also offers a wealth of nighttime activities. Don't go to bed early just because you're worn out from traipsing around museums and monuments all day. Take a nap before dinner and woo your second wind. In addition to perusing the following, check out the Friday "Weekend" section of the *Washington Post,* which will also tell you about children's theater, sports events, flower shows, and all else. *Washingtonian* magazine is another good source.

There is one show we particularly recommend, an only-in-Washington attraction. Stephen Wade's one-man, five-banjo folkloric show at the Arena Stage is one of the most magical and delightful entertainments we've ever had the pleasure of attending (and several times at that). It's called *Banjo Dancing,* and it's among the longest-running shows in the country. Wade spins yarns, plays virtuoso banjo, dances, and is, as *Time* magazine noted, "a wondrous artist."

THEATER

Except for New York, we can't think of another U.S. city that offers more first-rate theatrical productions than D.C. Almost anything on Broadway will eventually come to—or have previewed in —Washington. There are also several nationally acclaimed repertory companies here and a 16th-century-style Elizabethan theater for Shakespearean productions. Additional theater offerings, including the Kennedy Center, are listed under "Accent on Entertainment."

TICKETS: Similar to New York's TKTS discount ticket center is Washington's TICKET place on F Street Plaza between 12th and 13th Streets NW (tel. TICKETS), a service of the Cultural Alliance of Greater Washington. Here you can pick up half-price tickets—on the day of performance only—to productions at every major Washington-area theater and concert hall, not only for dramatic productions, but for opera, ballet, etc. If half-price tickets aren't available, you can also purchase full-price tickets in advance at this centrally located box office, not only for pop and cultural, but for sports events as well. You must pay in cash for half-price tickets, and there's a 10% service charge; full-price tickets can be purchased with credit cards as well. TICKET place is open Monday from noon to 2 p.m., Tuesday to Saturday from 11 a.m. to 6 p.m.; tickets to Sunday shows are sold on Saturday. Closest Metro: Metro Center, 12th Street exit. (While you're in the area purchasing tickets, stop in for lunch at Reeve's Bakery, 1209 F St. NW—details in Chapter IV.)

Full-price tickets for most performances in town can also be purchased through **Ticketron** (tel. 659-2601) or **Ticket Center at Hecht's Department Store,** 12th and G Streets NW (no phone; you have to go in person).

THE ARENA STAGE: Located at 6th Street and Maine Avenue SW (tel. 488-3300), Arena Stage, now in its third decade, is the home of one of the longest-standing acting ensembles in the nation. Under the superb guidance of director/founder Zelda Fichandler, several works nurtured here have moved to Broadway, and the company was the first outside of New York City to win a Tony award. They represented American theater on a 1973 State Department tour of Russia and performed at the International Arts Festival in Hong Kong. Several graduates—Ned Beatty, James Earl Jones, Robert Prosky, Jane Alexander, and George Grizzard among them —have gone on to commercial stardom. The National Endowment for the Arts (NEA) calls the Arena "the flagship theater of the not-for-profit professional theater movement, an immensely successful company with keen artistic vision, a large committed family of artists . . . the envy of and a beacon for the rest of the theater field." Having spent many stimulating and entertaining evenings here, we wholeheartedly agree, as does critic Clive Barnes ("American ensemble acting at its best").

The Arena's subscription-season productions, of which there are seven annually, are presented on three stages—the **Arena,** a theater-in-the-round; the smaller fan-shaped **Kreeger;** and the **Old**

Vat Room, a cabaret space where Stephen Wade's one-man, five-banjo American folklore show called *Banjo Dancing* has been playing since 1981. It has garnered unanimous critical raves. We've seen it three times, and in our opinion it's one of the not-to-be-missed sights of Washington.

A recent September-to-June season (sometimes shows are extended into summer) included productions of *Joe Turner's Come and Gone, All the King's Men,* adapted from Robert Penn Warren's novel, Moss Hart's *Light Up the Sky,* Pirandello's *Enrico IV,* Lorraine Hansberry's *Les Blancs,* Chekhov's *The Cherry Orchard,* and, to celebrate Irving Berlin's 100th birthday, George S. Kaufman's *The Cocoanuts.* In 1987, Arena initiated a new project, **Stage Four,** featuring four notable new American plays each year. Tickets are just $10. Some Stage Four plays have been developed in the theater's **PlayLab,** which features readings of new works followed by audience discussion. PlayLab readings are open to the public as well; call for details.

Ticket prices to regular season productions are in the $15 to $25 range, with discounts available for students and senior citizens.

NATIONAL THEATER: Renovated and refurbished at a cost of $6.5 million in 1982, the plush National Theater, 1321 Pennsylvania Ave. NW (tel. 628-6161), is the third-oldest continuously operating theater (since 1835) in the nation. Such venerables as Sarah Bernhardt and John Barrymore performed on its stage. The National is also called "the theater of the presidents," since every president from McKinley on has attended a performance here. The walls of the street-level lobby are covered with $40,000 worth of Italian marble; crystal chandeliers create an opulent mood within; and friezes, plasterwork, and moldings accent the theater's 19th-century origins.

Managed by New York's Shubert Organization, the National presents mostly star-studded pre- and post-Broadway shows such as Neil Simon's *Jake's Women, Cats, I'm Not Rappaport* with Judd Hirsch, and the 10th-anniversary revival of *Ain't Misbehavin'* with the original Broadway cast starring Nell Carter. Tickets range from about $20 to $45, with discounts available for students with ID, senior citizens, active-duty military personnel, and the disabled.

The National also offers free Saturday-morning children's theater (puppets, magicians, clowns, etc.), summer films, and Monday-night showcases of local groups and performers. Call 783-3370 for details.

THE SHAKESPEARE THEATRE AT FOLGER: Don't miss the opportunity to see Shakespearean plays performed in an Elizabethan inn courtyard setting at the internationally renowned Folger,

201 E. Capitol St. SE (tel. 546-4000). The **Folger Theatre Resident Acting Company** puts on four classical productions each October-to-June season, at least three of them Shakespearean. The 1988 roster included *Richard II, Richard III,* and *As You Like It.* Tickets are in the $15 to $32 range. Inquire about discounts for students and senior citizens.

Other Folger Entertainments

The **Folger Consort,** a Medieval- and Renaissance-music ensemble, performs about 24 concerts on six weekends between October and May. Tickets to hear their lute duos, troubadour songs, Gregorian chants, and court ensembles are about $12 to $14.

On Mondays at 8 p.m. there are often free evening lectures on Renaissance-related subjects. On selected evenings, poetry readings ($4) are scheduled at 8 p.m.; Joseph Brodsky, Seamus Heaney, Richard Wilbur, and Allen Ginsberg are among those who've read. And another exciting program is the Friday night series of fiction readings by noted authors—people like John Updike, Arthur Miller, Nadine Gordimer, John Irving, and Eudora Welty; admission is $10.

Finally, if you happen to be in town the Saturday closest to **Shakespeare's birthday** (April 23), join in the day-long celebrations here—free entertainment, Elizabethan fare, an appearance by "Queen Elizabeth I," even a birthday cake.

FORD'S THEATRE: At 511 10th St. NW, between E and F

Streets (tel. 347-4833). This is the actual theater where on the evening of April 14, 1865, actor John Wilkes Booth shot President Lincoln. The assassination marked the end of John T. Ford's till-then very popular theater for over a century. In 1968 Ford's reopened, completely restored to its 1865 appearance, based on photographs, sketches, newspaper articles, and samples of wallpaper and curtain material from museum collections. The presidential box is decorated and furnished as it was on the fateful night, including the original crimson damask sofa and framed engraving of George Washington.

Ford's season is more or less year round (summers are sometimes dark). Past productions—often experimental—have included several shows that went on to Broadway, e.g., *Your Arms Too Short to Box With God,* and off-Broadway, e.g., *Joseph & the Amazing Technicolor Dreamcoat.* More recent productions: *A Woman of Independent Means,* starring Barbara Rush, an encore presentation of the comedy *Greater Tuna,* Dickens' *A Christmas Carol* (more or less a yearly tradition here), a musical version of *Elmer Gantry,* and *Sammy Cahn: Words & Music.* Ticket prices range from about $22 to $26, with discounts available for senior citizens at matinee performances; both seniors and students with ID can also get "rush" tickets a half hour before performances.

A big event here is the nationally televised (CBS) annual fundraiser, always a celebrity-studded bash. A recent one was hosted by Mikhail Baryshnikov and Don Johnson and featured Bea Arthur, Glen Campbell, Art Garfunkel, Sammy Cahn, and David Copperfield, among others. The Reagans attended.

THE SOURCE THEATRE COMPANY: The Source (tel. 462-1073) presents top local artists in a year-round schedule of dramatic and comedic plays on its two stages and sometimes in other facilities around town as well. The **Warehouse Rep,** 1835 14th St. NW, between S and T Streets, is the larger space. Recent productions here have included Christopher Durang's *Beyond Therapy* and *Extremities*. And the Rep is also used for a Late Night Series (Friday and Saturday nights at 11:30 p.m.) of experimental or avant-garde productions, like the *Hitchhiker's Guide to the Universe* and a Paris mime ensemble called Théâtre Grottesco. The Washington-area première of Harvey Fierstein's *Safe Sex* was also at the Warehouse. On the smaller **Main-Stage,** 1809 14th St. NW, between S and T Streets, you might see anything from Sam Shepard's *Geography of a Horse Dreamer* to Charles Fuller's *A Soldier's Play.* Annual events include the Washington Theatre Festival each July, a four-week showcase of new plays.

The Source produces 30 to 50 plays a year—more than the Kennedy Center—and welcomes original scripts from unknowns. Twenty new plays are presented every July during the annual Theatre Festival here. Ticket prices for most productions are in the $13 to $16 range; Late Night shows are just $5.

NEW PLAYWRIGHTS' THEATRE: "There is no greater need in the American theater than for new writers who can record and reflect our times," says Joseph Papp. "New Playwrights' Theatre has responded to this need." A nationally acclaimed, fully professional theater involved in promoting the creation, development, and production of new works by American playwrights, NPT, 1742 Church St. NW (tel. 232-1122), premières four fully staged productions each October-to-June season, along with five staged readings. Under the direction of Peter Frisch, they evaluate some 400 scripts submitted annually from every state and return them to the playwrights with detailed critiques.

New works by established playwrights are also shown here occasionally, e.g., Larry King's *The Night Hank Williams Died* and Elizabeth Swados' *The Beautiful Lady.*

This is a vital and unique kind of theater. Show times are Tuesday to Saturday at 8 p.m., Sunday at 3 and 7 p.m. Tickets are $14 to

$17. To attend Monday-night rehearsed readings of new works and works in progress, followed by audience discussion, admission is $2.

ACCENT ON ENTERTAINMENT

The following listings are a potpourri of places offering a mixed bag of theater, headliners, jazz, classical music, rock, dance, comedy, etc. Here you'll find some of the top entertainment choices in the District.

THE JOHN F. KENNEDY CENTER FOR THE PERFORMING ARTS: At the southern end of New Hampshire Avenue NW and Rock Creek Parkway, this national cultural center is actually a composite of five facilities. You can find out what will be on during your stay before leaving home (and charge tickets) by calling a toll-free number, 800/424-8504. In town, call 254-3600 for information about current productions, 857-0900 to charge tickets. Half-price tickets are available for full-time students, senior citizens, enlisted personnel, and the disabled (call 254-3774 for details). Underground parking is $4 for the entire evening.

The Opera House

This plush red-and-gilt 2,200-seat theater is designed for ballet, modern dance, and musical comedy, as well as opera, and it's also the setting for occasional gala events such as the Kennedy Center Honors, which you've probably seen on TV (Lillian Gish, Cary Grant, Leonard Bernstein, and Bob Hope have been honorees). Other offerings have included performances by the Joffrey Ballet, the Bolshoi Ballet, the American Ballet Theatre with Baryshnikov, and the Metropolitan Opera, and theater productions such as the American première of *Les Misérables* and *Aren't We All*, starring Rex Harrison and Claudette Colbert. Call 254-3770 for information.

The Concert Hall

The National Symphony Orchestra under the direction of Mstislav Rostropovich has its home here and presents several concert series from September to June. Tickets are available by subscription and single sales; some are free. Guest artists have included Itzhak Perlman, Vladimir Ashkenazy, Daniel Barenboim, Aaron Copland, Jean-Pierre Rampal, and Leonard Bernstein. In addition, chamber music societies, orchestras, and choral groups from all over the world have performed in this space; there's an annual free Christmas concert, the *Messiah* Sing-Along; and rounding things out are headliner entertainers like Frank Sinatra, Johnny Mathis, Pearl Bailey, Steve Lawrence and Eydie Gorme, Neil Sedaka, Joel

Grey, Dionne Warwick, Engelbert Humperdinck, and Tony Bennett. Call 254-3776 for information.

The Terrace Theater

Small chamber works, operas, choral recitals, musicals, comedy revues, cabarets, theatrical and modern dance performances are among the varied provinces of the 500-seat Terrace Theater, a Bicentennial gift from Japan. It's been the setting for solo performances by people like clarinetist Richard Stolzman, pianists Peter Serkin and David Lively, tenor Robert White, cellist Thalia Moore, and folk singer Odetta. A recent production starred Al Pacino in a revival of *American Buffalo*. The Maria Benitez Spanish Dance Company has performed here, and cabarets have included *Some Enchanted Evening*, a delightful medley of Rogers and Hammerstein songs. Every spring the Terrace hosts productions of six finalists in the American College Theatre Festival competition. Call 254-9895.

The Eisenhower Theater

A wide range of dramatic productions can be seen in the Eisenhower Theater. Recent offerings have included Lily Tomlin's highly acclaimed show, *The Search for Signs of Intelligent Life in the Universe*, a revival of *Sleuth* starring Stacy Keach, Derek Jacoby in *Breaking the Code*, and a comedy called *Sullivan & Gilbert* with Fritz Weaver and Noel Harrison. The Eisenhower is also the setting for smaller productions of the **Washington Opera** from October to February. Tickets for most theatrical productions are in the $18 to $40 range. Opera seats soar higher. Call 254-3670.

Theater Lab Et Al

Many Kennedy Center events and performances are free, including the Theater Lab's full schedule of children's shows such as *Dick Wittington and His Cat* and *The Tale of Peter Rabbit*. In the evening Theater Lab becomes a cabaret, now in a long run of *Shear Madness*, a comedy whodunit, though this isn't gratis (tickets are $19 to $23). There are, however, free Family Concerts by the National Symphony Orchestra several times each year, not to mention clowns, jugglers, dance troupes, improvisational theater, storytellers, and films. Christmas and Easter are especially event-filled times.

The American Film Institute

This is your chance to see classic films, cult movies, themed film festivals, and the like in a 224-seat theater designed to offer the highest standard of projection, picture, and sound quality. There's something on almost every night and weekend afternoon, and tickets are only $5, less for members ($24 a year for one, $32 for two), who also receive other privileges. There are discounts for students with ID and senior citizens. The AFI also sponsors audience-participation discussions with major directors, film stars, and screenwriters—people like Alan Alda, Mike Nichols, Jack Lemmon, Frank Gilroy, and Donald Sutherland. Call 785-4600 or 785-4601.

THE WARNER THEATRE: Concerts, dance performances, and Broadway shows (coming or going) alternate with headliner entertainment at the Warner, a '20s vaudeville theater at 513 13th St. NW, between E and F Streets (tel. 626-1050). The Tuesday-to-Sunday shows (times vary) might be anything from the New York production of *Little Shop of Horrors* to The Stratford Shakespeare Festival. The last few years' productions have included a revival of *Fiddler on the Roof* with Herschel Bernardi, *Dreamgirls, La Cage aux Folles,* and *Lena Horne—The Lady and Her Music.* As for headliners, Ray Charles, Talking Heads, Patti LaBelle, Linda Ronstadt, and Miles Davis have all appeared on the Warner stage. Tickets for plays are $15 to $35; for concerts, $12.50 to $19.50.

WOLF TRAP FARM PARK FOR THE PERFORMING ARTS: The country's only national park devoted to the performing arts, Wolf Trap, just 30 minutes by car from downtown D.C. at 1624 Trap Rd., in Vienna, Va. (tel. 703/255-1860), offers a star-studded **Summer Festival Season** from late May to the beginning of September. Tickets can be purchased in advance by calling 432-0200 or via Hecht Ticket Center locations. Recent seasons have featured productions by the New York City Opera and the National Symphony Orchestra, jazz trumpeter Wynton Marsalis, the Kirov Ballet from Leningrad, *Camelot,* Benny Goodman, the Eliot Feld Ballet, the Paris Ballet, Ray Charles, Johnny Cash, Emmylou Harris, Natalie Cole, Johnny Mathis, Joan Baez, and Peter, Paul, and Mary. Talk about eclectic! Performances are held in the 6,900-seat Filene Center II theater, about half of which is under the open sky. Prices range from $12 to $38. Considerably cheaper are lawn tickets, $8 to $15, for which you'd best arrive good and early (the lawn opens an hour prior to the performance). Bring a picnic dinner; everyone does.

October to May is Wolf Trap's **Barn Season,** featuring jazz, pop, country, and bluegrass performers, chamber music, square dancing, etc., in the pre-Revolutionary, 350-seat German Barn. Tickets are $8 to $15. Call 703/938-2404 for information.

To get to Wolf Trap, take I-495 to Exit 12W (Dulles Toll Road); stay on local exits (you'll see a sign) until you come to Wolf Trap. Via public transportation: take the Wolf Trap Express Shuttle ($3 round trip) from the West Falls Church Metro station. Buses run every 20 minutes from 6:20 p.m.

CONSTITUTION HALL: Somehow we don't associate people like Rodney Dangerfield and Eddie Murphy with the Daughters of the American Revolution. Nevertheless, they've both appeared at Constitution Hall, the beautiful 3,746-seat Federal-style auditorium at the DAR's national headquarters at 18th and D Streets NW (tel. 638-2661). Others who've headlined here include Bob Hope, Barry Manilow, Alabama, Whitney Houston, Ricky Skaggs, Jay Leno, Suzanne Vega, James Taylor, Ray Charles, and Marilyn Horne. Tickets for most performers cost $12 to $20. They're usually sold through Ticketron and at Ticket Center.

THE PATRIOT CENTER: This 10,000-seat facility of George Mason University, 4400 University Dr. in Fairfax, VA (tel. 703/323-2672), opened in 1985 and has already hosted some major headliners. Conway Twitty, Hank Williams, Jr., Frankie Laine and Kay Starr, Andy Williams, Chicago, the Beach Boys, Billy Idol, and Kenny Rogers have all played here. To get to the Patriot Center take the Wilson Bridge to Braddock Road W (Route 623) and continue for about eight miles going west. Via public transportation take the CUE bus from the Vienna, Virginia, Metro station. Call 385-7859 for departure times. For ticket information and to charge tickets call 202/432-0200.

ROBERT F. KENNEDY MEMORIAL STADIUM: It takes superstars to pack this 55,000-plus facility at East Capitol and 22nd Sts. NE (tel. 547-9077). Michael Jackson, Bruce Springsteen, Bob Dylan, and Madonna are a few of those who've played here. Call 432-0200 to charge tickets.

MERRIWEATHER POST PAVILION: During the summer there's celebrity entertainment almost nightly at the Merriweather Post Pavilion, just off Rte. 29 in Columbia, Md. (tel. 301/730-2424), about 40 minutes by car from downtown D.C. There's seating in the open-air pavilion (roofed in case of rain) and on the lawn (no refunds for rain) to see performers like James Taylor, the Oak Ridge Boys, Crosby, Stills & Nash, Jackie Mason, John Cougar Mellencamp, Julio Iglesias, Joan Rivers, Willie Nelson, Jimmie Buffet, Elton John, Al Jarreau, and Barry Manilow. Pavilion tickets average about $19; lawn tickets, $13. Get your tickets—through Ticketron—early, since first buyers get the best seats. Parking is included in your ticket price. Call 800/233-4050 or 301/982-1800 to charge tickets.

THE CAPITAL CENTRE: Even closer to town, the Capital Centre, Exit 15 or 17A off the Capital Beltway in Landover, Md. (tel. 301/350-3400), hosts a variety of concerts and headliner entertainment in between sporting events. Frank Sinatra, Paul McCartney, Prince, Neil Diamond, Bill Cosby, Bob Dylan, the Rolling

Stones, and Diana Ross have all played this 20,000-seat theater. Ticket prices depend on the performer. To charge tickets, call 432-0200.

MOSTLY JAZZ: The following feature jazz artists exclusively or in conjunction with other entertainment.

Called "Blues in the Mews" because of its location in an alley behind M Street at 1073 Wisconsin Ave., **Blues Alley** (tel. 337-4141) is a top jazz club featuring artists like Sarah Vaughan, George Shearing, Ahmad Jamal, Stanley Turrentine, Freddie Hubbard, Maynard Ferguson, Carmen McRae, Dizzy Gillespie, Esther Phillips, and Stan Getz. There are shows nightly: three on Friday and Saturday, two the rest of the week. Reservations are essential, and since seating is on a first-come, first-served basis it's best to arrive no later than 7 p.m. and have dinner. Cover price ranges from $12 to $30, depending on the performer, and there's a $2 food or drink minimum, which you're bound to exceed since dinner entrees on the steak and Créole-seafood menu are in the $9 to $15 range and drinks are $3 to $5.

Dedicated to promoting the performance arts, **d.c. (district creative) space,** (a.k.a. "Soho on the Potomac"), 443 7th St. NW, at E Street (tel. 347-1445 or 347-4960), offers an exciting avant-garde mix of jazz, reggae, new wave, musical cabaret, comedy, and art theater. Many well-known jazz artists play the club—Abbey Lincoln, Don Cherry, Lester Bowie, Air, Sun Ra, Mal Waldron, Chico Freeman, etc.; productions have included Jacques Brel cabarets and a Kurt Weill revue, as well as *By George, by Ira, by Gershwin;* art performer Laurie Anderson has appeared here; and G.N.P., a group that does "Saturday Night Live"–style political comedy skits, performs here frequently. It's a comfortable, casual place with an eclectic assortment of furnishings. Ticket prices range from $3 to $10, and there's a food or drink minimum of $5 on Saturday nights at some shows. The food, by the way, is quite good and prices are reasonable.

While you're enjoying the artists on stage, you can also enjoy the art show on the walls at d.c. space; it secondarily functions as an art gallery.

CABARET: A hotel with a long history of providing great entertainment, the **OMNI Shoreham,** 2500 Calvert St. NW, at Connecticut Avenue (tel. 234-0700), today features talented ensembles in its plush art deco nightclub, the **Marquee Cabaret.** In the 1930s, people like Sinatra, Chevalier, Bob Hope, and Judy Garland performed at the Shoreham. And more recently, the elegant candlelit Marquee —with seating in Louis XV–style rose-velvet chairs and moss-green banquettes—has been offering some of Washington's most entertaining evenings. Mark Russell, the political satirist at the piano, played the room for many years before going on to TV fame. And subsequent shows have included *Forbidden Broadway*, Garry Trudeau's *Rap Master Ronnie*, Capitol Steps (a locally renowned group of political satirists made up of actual government bureaucrats and staffers), and a show called *Mrs. Foggybottom and Friends*. Drinks and light fare are available. There's one show a night Tuesday through Friday, two shows Friday and Saturday. Admission is $15 on weeknights, $18 weekends.

FREE SHOWS

In D.C. some of the best things at night are free—or so cheap they're as good as free in today's inflationary clime.

MILITARY BAND CONCERTS: The **U.S. Army Band, "Pershing's Own"** (tel. 696-3718), presents a mix of country, blues, Bach, choral music, jazz, pop, and show tunes every summer, all of it outdoors. There are performances at 8 p.m. every Friday on the west terrace of the Capitol and every Tuesday at the Sylvan Theatre on the grounds of the Washington Monument. Beginning early in July the band joins with the 3rd U.S. Infantry, "The Old Guard," on Wednesday at 7 p.m. to present Twilight Tattoo, a military pageant, on the Ellipse; it features the Old Guard Fife and Drum Corps, bayonet drills, flag presentations, and a musical salute to America's heritage. Arrive early to get a good seat at any of the above, and bring a picnic dinner. The season's highlight is a performance in August of Tchaikovsky's *1812 Overture* with real roaring cannons. There are some additional performances in winter. Call for details.

The **U.S. Navy Band, "The World's Finest"** (tel. 433-2525 for a 24-hour recording, or 433-6090), performs alternately at 8 p.m. Monday on the west terrace of the Capitol and Thursday at 8 p.m. at the Sylvan Theatre, June through August. The Navy Band highlight: the Children's Lollipop Concert of child-oriented music, in August, with elaborate sets, costumes, balloons, clowns, and free lollipops for the audience. And the band also features the Navy Summer Ceremony, a multimedia presentation tracing the history of the U.S. Navy, on Wednesday at 9 p.m. at the Washington Navy Yard Waterfront, 9th and M Streets SE. Performances take place June through August. Advance reservations are required; call 433-2678.

The **U.S. Marine Band, "The President's Own"** (tel. 433-4011 for a 24-hour recording, or 433-5809), alternates summer performances on the west terrace of the Capitol on Wednesday at 8 p.m. and the Sylvan Theatre on Sunday at 8 p.m. They also present the Evening Parade at the Marine Barracks, 8th Street SE, at I Street, on Friday at 8:20 p.m. between mid-May and early September. This military parade is free to the public, but you must make reservations three weeks in advance by calling 433-6060 or writing to Adjutant, Marine Barracks, 8th and I Streets SE, Washington, D.C. 20390.

Finally, there's the **U.S. Air Force Band and Singing Sergeants, "America's International Musical Ambassadors"** (tel. 767-4310). June through August they can be seen on the west terrace of the Capitol on Tuesday at 8 p.m. and at the Sylvan Theatre on Friday at the same time. And the Friday closest to August 25 is set aside for Christmas in August (carols and other Christmas music).

HEADLINER ENTERTAINMENT: Anheuser-Busch, along with local radio stations WDJY and WKYS, sponsors two fabulous outdoor summer concert series in conjunction with the National Park Service.

At the 4,500-seat **Carter Barron Amphitheatre,** Colorado Avenue and 16th Street NW, in Rock Creek Park (tel. 829-3200 or 485-9660), big names in jazz, pop, rock, Latin, and avant-garde music perform mid-June through the end of August on Saturday and Sunday nights at 8:30 p.m. Tickets are very low priced—about $10. They go on sale—at the box office and Ticketron outlets—about a week in advance and sell out fast. Seating is on a first-come, first-served basis, so arrive early and get on line. Who might you see here? Nancy Wilson, Phoebe Snow, the O' Jays, Stephanie Mills, Miles Davis, Diane Reeves, or B.B. King, among other stars.

Under the same sponsorship is a series of jazz concerts on the lawn in the **Fort Dupont Summer Theatre,** Randle Circle and Minnesota Avenue SE, in Fort Dupont Park (tel. 426-7723 or 485-9600), every Friday and Saturday at 8:30 p.m. from some time in June to the end of August. Bring a blanket and a picnic dinner; arrive early (by 6 p.m.) to get a good spot on the lawn. Past performers here have included Noel Pointer, Herbie Mann, the Motown Revue, Jimmy Witherspoon, Flora Purim, and Ahmad Jamal. Admission is free.

CONCERTS ON THE CANAL: Sponsored by the Mobil Corporation, these are free afternoon concerts right on the C&O Canal at 30th and Thomas Jefferson Streets NW, just below M Street (tel. 862-1300 or 778-6100). Featuring jazz, folk, Dixieland, bluegrass, country, and classical artists, they take place every other Sunday afternoon (1:30 to 4 p.m.) from early June to early September.

CONCERTS AT THE CAPITOL, AN AMERICAN FESTIVAL: Sponsored jointly by the National Park Service and Congress, free summer concerts with the National Symphony Orchestra take place at 8 p.m. on the west side of the Capitol on Memorial Day, July 4th, Labor Day, and a fourth date determined annually. Seating is on the lawn, so bring a picnic. Major guest stars like Leontyne Price, Sarah Vaughan, Henry Mancini, Peter Ustinov, and Mstislav

Rostropovich have participated. The music ranges from light classical to show tunes. For further information, call 485-9666.

DANCING IN THE PARK: From May through the end of September, you can attend Friday-night square dances, Saturday-night big-band concerts, and Sunday-night square or folk dances at the **Spanish Ballroom at Glen Echo Park,** MacArthur Boulevard and Goldsboro Road (tel. 492-6282). Admission is $4 to $7. Call for hours. There is usually also entertainment on other nights.

The Corporate Community Family (which is made up of organizations like Exxon and C&P Telephone) sponsors free **Big-Band Concerts** on Wednesday nights in summer at the Sylvan Theatre on the lawn south of the Washington Monument (tel. 485-9666). Once again, arrive early to snag a good seat, and bring a picnic dinner. Concerts begin at 7 p.m.

BARS AND DANCE CLUBS

It's often the case in Washington that the places offering the best singles action also have dance floors. Hence, we've grouped these categories together.

Isn't it romantic? The elegantly art deco **River Club,** 3223 K St. NW (tel. 333-8118), evokes the sophisticated dine-and-dance clubs that flourished in an earlier era ('20s and '30s). It brings unprecedented champagne-and-caviar glamor to the Washington nightlife scene. The clientele is glittery and gorgeous (wear your best), many with limos waiting out front. *Dossier* magazine described the River Club crowd as "the hungry moneyed and the money hungry." Among the former you'll often see local and visiting celebrities— Mayor Marion Barry, Ryan O'Neal, Merv Griffin, Eva Gabor, Lynda Carter, Senator John Warner, Sylvester Stallone. You can hang out in the large bar up front or have dinner (the food's superb) at the tables surrounding the circular dance floor. It's a great place to dance. The music runs the gamut from the swing era to jive, jitterbug, and '50s and '60's hits. If you can't manage sparkling repartee or kindle the spark of romance in this setting, you never will.

Open for dinner Sunday to Thursday 6 to 11:30 p.m., for dancing till 2 a.m., Friday and Saturday for dinner till midnight, for dancing till 3 a.m. See Chapter IV for a detailed description of the River Club and its culinary offerings.

D.C. has finally figured out what's hip and what's hot. Hence, **Cities,** 2424 18th St. NW (tel. 328-7194), a great new dance club where even Tama Janowitz might feel at home. Unlike so many clubs in this town, Cities' clientele isn't all white/all straight/all Yuppie. You're not in Kansas anymore.

Above a thrillingly innovative Adams Morgan restaurant/bar (details in Chapter IV), the club shares the eatery's post-industrial, crumbling-city-chic decor. The zigzag rooms, randomly lit by neon, are on the eerie side—like a street in a dream sequence. Cities' setting has been described as "concrete, scrap marble, concrete, local art, concrete. . . ." Slide shows and videos aren't of Michael Jackson; they're travelogues of the city currently being feted in the downstairs restaurant (the menu changes every six months to reflect the cuisine of a different city). The music is progressive/European, and the front room—with a wall of windows overlooking Adams Morgan's main drag—is a comfortable venue for champagne and conversation. Plan to dine downstairs earlier in the evening.

Open till 2 a.m. Wednesday and Thursday nights, till 3 a.m. Friday and Saturday. Admission is free on Wednesday, $5 Thursday, $8 Friday and Saturday. Average drink is $3.75. Minimum age: 21.

Note: Owner Saher Erozan plans to open a new place, the **Mountain Club**, 3065 M St. NW (no phone yet), featuring New American cuisine and major jazz artists, by the winter of 1989, shortly after we go to press. Check it out.

Champions, 1206 Wisconsin Ave. NW, down an alley just north of M Street (tel. 965-4005), is D.C.'s premier hangout for athletes and sports groupies. *Playboy* calls it Washington's best singles bar. Champions occupies two levels—the heaviest singles action is at the first-floor bar; the upstairs bar and glassed-in deck are more laid back. The attractive decor features numerous sports photos and artifacts such as Moses Mallone's sneakers, Joe Louis's headgear, and O.J. Simpson's football jersey. Of course, you're likely to see your favorite sports stars (particularly of Washington teams) at the bars or tables, and entertainment-world celebrities also drop by with some frequency. Speaking of those tables, they're hard to come by, unless you get here early; Champions is always packed, and they don't take reservations. If you do get a seat, you might order such fare as nachos, burgers, a Philly steak-and-cheese sandwich, or buffalo wings. And should you make your way through the crowd to the bar, you'll see that it's pasted over with $15,000 worth of baseball cards. Open Sunday to Thursday until 2 a.m., on Friday and Saturday until 3 a.m.

Clyde's, 3236 M St. NW (tel. 333-9180), is a New York–style bar complete with checkered tablecloths, gaslight sconces, and white tile floors. Its two bars are mobbed every evening with an upscale crowd of college students, political types, and Old Line Washingtonians. Should you desire solid rather than liquid refreshment, there are several dining areas, our favorite being the candlelit patio with numerous plants and a skylight ceiling. Or you can adjourn to the Omelette Room where a chef working in an open copper-canopied kitchen turns out such omelets as the Bonne Femme—stuffed with bacon, sautéed potatoes, onions, sour cream, and chives—till the wee hours. Drinks are served until 2 a.m. Sunday to Thursday, to 3 a.m. on Friday and Saturday.

F. Scott's, 1232 36th St. NW, between N and Prospect Streets (tel. 342-0009), attracts an Ivy League crowd that might indeed have stepped out of the pages of Fitzgerald. The upper-level bar is wall-to-wall preppies and post-preppies, and the decor evokes the '30s with Peter Arno cartoons and period art posters on the walls. Down a few steps is a small dance floor where taped music of the '20s through the '80s is played (eras progress as the evening wears on). There's no cover or minimum, but drinks begin at about $4 apiece, and the Northern Italian–influenced menu is on the expensive side with entrees ($10.50 to $18) like salmon baked in parchment and grilled breast of duck with fresh grilled duck sausage in Barolo wine sauce. On the other hand, you could opt for one of over 30 specialty drinks such as the Yellow Bird *("S'envoler dans la nuit* with a smooth blend of Galliano, fresh banana, ice cream, and vodka, highlighted with Tía Maria and orange juice" rhapsodizes the menu). There are also numerous desserts, including a delicious tira misu. Food is served until 12:30 a.m. Monday to Thursday, to 1 a.m. on Friday and Saturday; the bar closes at 2 and 3 a.m. respectively. Minimum age is 21, and jackets are required for gentlemen.

While we're on the subject of high-tone places, the **Old Ebbitt Grill,** 675 15th St. NW, between F and G Streets (tel. 347-4801), described in detail in Chapter IV, offers a good bit of glamor in its sumptuous turn-of-the-century bars and dining areas.

Along 19th Street NW (between M Street and Dupont Circle) is a lively singles strip with numerous clubs in close proximity. The set-up is perfect for an all-night debauch.

Beginning at 19th and M Streets NW is **Rumors** (tel. 466-7378), for many years *Washingtonian* magazine's choice as D.C.'s no. 1 singles bar. Rumors is mobbed even on Monday nights when other places offer all the excitement of a wake. In the California-style, neo-Victorian bar (overhead fans, ferns, and brass railings) and the dance floor area (featuring a DJ spinning contemporary dance tunes nightly, supplemented by live bands on Monday), unless you look like Quasimodo you're likely to score. Take your new love out for a daiquiri or a meal to the open-air café under a striped tent top, where conversation is possible and you can ascertain that you haven't snagged the Son of Sam. Food is served till midnight, with entrees in the $5 to $10 range. No cover or minimum. You must be 21 to get in. Open Sunday to Thursday until 2 a.m., on Friday and Saturday to 3 p.m.

Flaps Rickenbacker's, 1207 19th St. NW, between M and N Streets (tel. 223-3617), is a laid-back hangout housed in a white-shuttered, three-story brick town house. There's no dance floor, but a DJ plays records (mostly oldies and Motown) from 9 p.m. to closing Wednesday to Sunday. Here, people just boogey where they stand. All of the levels are decorated with aviation-themed photos and paraphernalia—airplane propellers overhead. There are two bars, one upstairs, one on the lower level, and nighttime promotions include the likes of outdoor barbecues, two-for-one Corona nights, and the Bahama Mama Party every May with a 15-piece steel band, tropical decorations, sand covering the floors, and goombay punch served in pineapples. Flaps features a reasonably priced menu listing items like a New York strip steak sandwich and a chef's salad. The nicest place to eat is the outside café, under umbrella tables. No cover or minimum. Flaps stays open till 2 a.m. Sunday to Thursday, till 3 a.m. Friday and Saturday.

One of the liveliest places in D.C., **Déjà Vu,** 2119 M St. NW (tel. 452-1966), is an eight-room Victorian extravaganza with three dance floors, six bars, and Blackie's House of Beef (details in Chapter IV) on the premises. The dance floors have working fireplaces, which, along with stained-glass paneling, lots of plants, fountains, and Victorian furnishings, make for a cozy setting. A DJ plays mostly oldies. Minimum age is 21. No cover or drink minimum. Every Thursday there's a jitterbug contest at midnight (first prize is $50), and there are frequent theme parties such as Christmas in July and New Year's in August. Open Sunday to Thursday to 2 a.m., on Friday and Saturday to 3 a.m.

Samantha's, 1823 L St. NW (tel. 223-1823), is an exceptionally cozy hangout with oak-paneled and exposed brick walls hung with French posters from the '20s, stained-glass panels, art nouveau wall sconces, sienna tufted-leather banquettes, and a working fireplace (filled with plants and flowers in summer) on the dance floor. A DJ is on hand Wednesday to Saturday (Wednesday to Sunday in summer). The menu features typical American fare (eight-ounce burgers, omelets, spinach salad, and quiches, along with more ambitious American nouvelle daily specials like hickory-smoked chicken breast with rotini pesto); prices are moderate. Open Monday to Thursday till 2 a.m., on Friday and Saturday till 3 a.m. Closed Sundays except in summer when open till midnight.

COMEDY

Though big-name comedians perform around town at places like Constitution Hall, and lesser-known comedians and groups at places like d.c. space, there are two clubs in town totally devoted to comedy. **The Comedy Café,** 1520 K St. NW (tel. 638-JOKE), is a club modeled after places like L.A.'s famous Comedy Store and New York's Catch a Rising Star. Shows feature about three acts nightly—both local talent and nationally known comics you might have seen in movies or on TV (like Jay Leno, Larry "Bud" Melman, Yakov Smirnoff *(Moscow on the Hudson),* Shirley Hemphill *(What's Happening?),* and Soupy Sales. Reservations are recommended, and it's a good idea to arrive early to get a good seat. There are two shows every Friday night (8:30 and 10:30 p.m.) and three every Saturday night (7:30, 9:30, and 11:30 p.m.); admission is $15.95 with dinner (soup or salad and an entree such as deep-fried butterfly shrimp),

$7 without dinner. Thursday night is open-mike night from 8:30 p.m. to midnight; that means people are auditioning or, occasionally, pros are working out new material (cover is $3.49, no minimum).

Then there's **Garvin's,** presently residing at 1335 Green Court (on L Street NW, between 13th and 14th Streets; tel. 726-1334). Garvin's is likely to have moved on by the time you read this; it's had about six locations in as many years. Not to worry—if you call the above number and they don't know where Garvin's is just check the local paper; it's always somewhere. And its well worth looking for.

Owner Harry Monocrusos books lots of big names. People like Charley Barnett, Marcia Warfield *(Night Court),* Yakov Smirnoff, Emo Phillips, and Joe Piscopo have all played his D.C. clubs, and even when lesser lights are onstage major comedy stars (Eddie Murphy, Redd Foxx, Rodney Dangerfield, to name a few) have dropped in and grabbed the mike for a spell.

Monday and Tuesday are open-mike nights when people audition ($3 cover is charged), Wednesday nights feature improvisational performers taking audience suggestions ($3 cover), Thursdays national and local pros perform ($4 cover), and Friday and Saturday nights feature established pros from New York and Los Angeles ($7 cover). There's no drink minimum. Monday through Thursday the show begins at 8:30 p.m., Friday and Saturday nights there are two shows (8:30 and 10:30 p.m.), in winter three Saturday night shows (7:30, 9:30, and 11:30 p.m.). Continental/Créole fare is available, with entrees priced from $7.50 to $14.

Garvin's has another comedy club in Arlington at 2700 Jefferson Davis Hwy., near Crystal City (tel. 703/684-3354).

CHAPTER VIII

SHOPPING IN WASHINGTON

□ □ □

Shopping in Washington gets better and better all the time. The District has its share of classic department stores and classy boutiques, suburban shopping centers and tiny crafts and gift shops, plus some surprisingly good discount stores. In addition, it has something unique to its status as the capital city: stores at museums and other sightseeing attractions.

Washington's traditional downtown shopping area runs from F and G Streets between 7th and 14th Streets NW, and it is here that the city's top three department stores—Garfinckel's, Woodward & Lothrop, and Hecht's—are located.

Moving uptown a bit to the area around Connecticut Avenue and K Street, the climate turns to posh boutiques and specialty shops. And our favorite area for relaxed browsing—antique stores, craft shops, design centers, and gourmet marts abound—is the Wisconsin Avenue and M Street area in Georgetown. Let's begin, however, with a look at the major department stores.

THE DEPARTMENT STORES

Garfinckel's, at the corner of 14th and F Streets NW (tel. 628-7730), is perhaps the area's most prestigious specialty store. The newest fashions for women, men, and children are elegantly displayed in a graceful setting. Christian La Croix, Tiktiner, Gloria Sachs, Armani, Chanel, Calvin Klein, Sonia Rykiel, Anne Klein, Ellen Tracy, Ungaro, and Krizia are just a sampling of the top designers whose creations for women are shown in their own boutiques. Designers of men's clothing represented here include Valentino, Polo, Hugo Boss, and Gieves and Hawkes. Garfinckel's brings the finest to Washington homes too, with a choice selection of china (including Picard, the firm that produces china for the White House), crystal (Lalique, Baccarat, Waterford, Orrefors),

Christofle silver, and dry goods, including exquisite imported French linens.

Other branches of Garfinckel's are at 4280 Massachusetts Ave. NW (tel. 363-7700) and the Georgetown Park Mall (tel. 628-8107).

Woodward & Lothrop, 11th and F Streets NW (tel. 347-5300), specializes in clothing for the whole family, plus gifts, stamps and coins for collectors, housewares, and furniture. There's a large bridal department on the fifth floor. Woodies—that's how this store is known among Washington families, who have been coming here for several generations—has an excellent reputation for fine service and quality merchandise at reasonable prices. There are several eating places, including the archetypical department store tea room, on the premises. Designer showrooms here include Fendi, Calvin Klein, Oscar de la Renta, and Ralph Lauren. Celebrity promotions—Elizabeth Taylor hawking her new fragrance, Greg Louganis for Speedo, and Debbie Reynolds for Leslie Fay—are part of the fun. Altogether, there are 16 Woodward & Lothrop stores in the D.C. area; check your phone book for locations.

Hecht's, 12th and G Streets NW, at Metro Center (tel. 628-6661), like Woodie's, has been in Washington for about a century. But it's not fusty. In fact this brand-new branch is a fun store—kind of a mini-Macy's—with five floors of moderate- to higher-priced merchandise and lots going on. You might happen on cooking and merchandise demonstrations here, a contest (win a car or a trip to Buenos Aires), or an in-store personality appearance (in the past these have included Jane Powell, Paloma Picasso, Liz Claiborne, Richard Simmons, soap opera stars, and the cast of *42nd Street)*. It's a full-service department store, featuring brand names in clothing and footwear for the whole family, contemporary and traditional home furnishings, and numerous specialty shops. In addition all Hecht's stores house **Ticket Center** outlets selling tickets to most major shows, concerts, and sports events in town; you get the best available seats for the price at the time you buy. There are 14 Hecht's stores in the D.C. area.

In addition to these local stores, Washington boasts branches of several prestigious New York and West Coast stores. **Lord & Taylor** is at 5255 Western Ave. NW (tel. 362-9600); **Saks Fifth Avenue** can be found at 5555 Wisconsin Ave. in Chevy Chase, Md. (tel. 657-9000); and **Neiman-Marcus** is located in Mazza Gallerie on upper Wisconsin Avenue (tel. 966-9700); see ahead. You'll find a branch of **Bloomingdale's** at Tysons Corner Center in McLean, Va. (tel. 556-4600). **I. Magnin** has set up shop at the White Flint Mall in Kensington, Md. (tel. 468-2900). And good old plebeian **Sears Roebuck & Co.** has a branch at 4500 Wisconsin Ave. NW (tel. 364-1299).

GOOD SHOPPING AROUND THE TOWN

ART REPRODUCTIONS, PRINTS, AND ENGRAVINGS:
All the art museums detailed in Chapter V are good bets, especially
the **National Gallery of Art** (tel. 737-4215), with several shops featuring a wide choice of prints, posters, art reproductions, Christmas
cards, and art books. The West Building shop is the largest; the special Exhibition desk in the East Building deals with current exhibit-
related books and art.

Good reproductions of engravings can be had, by mail, from
the **Bureau of Engraving and Printing** at 14th and C Streets SW,
Washington, D.C. 20228 (tel. 447-0326), including presidential
portraits, portraits of government officials, scenes of Washington
landmarks, government seals, and prints of the Gettysburg Address
and the Bill of Rights; the list goes on and on. The Bureau also sells
sheets of uncut currency. Write for a free brochure or stop by the
store on the premises (details in Chapter V).

BOOKS AND RECORDS: Crown Books, with seven D.C.
locations and many more in suburbia, offers 35% off *New York
Times* fiction and nonfiction paperback bestsellers, 40% off hard-
covers. Other books—on all subjects running the gamut from
gardening to philosophy—are discounted at least 10%. Even magazines are reduced. Centrally located stores include branches at
3131 M St. NW (tel. 333-4493), 1710 G St. NW (tel. 789-2277),
New Hampshire Avenue and M Street NW (tel. 822-8331), and
2020 K St. NW (tel. 659-2030), among others; check your phone
book. Both the K and G Street locations also sell discounted computer software. All the above except G Street are open seven days a
week.

Bookstore buffs will enjoy a browse in **Estate Book Sales**,
2824 Pennsylvania Ave. NW (which merges with M Street here; tel.
965-4274), which, as its name implies, buys up estate libraries.
There are three floors chock-a-block with first editions, rare books,
prints, and low-priced paperbacks. The owners play classical music
too, which makes things just about perfect.

Both locations of **Olsson's Books & Records**, 1307 19th St.
NW, just off Dupont Circle (tel. 785-2662 for records, 785-1133
for books), and 1239 Wisconsin Ave. NW, between M and N
Streets (tel. 338-6712 for records, 338-9544 for books), offer discounts on all records and tapes (of which they offer an immense variety) and have about 50,000 to 60,000 books on their shelves
focusing on every possible area except romance and porn. *Washington Post* hardcover bestsellers are reduced 30%; other books are sold
at regular prices. Especially at the Georgetown store, book signings
are frequent events; among the authors who have appeared are Tom

Wicker, Anthony Burgess, Maurice Sendak, Garrison Keillor, P. D. James, Joan Baez, and Liv Ullmann.

CHILDREN'S CLOTHING: 7th Heaven, 1110 F St. NW (tel. 638-5264), is every indulgent grandma's idea of paradise. Imagine being let loose in a place stocked with tons of bargains on first-quality merchandise by leading brand-name manufacturers and designers of children's clothing—names like Oshkosh, Levi's, Lee's, Jordache, Izod, Buster Brown, and Healthtex, to name just a few. Discounts run from 20% to 40%, but prices may plummet even lower when a special sale is on—which happens frequently.

CRAFTS: Save the Children, the marvelous organization that helps needy children throughout the world, runs **The Craft Shop,** 1341 Connecticut Ave. NW (tel. 822-8426), to raise money for their very worthwhile cause. If you're looking for gifts to take back home, or care to do your Christmas shopping early, you can at the same time, by doing your shopping here, put food into the mouths of hungry children from Appalachia to Africa. And the money you spend here helps in another way. The store's craft items are purchased from people in Save the Children's project areas, thus helping adults in poor countries to augment their meager incomes. The organization's far-reaching programs also include day-care centers, health care, schools, and other desperately needed facilities. By stressing community projects that encourage self-sufficiency, they provide a means by which parents can break the cycle of suffering and poverty and establish a more meaningful life for their children.

However, you'd be thrilled to shop here, even if your money weren't going to a good cause. Prices are very reasonable, and the ever-changing array of festive merchandise is of the highest quality. Prices begin at just 50¢ for delightful little wooden animals from Sri Lanka. On my last visit there were Bolivian flutes, soapstone animals and candlesticks from Kenya, wooden dragon masks and puppets from Nepal, jewelry and painted fish from India, Mexican dolls and candleholders, stuffed hanging birds from El Salvador, Colombian and Peruvian wall hangings, and papier-mâché boxes from Kashmir. That's just a small sampling—there's much more. Everything you buy is wrapped in brightly colored tissue paper.

And while we're on the subject of doing some good in the world—pleasantly enough while increasing one's own stock of material goods—don't forget the museum shops all over town. The Smithsonian museums, especially, all have sizable shops filled with thrilling merchandise (the Arts and Industries Building's country store and the National Museum of American History's emporium of Americana are our favorites). They, too, are worthy sources for your do-gooder dollars.

Many fine Indian crafts are for sale at the **Indian Crafts Shop** at the Department of the Interior, 18th and C Streets NW (tel. 343-4056). Work here is generally of a higher quality than those items sold at the Grand Canyon and other locations closer to Indian reservations. The price range is wide: we found many lovely small Navajo weavings in the $15 to $18 range (larger rugs can go up to $2,000), squash blossom necklaces from $300 to $3,000, and many attractive pieces of jewelry—Navajo, Zuni, and Hopi—in varied price ranges. The store also offers Navajo sand paintings and an outstanding selection of Hopi, Santa Clara, San Ildefonso, Jemez, Acoma, Taos, Cochiti, and Navajo pottery. *Note:* You need photo ID to enter the building.

DRUGSTORES: The major chain in D.C. is called **Peoples.** Check your phone book for convenient locations. Most branches carry just about everything from the kind of stuff you expect (cosmetics, medicines, etc.) to frozen foods and appliances. Peoples has a 24-hour store at 7 Dupont Circle (tel. 785-1466), another at 14th Street and Thomas Circle NW, off Vermont Avenue (tel. 628-0720).

MEN'S CLOTHING: Dash's Designer, 1111 19th St. NW, at L Street (tel. 296-4470), buys large quantities of current designer styles in suits, slacks, blazers, ties, shirts, rainwear, and accessories and sells them at discounts of 30% to 50%. Oleg Cassini, Givenchy, Tiger, Ted Lapidus, Phoenix, Enrico Ferrini, Tallia, and Adolfo are among the labels you'll find here. Special sales in the fall, spring, and August offer even better bargains. Alterations are reasonably priced, and husky guys will find extra-large sizes here. Other locations at 1309 F St. NW (tel. 737-6008) and 3229 M St. NW (tel. 338-4050).

NEWSPAPERS AND MAGAZINES: At 3109 M St. NW, **Periodicals** (tel. 339-2955), in the heart of Georgetown, carries a very wide array of magazines. Certainly we've never failed to find any journal, however esoteric, on this store's copious racks. There are Russian-language magazines, *Pravda* (in English), hometown newspapers from all major U.S. cities, literary journals, comic books, foreign papers, and periodicals to suit every variety of enthusiast, including over 100 car magazines, wide selections on guns, computers, cooking, health, cycling, sports, photography, fishing, muscle building—even one about mules and donkeys called *The Brayer!* Of course, you can also get *Time, People,* or any other mundane mag here too.

An even more extensive source (they stock over 4,000 different magazines) is **World News,** 1825 I St. NW, at the Farragut West Metro (tel. 223-2526).

RESALE SHOPS: Once Is Not Enough, 4830 MacArthur Blvd. NW, near Reservoir Road (tel. 337-3072), has super high-fashion finds. Washington society women must change their wardrobes frequently: what do they do with the lovely clothes they've worn only once or twice? Some of them find their way to this resale shop, which specializes in top-quality women's clothing. We've seen names here like Halston, Nippon, Perry Ellis, Anne Klein, and Calvin Klein, to mention just a few. On our last visit we picked up a black voile Chanel gown for $150 (it retailed for $2,500), a Perry Ellis sweater for $40, and a Valentino white leather pantsuit for $80. Many items were much less. The store sometimes scoops up brand-new clothing too, and sells it at unfancy prices, averaging 40% off regular store tabs. You'll also find new imported French clothing and designer shoes for children here at 30% off. And there are terrific bargains in used men's clothing; some examples: a $400 camel's-hair coat for $75, an $800 sheepskin coat for $150, and a Polo raw-silk blazer for $75. Brooks Brothers suits, Sulka shirts, tuxedos, and Liberty ties are other frequent finds.

WOMEN'S CLOTHING: T. H. Mandy, 1118 19th St. NW, between L and M Streets (tel. 659-0024), is the place where Washington women on a budget manage to look like they're not. It sells brand-name women's clothing, mostly better sportswear, at discounts of 20% to 50% below retail, plus a good selection of jewelry and accessories. You'll find Kasper, Liz Claiborne, Gianni Sport, Kitty Hawk, Chaus, S & K, Cherokee, and Carole Little among the labels here. The store is tightly packed with merchandise—in fact, a fat person probably couldn't make it through the aisles—but the dressing area, with individual booths, is nice and roomy.

GEORGETOWN SHOPPING

In Georgetown you can combine shopping and browsing (there are hundreds of stores) with a meal at a good restaurant, crowd-watching over cappuccino at a café, even a little sightseeing. The hub is at Wisconsin Avenue and M Street, and most of the stores are on those two arteries. Also at that intersection is **Georgetown Park** (tel. 342-8190), a four-story 120-shop complex that, architecturally, belongs to two worlds: outside, quietly Federal, in keeping with the character of the neighborhood; inside, flamboyantly Victorian, with a huge skylight, fountains, many plantings, and ornate chandeliers. You could spend hours wandering around here exploring the shops, but be sure to have plenty of green stuff with you—there are branches of the nation's most exclusive specialty stores, like **Le Sac** from New Orleans and **Caché** from Miami. Washington's own **Garfinckel's** is here, and so are **Ann Taylor, Mark Cross, Crabtree & Evelyn, Liberty of London, Conran's,**

Abercrombie & Fitch, Polo, Uzzolo, Godiva Chocolatier, and other posh names. If you have kids with you, take them to admire the adorable stuffed animals at the **Georgetowne Zoo** or to **F.A.O. Schwarz.** Several restaurants, including **Clyde's** are on the premises.

An archeological exhibit of artifacts found during the complex's excavation is on display on the Canal level. It includes many historic photos and maps of the Georgetown area.

At this writing the mall is in the process of incorporating the adjacent 18th-century Market House as a gourmet food emporium. It's also offering a gratis package of premiums; to get one, write to Charlotte Sykes, Georgetown Park, 3222 M St. NW, Washington, D.C. 20007.

Many of our favorite Georgetown shops, however, are outside Georgetown Park's walls and right on the street. Look in, for starters, at—

Appalachian Spring, 1415 Wisconsin Ave. NW, at P Street (tel. 337-5780), brings country crafts to citified Georgetown. They sell pottery, jewelry, newly made patchwork quilts in traditional and contemporary patterns, stuffed dolls and animals, glorious weavings, and simple country toys. Everything in the store is made in the U.S.A., all of it by hand. We especially like the selection of wooden boxes; they range from about $30 for a simple box to $700 for ornate marquetry and polished maple burl creations.

Georgetown Coffee, Tea, & Spice, 1330 Wisconsin Ave. NW, between N and O Streets (tel. 338-3801), features a collection of more than 70 different coffees from about $6 a pound—everything from Jamaican Peaberry to Tanzanian Kilimanjaro and Ethiopian Harrar, plus a choice of about ten decafs. Then there are some 85 varieties of tea—plum from Ceylon, Japanese basket-fired green, China black, Assam, Kenyan broken-leaf orange pekoe, and many less exotic varieties. There are also decaffeinated teas. The spice selection is equally wide-ranging, and in addition, this gourmet emporium sells cookware, coffee and tea pots and accessories, Quimperware, fancy chocolates (including the yummy Lindts), and French candies made with real fruit.

Be sure not to miss the **Yes! Bookshop,** 1035 31st St. NW, just below M Street (tel. 338-7874) the unique creation of Ollie and Chris Popenoe. A wealth of literature on personal-growth-and-transformation subjects can be found on the store's shelves, along with books on international travel, Asia, mythology, philosophy, ancient history, and Native American traditions. CDs and cassettes include non-Western music (Asian, African, Chinese, Indonesian, and Native American), instrumental music, new age music (meditation cassettes with names like *Visions of a Peaceful Planet*), light jazz, sounds of nature (English songbirds in a meadow, sounds of the womb, whale records, etc.), and instruction in everything from quitting smoking to astral projection hypnosis. The Popenoes also carry 2,000 nontheatrical video cassettes—travelogues, opera, dance, fine arts, and instructionals—for sale or rental.

Yes! Natural Gourmet, 1015 Wisconsin Ave. NW (tel. 338-1700 or 338-0883), another Popenoe venture, sells health-food items in bulk at money-saving prices, natural vitamins, organic produce, baked goods, beans, nuts, grains, pastas, Shakti shoes, Asian/macrobiotic foods, imported honeys and crackers, Dimpflemeyer sourdough bread, nonalcoholic beers, natural cosmetics, soaps, body oils, and much more. And there are a few tables where you can enjoy fresh-squeezed juices, sandwiches, healthy smoothies, and Tofutti (tofu ice cream).

The **Spectrum Gallery, Inc.,** 1132 29th St. NW, at M Street (tel. 333-0954), is a cooperative venture in which 29 professional Washington-area artists—painters, potters, sculptors, and print-makers—share in shaping gallery policy, maintenance, and operation. Art is reasonably priced. The Spectrum has been going since 1966.

The **Irish Corner at the Threepenny Bit,** 3122 M St. NW (tel. 338-1338), sells Irish imports—beautiful mohair scarves, linen clothing, ladies' wool tweeds (coats, capes, and suits), Irish records and tapes, shamrock-motif clothing, hand-knit fishermen's sweaters, delicate hand-painted Belleek china, Cavan crystal, hand-painted coats-of-arms on parchment, Claddagh rings (Irish friendship rings in sterling or gold), 100% wool tartan blankets, and Irish jams, jellies, biscuits, and fruitcakes.

You probably need no introduction to **Laura Ashley,** 3213 M St. NW (tel. 338-5481), and her romantic-look 100% cotton clothing, very feminine lingerie, floral-design fabrics and wallpapers, etc.

There's a **Conran's** store in (actually it's sort of behind) the Georgetown Mall, but since its main entrance is over at 3227 Grace St. NW, across the C&O Canal (tel. 298-8300), it's easy to miss. This London-based home furnishings chain, now with over a dozen stores in the U.S., is great fun. They carry beautiful bedding and linens, a full line of furniture for the entire house and the outdoors (striking canvas beach chairs and umbrellas here), exciting fabrics, kitchenware, lighting fixtures, shelving, Indian Dhurrie rugs, fine English jams and jellies, and much more.

The **French Market,** 1626–32 Wisconsin Ave., between Q Street and Reservoir Road (tel. 338-4828), is so French they answer their phone "Le Marché Français. Bonjour!" Since 1948 (a time in America predating even women eating quiche) they've been supplying Washingtonians with pâtés en croûte, escargots, baguettes, croissants, Camembert (they stock about 50 French cheeses), crème de marrons, French-roast coffees, even imported wines and champagnes. The *boucherie* section carries pheasant, quail, partridge, guinea hens, and mallards, along with less exotic European-cut meats, and French pastries are featured in the *boulangerie*. The market makes up fabulous sandwiches to go, too, on croissants or baguettes.

Secondhand Rose, 1516 Wisconsin Ave., at P Street (tel. 337-3378), is a consignment shop where you'll find beautiful designer clothing, furs, designer bags and shoes, and costume jewelry priced at about a third of what you'd pay for new merchandise. Of course, you're the only one to know these oft once-worn garments aren't new. Last time we looked in, we noted a pair of gray Charles Jourdan pumps for just $35, a black lace Chloe gown for $165, and a black-and-white linen Mary McFadden suit for $210—the kind that would cost over $1,000 new. And there's usually a good selection of Ralph Lauren and Calvin Klein sportswear.

Take the kids over to the **Red Balloon,** 1073 Wisconsin Ave. NW, below M Street (tel. 965-1200), an old-fashioned toy store jam-packed with the kind of inexpensive little items you played with as a kid—finger traps, tin tea sets, water guns, squirt flowers, Mexican jumping beans, etc. There are 687 items priced under $4! There's also a large selection of carefully chosen children's books, as well as pricier, but still innovative, toys, games, stuffed animals, kaleidoscopes, etc. It's a very friendly place, and everyone—kids and adults—plays with the toys. Owner Linda Joy and manager Dennis Baker travel all over the world seeking intriguing playthings.

THE MALLS

There are several large shopping malls in the D.C. area, including the above-mentioned **Georgetown Park.**

Very popular is the *très chic* **Mazza Gallerie,** 5300 Wisconsin Ave. NW, between Western Avenue and Jenifer Street at the D.C./Maryland border (tel. 966-6114). Billing itself as "Washington's answer to Rodeo Drive," this four-level mall has 55 boutiques under a skylit atrium, including a branch of Neiman-Marcus and a Raleighs, a smaller luxury department store specializing in top-quality men's and women's clothing. And though it's not part of the mall, a Lord & Taylor adjoins. Other classy boutiques here are Ted Lapidus, F.A.O. Schwarz, Pierre Deux (French antiques and 18th-century country French-print fabrics), Pampillonia Jewelers (estate jewelry and one-of-a-kind creations), Kron Chocolatier, Williams Sonoma (gourmet cookware and foods), and Saville of London. There is a formal restaurant, the Pleasant Peasant, plus three movie theaters featuring the hottest new American films and award-winning international films.

The newest D.C. mall has the oldest location. It's the **Pavilion at the Old Post Office,** 1100 Pennsylvania Ave. NW (tel. 289-4224), a stunning three-level retail and restaurant complex under a 196-foot skylight canopy that opened in the fall of 1983 in the capital's most venerable federal building—the Old Post Office. Topped by a 315-foot clock tower, it's the tallest structure in town, save for the Washington Monument. It was built in 1899 to house the federal postal department and has happily managed to escape the wrecking ball throughout this century. Its rough stonework, turrets, and massive arches were inspired by the 12th-century Romanesque cathedrals of France. The atrium is lined with balconied corridors reminiscent of an Italian palazzo, and the arched galleries of the upper floors overlook a magnificent inner court 99 feet wide and 184 feet long. In the tower are ten great bells (a Bicentennial gift from England, they duplicate those at Westminster Abbey) that ring out from time to time.

Today completely renovated and restored, the building is boutiqued and restauranted (about 25 of each), and its hub is a performing arts stage with a three-tier arena, the scene of daily lunchtime, afternoon, and early-evening free entertainment. You can take a break from shopping to enjoy clowns, symphony orchestras, jazz ensembles, bluegrass groups, dance performances, or whatever else might be going on. On Saturday much of the entertainment is especially geared to children. Call the above-listed phone number to find out what the entertainment will be on any given day. The shops on the premises carry everything from Christmas ornaments to puppets and marionettes, from papier-mâché birds and clowns to heart-themed pocketbooks; they're a tad frivolous, but lots of fun. And the novelty shops are balanced a bit by fine men's and women's sportswear and women's shoe emporia. While you're here, ride the windowed elevator to the tower observation deck for a lofty 360° vista. You can climb down a flight and see the bells themselves. If you'd like to hear them, the bellringers practice on Thursday evening between 6:30 and 9:30 p.m.; otherwise they're only played for state occasions. Plan a meal here too—your options range from every kind of fast food to new American cuisine.

A major shopping complex is the **Springfield Mall** (tel. 971-3000), about ten miles from the downtown area in Springfield, Virginia (take I-95 south to the Franconia exit and stay in the right lane). The mall has 225 shops plus 23 restaurants (including a food court) and 10 movie theaters. Major stores here include branches of Garfinckel's, Raleighs, J. C. Penney, Lane Bryant, Benetton, Britches of Georgetowne, and Montgomery Ward. There are over a dozen shoe stores; other shops and boutiques carry clothing for the entire family, athletic footwear, audio equipment, telephones, bicycles, books (there's a B. Dalton), toys, jewelry, health foods, gourmet foods, sporting goods (Herman's, among others), maternity wear, records and tapes, and just about anything else you might need or desire. While you're here you can have your hair done (several salons vie for your patronage), work out at the Holiday Spa, even have your eyes examined at any of four opticians.

Another biggie is **Tysons Corner Center** (tel. 893-9400),

about 15 minutes from town in McLean, Va. (take the Beltway I-495 to Exit 11B). Among the 250 shops here are such well-known emporia as Bloomingdale's, Garfinckel's, Woodward & Lothrop, Hecht's, Lord & Taylor, Nordstrom, Banana Republic, Raleighs, Lane Bryant, Brooks Brothers, F.A.O. Schwarz, Hoffritz for Cutlery, Waldenbooks, Britches of Georgetown, Ann Taylor, Crabtree & Evelyn, Radio Shack, Woolworth's, and The Gap. Once again, there are about a dozen shoe stores, hair salons, a spa, several banks, and—very convenient—a U.S. Post Office. Over 20 restaurants run the gamut from Magic Pan to Wendy's, and 12 movie theaters make this a good choice for an afternoon shopping spree followed by a relaxing dinner and a film. There's free parking for 10,000 cars.

The Shops at National Place, entrance on F Street NW, between 13th and 14th Streets, or via the J. W. Marriott at 1331 Pennsylvania Ave. NW (tel. 783-9090), is an exciting part of the revitalization of Pennsylvania Avenue. Opened in April 1984, it soon became a favorite shopping stop for Washingtonians. A Rouse Company project (like South Street Seaport, Baltimore's Harborplace, and Faneuil Hall), this four-tiered, 125,000-square-foot retail complex houses over 85 stores and eating places in the renovated National Press Building, a worldwide media nerve center that is, among other things, headquarters of the National Press Club. With its terracotta floors, balconies, columns, and fountains, it's a most attractive setting for serious shopping. All the mall regulars are here —Banana Republic, B. Dalton, Esprit, The Sharper Image, The Limited, Benetton, etc. You can also shop for candy, leather goods, lingerie, clothing and shoes for the entire family, gifts, records and tapes, home furnishings, etc. On the top level is the Food Hall, with plenty of seating and walls lined with fast-food vendors of every stripe—sushi, lo mein, stuffed potatoes, hot dogs, pizza, ice cream, salads, subs, you name it. We prefer the complex's sit-down eateries like A Bagel Place (any topping you can think of on a fresh-baked bagel, plus a salad bar), Le Café (croissant sandwiches and homemade desserts), the Boston Seafood Company (raw bar and seafood entrees), and a branch of the American Café (see Chapter IV), among them. And if you really want to get down to some serious eating, there are excellent restaurants in the adjoining Marriott (see Chapter III).

CHAPTER IX

DAY TRIPS TO HISTORIC VIRGINIA

□ □ □

If possible, consider planning a few days away from Washington, visiting pre-Revolutionary America and other close-to-the-capital attractions. All of the below-listed destinations can be visited on one-day trips, keeping your Washington, D.C., hotel base.

ARLINGTON

ARLINGTON NATIONAL CEMETERY: Arlington occupies some 612 acres on the high hills overlooking the capital from the west side of the Memorial Bridge. Our most famous national shrine, it honors many of our national heroes and more than 210,000 of our war dead.

The **Tomb of the Unknown Soldier,** with the unidentified remains of soldiers from both World Wars, the Korean War, and the Vietnam War, is located here. It's an unembellished 79-ton white-marble block, moving in its simplicity. Inscribed are the words "Here rests in honored glory an American Soldier . . . known but to God."

Soldiers stationed at Fort Myer, specially selected and trained for duty here, guard the tomb day and night. Changing of the guard is performed every half hour from April through September and every hour on the hour from October through March—a ceremony that requires the most meticulous presentation of arms.

Many graves of the famous bear nothing more than simple markers in Arlington. Gen. John J. Pershing's is one of those. Secretary of State John Foster Dulles is buried here. So is President William Howard Taft.

Below Arlington House, the Robert E. Lee Memorial, is the

Gravesite of John Fitzgerald Kennedy. Simplicity is the key to grandeur here too. John Carl Warnecke designed a low crescent wall embracing a marble terrace, inscribed with memorable words of our 35th president, including his most famous utterance, "And so my fellow Americans, ask not what your country can do for you, ask what you can do for your country. . . ." Low steps and rough field-stone from Cape Cod, in contrast to the marble, set off the grave plot with its eternal flame. Senator Robert Kennedy is buried near-by, his grave marked by a simple white cross. The Kennedy graves attract streams of visitors. Arrive as close to 8 a.m. as possible to ex-perience the mood of quiet contemplation the site evokes when it's not mobbed with tourists. Looking north, there's a spectacular view of Washington.

Arlington House (tel. 557-0613), was for 30 years (1831–1861) the residence of Gen. Robert E. Lee. Lee married the great-granddaughter of Martha Washington, Mary Randolph Custis, who inherited the estate upon the death of her father. It was at Ar-lington House that Lee received the news of Virginia's secession from the Union and decided to resign his commission in the U.S. Army. During the Civil War the estate was taken over by Union forces, and troops were buried there. Soon after the defeat of the Confederate forces at Gettysburg, the estate was bought by the gov-ernment. A fine example of Greek Revival architecture combined with many features of the grand plantation houses of the early 1800s, it has been under the National Park Service since 1933.

You can take a self-guided tour of the house; hostesses in pre–Civil War dress give an orientation talk, hand out brochures, and an-swer questions. About 30% of the furnishings are original. Servants' quarters and a small museum adjoin. Admission is free. It's open daily from 9:30 a.m. to 4:30 p.m. October to March, till 6 p.m. April through September.

L'Enfant's Grave was placed in Arlington near Arlington House at the point that is believed to offer the best view of Washing-ton.

The Iwo Jima Statue and The Netherlands Carillon

The famous statue of the marines raising the flag on Iwo Jima, the **Marine Corps Memorial,** stands near the north (or Orde-Weitzel Gate) entrance to the cemetery as a tribute to marines who died in all wars. In summer there are military parades on the grounds on Tuesday evening at 7 p.m.

Close to the Iwo Jima statue is the **Netherlands Carillon,** a gift from the people of Holland with 49 bells. Every spring over 15,000 tulip bulbs are planted on the surrounding grounds. Carillon con-certs take place from 2 to 4 p.m. on Saturday and national holidays from April through September. (Sometimes hours change; call 703/485-9666 before you go.) Visitors are permitted into the tower to watch the carillonneur perform and enjoy panoramic views of Washington.

Getting There and Getting Around

Walk or drive over the beautiful Arlington Memorial Bridge from the base of the Lincoln Memorial, or take the Metro to Arlington Cemetery. If you're driving, park in the lot (you're not allowed to drive around the cemetery). Upon arrival, head over to the **Visitor Center,** where for $2.25 ($1 for children 3 to 11) you can purchase a Tourmobile ticket that allows you to stop at all major sights and reboard when you like. Service is continuous, and the narrated commentary is informative. However, if you've ample stamina, consider doing at least part of the tour on foot. There's something jarring about seeing a cemetery with a rambunctious crowd of tourists; walking makes for a more contemplative experience. Maps are available at the Visitor Center.

Arlington Cemetery is open to visitors April through September from 8 a.m. to 7 p.m., until 5 p.m. the rest of the year. Call 692-0931 for further information.

THE PENTAGON: Built during World War II, the massive five-sided fortress-like headquarters of the American military establishment is actually open to the public. Free hour-long tours, of certain areas only, of course, are given weekdays between 9:30 a.m. and 3:30 p.m., except on national holidays. Departure is from the Concourse area, and the line (a long one in tourist season; arrive early) forms at the Corridor No. 1 Visitor's Entrance, located off Pentagon South parking. Actually you won't stay on the line very long in any case; you're assigned a tour time, and you can sit in the waiting area.

The best way to get to the Pentagon is via Metro, which lets you off right in the Concourse area. If you drive, take I-395 south to the Boundary Channel Drive exit. The visitor's parking lot is directly on your left, and a free shuttle from this lot (running about every 15 minutes in both directions) takes you to and from Corridor No. 1. *Note:* You will have to go through a metal detector and have your bags searched, so leave anything dubious at your hotel. Also realize before leaving home that there are no food facilities or public rest rooms at the Pentagon.

The tour begins with an introductory film, after which a crew-cut military guide, walking backward to see that you don't wander off into restricted areas, takes you around.

A lot of what you see is military-themed art—works commemorating historical events of the U.S. Air Force, some of them done by Walt Disney when he was a World War I ambulance driver; the Coors' collection depicting the suffering and pain in all wars, especially Vietnam; portraits of all past presidents; artists' conceptions

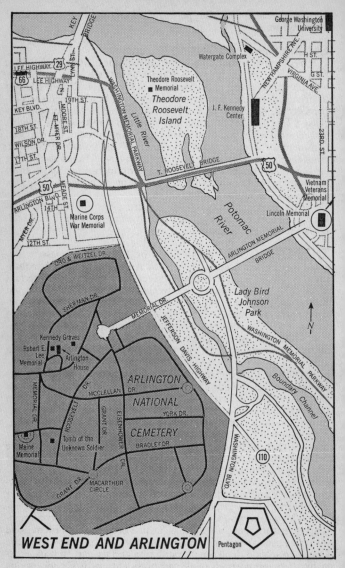

WEST END AND ARLINGTON

of life in POW camps; war photographs; British artist John Hamilton's paintings of World War II navy battle scenes; and *Time/Life* art depicting battle scenes during World War II. You'll also see models of past and present Air Force craft; a replica of *Lady Luck,* one of the navy's most popular ship figureheads; army command and divisional flags, plus 168 army campaign streamers from 1775 through the U.S. involvement in Grenada; a corridor honoring Gen. Douglas MacArthur; and state and territorial flags from the first Union Jack to the 50-star flag of today. A Women in the Military Corridor honors the contributions of women to America's armed forces from Revolutionary days to the present.

Call 695-1776 for further information.

MOUNT VERNON

No visit to Washington is complete without a trip to Mount Vernon, the estate of George Washington. Only 16 miles away from the hubbub of the capital, this southern plantation dates to a 1674 land grant to Washington's great-grandfather.

Mount Vernon was purchased for $200,000 in 1858 by the Mount Vernon Ladies' Association from John Augustine Washington, great-grandnephew of the first president. Without them, the estate might have crumbled and disappeared, for the federal government and the Commonwealth of Virginia both refused to buy the property when it was offered for sale in 1853. The restoration is an unmarred beauty; many of the furnishings are original pieces acquired by Washington, and the rooms have been repainted in the original colors favored by George and Martha.

Mount Vernon's manor house and grounds are stunning. Some 500 of the original 8,000 acres (divided into five farms) over which Washington presided are still there. Washington delighted in riding horseback around his property, directing planting and other activities; he was a fine agriculturist, and one of the first people to realize the importance of crop rotation and soil conservation. The Bowling Green entrance still contains some of the trees he planted. The American Revolution and his years of the presidency took Washington away from his beloved estate most of the time. He finally retired to Mount Vernon in 1797, just two years before his death, to "view the solitary walk and tread the paths of private life with heartfelt satisfaction." He is buried on the estate. Martha was buried next to him in May 1802. Public memorial services are held at the estate every year on Washington's Birthday.

Mount Vernon has been one of the nation's most visited shrines since the mid-19th century. Today over a million people tour the property annually. There's no formal tour, but attendants stationed throughout the house and grounds provide brief orientations and answer questions. Best time to visit is off-season; in heavy tourist months avoid weekends and holidays if possible, and year round, try to arrive at 9 a.m. sharp to beat the crowds. Late afternoon is also usually a good time to visit.

The house itself is interesting as an outstanding example of colonial architecture, as an example of the aristocratic lifestyle in the 18th century, and of course, as the home of our first president. A key to the Bastille presented to Washington by Lafayette in 1790 (via messenger Thomas Paine) hangs in the central hall. There are a number of family portraits, and the rooms are appointed as if actually in day-to-day use.

After leaving the house, you can tour the outbuildings or "dependencies"—the kitchen, slave quarters, storeroom, smokehouse, overseer's quarters, coachhouse, and stables. A museum on the property contains Washington memorabilia, and details of the restoration are explained in the adjoining annex; there's also a gift shop on the premises. You'll also want to walk around the grounds (most pleasant in good weather), see the wharf, the slave burial ground, the greenhouse, the tomb containing George and Martha Washington's sarcophagi, the lawns, gardens, and greenhouse.

The house and grounds are open to the public daily from 9 a.m. to 5 p.m. March to October, till 4 p.m. the rest of the year. Adults pay $5; senior citizens $4; children 6 to 11, $2; under 6, free. A map is provided at the entrance. For further information call 703/780-2000.

GETTING THERE: There are several ways to get to Mount Vernon. It's a scenic 16-mile drive via the George Washington Parkway/Mount Vernon Memorial Highway.

At 10th Street and Pennsylvania Avenue NW you can catch the **no. 11A bus** to Mount Vernon at 35 minutes past the hour.

Tourmobile buses (tel. 554-7950) depart daily from Arlington Cemetery, the Lincoln Memorial (summer only), and the Washington Monument at 10 a.m., noon, and 2 p.m. April through October. Round-trip fare is $13.50 for adults, $6.25 for children under 13, including admission to Mount Vernon. Make reservations at any of those departure sites at least an hour in advance.

Finally, from late March through the first week in November, **Washington Boat Lines** riverboats travel up the Potomac from Pier 4, at 6th and Water Streets SW (tel. 554-8000 for departure hours) twice a day. Fare for the 1½-hour trip is $12.75 for adults, $7.50 for children 2 to 11; round-trip fares are $15.75 and $8.50, respectively. Either way, your fare includes entrance to Mount Vernon.

WHERE TO EAT: At the entrance to Mount Vernon you'll find a snackbar serving light fare, and picnic tables outside. However, if a picnic is what you have in mind, drive a mile north on the parkway to **Riverside Park,** where you can lunch at tables overlooking the Potomac.

Very much in the spirit of the day is lunch at the charming **Mount Vernon Inn** (tel. 703/780-0011), also right on the premises. Its interior is quaintly colonial, with period furnishings and fare. Three working fireplaces further enhance this cozy setting. At lunch, served daily from 11 a.m. to 4:45 p.m., try peanut-and-chestnut soup, followed by quiche with fresh fruit (about $7). Dinner, served Monday to Saturday from 5 to 9:30 p.m., features a more serious menu. An à la carte meal here might consist of an appetizer of artichoke hearts and shrimp with a caper sauce, followed by mesquite-grilled capon stuffed with prunes and apples, and a dessert of deep-dish pecan pie with coffee. Entrees are in the $12 to $17 range. A $13 prix fixe meal is a good bet. Reservations advised at dinner.

ALEXANDRIA, VIRGINIA

History thrives in Alexandria. This colonial port town is so proud of its heritage—it is the hometown of both George Washington and Gen. Robert E. Lee—that it has spruced itself up and restored over 2,000 18th- and 19th-century buildings—especially in the harbor area called Old Town. Here, the past is being increasingly restored year after year in an ongoing program of archeological and historical research. There are about a dozen major sightseeing attractions—from a restored Georgian tavern (George and Martha Washington danced in the upstairs ballroom) to the boyhood home of Robert E. Lee. And capitalizing on the great volume of tourism generated by these restorations are hundreds of restaurants, shops, and boutiques, for the most part of a very high quality. A day in Old Town is a delight.

GETTING THERE: If you're driving, take the Arlington Memorial or the 14th Street Bridge to the George Washington Memorial Parkway; it leads right to King Street, Alexandria's main thoroughfare. Parking permits are available (details below). However, the easiest way to do this 7½-mile trip is via Metro. Take the Yellow Line to the King Street station. From the station (actually a walkable distance, but you might as well save your feet for sightseeing) you can catch a 50¢ DASH shuttle bus to King and Fairfax, where you should begin your tour.

Note: Many Alexandria attractions are closed on Monday, so it's not the best day to come.

FIRST STOP: Upon arrival in Alexandria, make a beeline for the **Ramsay House Visitors Center,** 221 King St. (tel. 703/549-0205). Pick up a self-guided walking-tour map, and find out if any special events will take place during your visit (there's almost always something going on—colonial games for children, Celtic festivals, Scottish Highland dancers in Market Square, parades, battle reen-

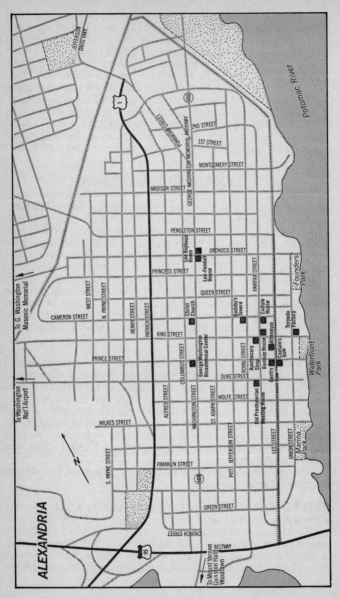

actments, garden tours, etc.). The very knowledgeable staff can answer all queries about accommodations, dining, sights, and shopping. Numerous brochures about the area are free for the taking. And weekdays, Memorial Day through Labor Day, "Doorways to Old Virginia" **guided walking tours** depart from this office.

If you came by car, get a free **three-day parking permit** that will allow you to park at any two-hour meter for as many hours as you like at no charge. You won't need your car much. Old Town is pretty compact, and you can see everything on foot.

Also available here: a **Block Ticket** for admission to four historic Alexandria properties — Gadsby's Tavern, Lee's Boyhood Home, Carlyle House, and Lee-Fendall House. It costs $5 for adults (a $3 saving over buying the tickets separately), $3 for children 6 to 17 (a $1 saving); under 6, free. The Block Ticket may also be purchased at any of those four sights.

Ramsay House (a reconstruction of the first house in Alexandria, and itself a historic attraction) is open daily from 9 a.m. to 5 p.m. except on Thanksgiving, Christmas, and New Year's Day.

SEEING THE SIGHTS: The third-largest seaport in the colonies during the 18th century, Alexandria was founded by a group of Scottish tobacco merchants. It became a city in 1749, when a 60-acre tract of land was auctioned off in half-acre lots. George Washington, then 17, was the surveyor's assistant. Today those 60 acres form the heart of Old Town, a restored historic district with cobblestone streets bearing colonial (King, Queen, Princess, Royal) or post-Revolutionary (Jefferson, Patrick Henry) names.

The streets are laid out on a simple grid system. It's helpful to know, when looking for addresses, that Union to Lee Street is the 100 block, Lee to Fairfax the 200 block, and so on up. Cross streets (going north and south) are divided by King Street. King to Cameron is the 100 block north, Cameron to Queen the 200 block north, and so on. King to Prince is the 100 block south, etc. A glance at the map from the Visitors Center will make all this crystal clear.

This same walking-tour map lists many attractions. The following, beginning with the four on the Block Ticket, are highlights. Remember, many attractions are closed Monday. Sometimes restored mansions are also hired out for weddings and closed to the public; inquire at the Visitors Center. If you don't have a Block Ticket, admission to each attraction is $2 for adults, $1 for children.

Gadsby's Tavern Museum, 134 N. Royal St. (tel. 703/838-4242), consists of two Georgian buildings dating from 1770 and 1792 respectively, which innkeeper John Gadsby combined in 1796 to create a "gentleman's tavern" offering comfort and elegance. Rooms are today restored to their 18th-century appearance. In addition to the restaurant, which serves authentic 18th-century food and drinks, there is a museum with an extensive collection of period furnishings and artifacts. George Washington was a frequent dinner guest; the Tavern was visited by Lafayette, James Madison, and Thomas Jefferson; and George and Martha Washington danced in the second-floor ballroom (since 1797 an annual George Washington's Birthday ball has taken place here). It was the scene of lavish parties, theatrical performances, and concerts. Itinerant merchants used the tavern to display their wares, and doctors and dentists treated an unfortunate clientele (these were rudimentary professions in the 18th century) on the premises.

Gadsby's Tavern Museum is open from 10 a.m. to 5 p.m. Tuesday through Saturday, from 1 to 5 p.m. on Sunday. Thirty-minute tours depart throughout the day at 15 minutes before and 15 minutes past the hour; last tour is at 4:15 p.m. Every Wednesday at 2 p.m. there's a special "living history" tour led by a costumed personality representing Mary Hawkins, who ran the tavern in the 1770s.

The **Boyhood Home of Robert E. Lee**, 607 Oronoco St. (tel. 703/548-8454), was built in 1795. Lee's father, Revolutionary cavalry hero Gen. "Light Horse Harry" Lee, brought his wife, Ann Hill Carter, and their five children to live in the early Federal-style mansion in 1812; at that time the future Confederate military leader was just a boy of five. Earlier residents, Col. and Mrs. William Fitzhugh, were friends of George Washington, an occasional guest. Their daughter married Washington's grandson, George Washington Parke Custis, in the drawing room, and their granddaughter (G.W.P.C.'s daughter) married Robert E. Lee. In 1824 General Lafayette visited Anne Hill Carter Lee, by then a widow, at the house. The drawing room has ever since been known as the Lafayette Room to commemorate his visit. Tours of the house depart from 10 a.m. to 3:30 p.m. Monday to Saturday, from noon to 3:30 p.m. on Sunday.

The **Lee-Fendall House**, 614 Oronoco St. (tel. 703/548-1789), was home to many others of the Lee family and is now a repository of their documents, furniture, and precious memorabilia. Robert E. Lee never lived here—though he was a frequent visitor—but 37 other Lees did over a period of 118 years. And George Washington was a frequent guest. The house was built in 1785 by Phillip Richard Fendall, a Lee on his mother's side, who married three Lee wives! Here "Light Horse Harry" penned Alexandria's farewell address to George Washington and the town's mayor delivered it the next day as Washington passed through on his way to assume the presidency.

On the 30-minute tour you'll see much original woodwork and glass, a delightful antique dollhouse collection, and a period garden with boxwood-lined paths and magnolia trees. Open Tuesday to Saturday from 10 a.m. to 4 p.m., on Sunday from noon to 4 p.m. Occasionally the house is closed on weekends for private parties.

Carlyle House, 121 N. Fairfax St. (tel. 703/549-2997), is an imposing Georgian mansion built in 1752 by John Carlyle, a prosperous Scottish merchant and an Alexandria city trustee. Its design is reminiscent of the luxurious manor houses in Scotland which Carlyle likely saw as a boy. In April 1755 governors of five royal colonies met here with the commander-in-chief of British forces, General Braddock, to plan the early campaigns of the French and Indian War. Braddock asked the governors to tax colonists in order to finance the defense effort, but they refused—a forerunner of later British-American conflict over taxation without representation. Braddock did, however, make Carlyle House his headquarters during the war. On a 40-minute tour you'll see two rooms that have survived intact—the main parlor and the study; in the former, where Braddock met with the governors, you'll see original woodwork, paneling, and pediments. Some of Carlyle's furniture and paintings also remain. Upstairs is an area used for special exhibits on the architecture of the house. Tours are given every half hour on the hour and half hour between 10 a.m. and 4:30 p.m. Open Tuesday through Saturday from 10 a.m. to 5 p.m., on Sunday from noon until 5 p.m.

If time allows, also visit the following:

Christ Church, Cameron and Washington Streets (tel. 703/549-1450), is where George Washington and Robert E. Lee both worshipped (you can sit in their pews). The church dates from 1773 and it has been in continuous use ever since. Though there have, of course, been changes over the years, the original structure, including hand-blown windows, remains intact. Originally called "The Church in the Woods" because of its rural setting, it is now in the heart of town. In the 18th century Washington and others discussed revolution in the churchyard, and Robert E. Lee met here with Richmond representatives who offered him command of Virginia's military forces at the start of the Civil War. U.S. presidents generally attend a service here on a Sunday close to Washington's birthday and sit in his pew. Shortly after Pearl Harbor Franklin Delano Roosevelt and Winston Churchill attended services at Christ Church on the World Day of Prayer.

Christ Church is open to visitors Monday to Saturday from 9 a.m. to 5 p.m., on Sunday from 2 to 4:30 p.m. A docent gives a brief lecture. Donations are appreciated.

The **Stabler-Leadbeater Apothecary Shop,** 105–107 S. Fairfax St. (tel. 703/836-3713), was one of America's oldest drugstores, in continuous operation from 1792 until the early 1930s. Now it is a quaint museum that retains the character of the days when George Washington and Robert E. Lee were among its customers. There's a letter on display from Martha Washington requesting cod liver oil. The shelves are aclutter with original hand-blown medicine bottles from the 18th century, patent medicines, blood-letting equipment, and antique mortar and pestle sets, all in their original locations. Note the two marble slabs, on one of which medicines were prepared for people, the other for animals. There's no tour, but a ten-minute recording enhances your understanding of the displays. Antiques, postcards, and other gift items are on sale in a small and tasteful shop that helps support the museum. Open Monday to Saturday from 10 a.m. to 4 p.m.; admission is free, but voluntary contributions are most welcome.

The **Torpedo Factory Art Center,** 105 N. Union St. (tel. 703/838-4565), houses 165 artists and craftspeople who create and sell their works on the premises of this converted torpedo shell-case factory. There are painters, printmakers, potters, sculptors, and photographers, and artists engaged in working with fibers, making jewelry, and creating stained-glass windows. In addition the Torpedo Factory is headquarters for **Alexandria Archeology,** the city's center for archeological discovery and research. Many artifacts unearthed in excavations are on display, and the organization's research lab, open to the public Tuesday to Thursday 10 a.m. to 3 p.m., Friday and Saturday from 10 a.m. to 5 p.m., is on the third floor. The Torpedo Factory is open daily from 10 a.m. to 5 p.m. Admission is free.

SHOPPING: In addition to its historic attractions, Alexandria has numerous boutiques, gift shops, and most of all, antique stores—the latter purveying everything from 17th-century American furniture to Orientalia. A shopping guide and a directory of antique shops are available at the Visitors Center. Plan your day to allow plenty of time for browsing.

WHERE TO EAT: There are so many fine restaurants in Alexandria that Washingtonians often drive over of an evening just to dine here and stroll the cobblestone streets.

The Top Choices

At **Gadsby's Tavern,** 138 N. Royal St. (tel. 703/548-1288), you can eat 18th-century fare in a thoroughly authentic—and very charming—setting, a registered historic landmark complete with period music, wood-plank floors, hurricane lamp wall sconces, and a rendition of a Hogarth painting over the fireplace (one of several). Servers are dressed in authentic colonial attire, and you dine off pewter and china as our forefathers did. At night appropriate entertainment—a strolling minstrel or balladeer—adds to the ambience. A flagstone courtyard edged with flower beds serves as an outdoor dining area in good weather.

All the food is homemade, including the fresh-baked Sally

Lunn bread. A lunch in the $10 range might consist of an appetizer of shrimp and clams in a puff pastry, chicken roasted on an open fire served with fried potatoes, and a dessert of buttermilk "pye." In winter, warm yourself with drinks like hot buttered rum and Martha's Remedy—coffee, cocoa, and brandy. Children's portions are available at half price. Sunday and Monday evenings at 6:30 p.m. (and Sunday afternoons at 3:30) there's a "Publick Table," described as an "authentic 18th-century bountiful board." A feast of the season's victuals—meats, fishes, fowl, fresh vegetables, relishes, homemade bread, dessert, and port wine—it costs $20 per person. A serving wench entertains with toasts, song, news, and humor. Reserve well in advance. Otherwise, dinner entrees are in the $11.50 to $17.95 range, like George Washington's favorite—a roast half duckling served golden brown with fruit dressing and madeira sauce.

Open for lunch/brunch daily from 11:30 a.m. to 3 p.m., for dinner from 5:30 to 10 p.m. Reservations suggested.

Though a meal at Gadsby's is most definitely in the spirit of historic Alexandria—and a great choice for families—there are other dining facilities in town featuring more haute-cuisine fare. High on our list of recommendables is the enchanting **East Wind,** 809 King St. (tel. 703/836-1515). Its decor is very appealing, the sienna stucco and knotty-pine-paneled walls adorned with works of Vietnamese artist Minh Nguyen. There are planters of greenery, a lovely flower arrangement decorates each table, and there's a large floral display up front. Very cozy, too, is the downstairs dining room, which is more Oriental in feel. Owner Khai Nguyen personally visits the market each morning to select the freshest fish.

An East Wind lunch might begin with an appetizer of cha gio (delicate Vietnamese eggrolls) or a salad of shredded chicken and vegetables mixed with fish sauce. One of our favorite entrees is bo dun—beef tenderloin strips marinated in wine, honey, and spices, rolled in fresh onions, and broiled on bamboo skewers. Also excellent is grilled lemon chicken or char-broiled shrimps and scallops served on rice vermicelli. And there's refreshing ginger ice cream for dessert. A typical three-course lunch is about $15. Most dinner entrees are in the $11 to $15 range. East Wind will delight all your senses.

Open weekdays for lunch from 11:30 a.m. to 2:30 p.m., nightly for dinner from 6 to 10 p.m. Reservations suggested. There's a full bar, though you can also order fresh-squeezed lemonade.

La Bergerie, 218 N. Lee St., on the second floor (tel. 703/683-1007), features Basque specialties in a fittingly provincial setting with oil paintings of pastoral scenes adorning exposed brick walls. Plush royal-blue and sienna-leather furnishings and mauve-linened tables, the latter adorned with a sprays of fresh flowers in silver vases, add an elegant note. Exquisite desserts and larger floral arrangements grace an antique dresser, and there are crystal chandeliers overhead.

Everything here is just delicious. It's easy to see why a local paper has voted La Bergerie Alexandria's favorite restaurant every year for a decade. Luncheon fare includes hors d'oeuvres ($5.50 to $8.50) like boneless duck with fresh fruits, escargots in garlic and walnut butter, and Norwegian smoked salmon. Among the entrees ($10 to $15) are filet of mountain trout with crabmeat and lobster sauce, and sautéed scallops with a coulis of fresh tomatoes and garlic. Leave room for one of those beautifully displayed desserts. The Basque almond tart with sabayon sauce is heavenly, as is a chocolate mousse cake dubbed le gâteau des prélats. But you don't have to order à la carte. A three-course table d'hôte meal is $11.95 at lunch, $18.95 at dinner. Otherwise, dinner entrees such as roast rack of lamb with fresh vegetables and duck baked in its own juices with sautéed potatoes, fresh mushrooms, and a rich brown sauce are in the $12 to $20 range. Lunch and dinner menus are supplemented by daily specials reflecting fresh market fare.

Open Monday to Saturday for lunch from 11:30 a.m. to 2:30 p.m. and for dinner from 6 to 10:30 p.m. Reservations advised.

The classic, delicate cuisine of Tuscany is featured at **Landini Brothers,** 115 King St. (tel. 703/836-8404), a rustic, almost grotto-like restaurant with stone walls, a flagstone floor, and rough-hewn beams overhead. Diners sit in wicker-seated chairs at flower-bedecked tables covered with cheerful pink cloths. It's especially charming at night by candlelight. Everything is homemade—the pasta, the desserts, and the crusty Italian bread. At lunch you might choose lighter entrees like a cold seafood salad ($7.50) or spinach-and ricotta-stuffed agnollotti in a light cream sauce ($8.95), thus leaving room for a dessert of coccoto—creamy frozen zabaglione. More substantial veal/steak/seafood entrees are in the $7.95 to $11.95 range. At dinner, get things under way with an order of prosciutto and melon ($6.50) or shrimp sautéed in garlic-butter/lemon/wine sauce ($6.95). Then you might proceed to an order of veal scaloppine sautéed with mushrooms in a cream sauce (entrees are $13.50 to $17) with a half order of pasta—perhaps the penne salsicce, sautéed with homemade Italian sausage in tomato sauce (pastas cost $9.50 to $11.25 for a full order). Friendly waiters are in the Italian tradition, even when they're from Thailand.

Open Monday to Saturday from 11:30 a.m. to 11 p.m. Reservations suggested.

Medium-Priced Dining

Thus far we've been concentrating on upper-bracket eateries. The following medium-priced restaurants are all excellent choices as well.

Bilbo Baggins, 208 Queen St. (tel. 703/683-0300), named after a character in Tolkien's *The Hobbit,* is indeed a Middle Earth–like environment. The downstairs dining room has rustic pine plank floors, rough-hewn wood walls, oak tables, and a brick oven centerpiece. Upstairs is another cozy room with stained-glass panels and seating in old church pews. It adjoins the wine bar (in fact that stained glass has a grape motif and is also seen here), a light and airy white-walled room with skylights and windows overlooking the treetops. The background music—classical, Jean Michel Jarre, etc.—is always perfect.

Entrees are served with chunks of crusty raisin-studded whole-wheat bread (it's delicious) and small dishes of butter. The eclectic menu changes daily to reflect seasonal specialties. On a recent visit lunch fare included entrees of fresh softshell crab sautéed in beurre blanc with almonds, blackened redfish sautéed in Créole spices, and salmon/Swiss cheese quiche, all in the $7 to $9 range. Dinner entrees ($12 to $17) included ocean scallops sautéed with pesto cream sauce over capellini pasta and thinly sliced peppercorned chateaubriand served with chilled marinated potatoes. There's an extensive wine list, and fresh-from-the-oven desserts include the luscious likes of a cake consisting of two layers of chocolate genoise sandwiching a chocolate mousse center and iced with a papery thin layer of buttery-rich chocolate. Or you might opt for a praline charlotte—vanilla genoise and brown sugar-flavored praline mousse topped with chocolate shavings. In the wine bar, light fare and over 30 wines are available by the glass.

Open for lunch Tuesday to Saturday from 11:30 a.m. to 2:30 p.m., for Sunday brunch from 11 a.m. to 2:30 p.m., for dinner Tuesday to Saturday from 5:30 to 10:30 p.m. and on Sunday from 4:30 to 9:30 p.m. Reservations suggested at dinner; at lunch, get here early—or late—if you don't want to wait in line.

We're great fans of the **Hard Times Cafe,** 1404 King St., near West Street (tel. 703/683-5340), and since it's close to the Metro station, we often stop by for a bowl of chili to fortify us for the journey back to D.C. It's a laid-back hangout where waiters and waitresses wear jeans and T-shirts, country music is always playing on the jukebox, seating is in roomy oak booths, and the Texas decor features Lone Star flags, a longhorn steer hide overhead, and historic photos of the Old West on the walls. The chili is made from a top-secret recipe, and it's some of the best we've ever tasted. It comes in three varieties—Texas, Cincinnati (cooked with sweeter spices, including cinnamon), and vegetarian (made with soy protein). We favor the Texas style—coarse-ground chuck simmered for six hours with special spices in beef sauce. A big serving of chili with or without beans, served with homemade corn bread, cheddar cheese, and chopped onions, is $4.50. A side order of steak fries cooked with the skins ($1.55) or deep-fried onion rings ($2.75) is ample for two. The chili cheeseburgers ($4.50) are also a good choice. Wash it all down with a bottle of Coors or Lone Star. The Hard Times has garnered many a chili cookoff award, and Chili-U.S.A., a resolution before Congress "to make chili the official food of this great nation," was conceived by Oklahoma lobbyists over a "bowl of red" here. There's additional seating upstairs, by the way, where the Colorado flag overhead was brought in by a senator from the Rocky Mountain state.

Open Monday to Thursday from 11 a.m. to 10 p.m., on Friday and Saturday from 11:30 a.m. to 11 p.m., and on Sunday from 4 to 10 p.m. They don't take reservations; arrive at off-hours to beat the crowds.

CHAPTER X

DAY TRIPS TO MARYLAND

□ □ □

The District's other bordering state also beckons tourists—to quaintly charming historic Annapolis and the up-to-date excitement of Baltimore's Inner Harbor area.

ANNAPOLIS, MARYLAND

Annapolis, 30 miles from the District of Columbia, can easily be visited and explored in one day with a return to Washington the same night. Or if you're driving home to points north of Washington, it makes a pleasant few hours' break in your journey. To get there, take Rte. 50 out of D.C. to Rowe Boulevard (Rte. 70) and make a right.

There are more than a few reasons for visiting the capital of Maryland: to soak up some history (it was the nation's capital and home to the Continental Congress from November 1783 to midsummer 1784, and it was here that Washington resigned his commission as commander-in-chief of the Continental Army and that the Treaty of Paris was signed); to visit to the U.S. Naval Academy; to shop for antiques; to explore 18th-century architecture and stately Georgian mansions in a well-preserved historic district (Colonial Annapolis was designated a registered national historic landmark in 1965); and in general to enjoy the sporty nautical flavor of this boat-minded community. Come in summer and you can even have a swim at nearby Sandy Point State Park.

If you don't have a car, bus transport is available via **Carolina Trailways** (tel. 202/565-2662), departing from the terminal at 1st and L Streets NE. There are several daily departures; the fare is $9 each way, $17.10 round trip, half price for children 5 to 11; under 5, free. A shuttle from the bus stop in Annapolis takes you to the heart of town.

SEEING THE SIGHTS: April through October, make your first

stop the **Visitor Information Center** at the City Dock (tel. 301/
268-TOUR), a full information service offering maps, brochures,
and help with accommodations, sightseeing, etc. It's open from 10
a.m. to 5 p.m. daily. The rest of the year the same services are offered
at the **State House Visitor Center,** State Circle (tel. 301/269-
3400), open from 9 a.m. to 5 p.m. daily.

Since the Historic District sights are so compact, best bet is to
park your car for the day and proceed on foot. Otherwise you'll find
yourself constantly feeding meters that, at best, have a two-hour duration. You can park free at the **Naval Academy Stadium,** just off
Rowe Boulevard at Taylor Avenue. From there an old-fashioned
Victorian trolley (fare: 60¢) takes you into the Historic District,
making several stops en route. It runs about every 15 minutes in
both directions between 6:30 a.m. and 7 p.m. Monday to Saturday.
Call 301/268-TOUR for details.

A money-saving **Ring Ticket** to three attractions—the William
Paca House, the William Paca Garden, and the Victualling Warehouse Maritime Museum—can be purchased from Historic Annapolis headquarters at the Old Treasury Building in State Circle, at
Paca House, or at the Victualling Warehouse. It costs $4.50 for
adults, $4.25 for senior citizens, and $2 for students. We'll be providing details shortly, but first, Annapolis' major sightseeing attraction.

The United States Naval Academy

Attracting more than a million visitors a year, the **U.S. Naval
Academy** covers more than 300 acres and has over 200 buildings
on a park-like site.

The most convenient entrance is Gate 1, where you will be directed to the **Visitor Information Center** (tel. 301/263-6933) at
Ricketts Hall, starting point for one-hour guided tours. These leave
on the hour between 10 a.m. and 3 p.m. March 1 through the end of
May, on the half hour between 9:30 a.m. and 4 p.m. June 1 through
Labor Day weekend, and on the hour between 10 a.m. and 3 p.m.
Labor Day weekend through Thanksgiving weekend. Cost is $2 per
adult, $1 for children 5 to 12; under 5, free. The rest of the year
there are no guided tours, but a comprehensive walking-tour brochure is available. Or you can arrange a private tour if you call in
advance. While waiting for your tour to depart, you can watch a
half-hour film on the life of a midshipman and examine a scale model of the academy grounds. A souvenir shop and cafeteria are also on
the premises.

The present academy dates to 1845, the U.S. Navy itself to
1794. Six years after the navy was established, President John Adams proposed to Congress that a training school be founded in conjunction with it. The first such navy school, established in 1821, was

in New York aboard the U.S. frigate *Guerrière*. A second school opened the same year aboard the *Java* in Norfolk, Virginia, and a third in 1833 at the Boston Navy Yard. All three of these schools were closed in 1839 and naval training was concentrated in a single school in Philadelphia, later moved to the present site. It has operated here continuously ever since, except during the Civil War when Union forces seized the property for use as a campground and military hospital. The first Annapolis class had only 50 students and a faculty of seven. Today students number about 4,600, 9% of them women. During nine months of the year they work toward a Bachelor of Science degree, majoring in subjects like aerospace, naval architecture, and oceanography, and taking advanced courses in the likes of nuclear power and surface warfare. Summer months are spent acquiring professional training in all aspects of navy and Marine Corps life. Upon graduation, five years on active duty as a commissioned officer is required.

Your tour begins, after a brief orientation, at **Lejeune Hall,** the physical-education center. Here midshipmen take four years of swimming (to graduate, they have to be able to dive from a 17-foot board for abandon-ship drill) and otherwise get themselves into fighting shape. Athletics are much stressed at the academy. It includes facilities for golf, ice skating (hockey is played), football, track, baseball, and tennis, among other sports. At Lejeune you'll see sports trophies representing victories over Army on display.

You'll next pass the **Captain's Homes** on Porter Road, occupied by the senior officers who are heads of academic divisions. They live quite nicely in turn-of-the-century homes with awninged patios. And your guide is sure to point out **Tecumseh,** a bronze replica of an Indian figurehead that once graced the *Delaware III*, a 74-gun ship launched in Norfolk in 1820. The Delaware chief, who is actually Tamanend, is known on campus as the "God of Passing Grades." During exam weeks students toss pennies at him; if a penny falls into his quiver, a passing grade is indicated.

The tour continues to **Bancroft Hall,** the world's largest dormitory accommodating all 4,600 students under one roof. It also contains a dining hall ample to feed them all at one sitting. It's quite a grand building in the beaux arts style, built in 1901 with later additions and replete with rotundas, columns, and expanses of gleaming marble. You'll get to examine a typical dorm room—not too bad compared to other college digs we've seen, because students are compelled to keep them much cleaner than the norm. On the premises are a small department store, a barber, shoe-repair, naval uniform shop, medical and dental facilities, and a post office. Out front are a 15th-century Japanese bell brought back from Okinawa by Commodore Perry and a bell from the U.S.S. *Enterprise,* a World War II fighting ship. When Navy defeats Army at football, the Japanese bell tolls; the *Enterprise* bell is rung for all other wins over Army. The four bronze guns flanking the steps were also Commodore Perry's. A room in Bancroft called Memorial Hall is dedicated to all the Annapolis graduates who lost their lives in conflicts from the Civil War through Vietnam. Here a flag from the War of 1812, bearing the legend "Don't Give Up the Ship," is displayed, along with other memorabilia.

En route to the Chapel you'll pass the **Herndon Monument,** a granite obelisk dedicated to Commander William L. Herndon, first man to explore the Amazon to its headwaters. Herndon went down with his ship, the *Central America,* in 1857 off Cape Hatteras after rescuing 152 passengers and crewmen. During the Plebe Recognition Ceremony each May, this hero's monument is greased and plebes are required to climb it and remove a midshipman's cap that upperclassmen have glued to the top. According to tradition, the plebe removing the cap is destined to become the class's first admiral.

The **Chapel** itself is flanked by immense anchors from the armored cruiser *New York* that sailed during the Spanish-American War. It is entered via massive bronze doors embellished with figures symbolizing Patriotism, Peace, Invention, and Prosperity, and bearing the motto "Non Sibi Sed Patriae" ("Not for Self but for Country"). Built between 1904 and 1908, the building stands 210 feet from floor to dome top and contains notable stained-glass windows including an arch-framed Tiffany showing Christ walking on the water. The church is nondenominational. Under it is the crypt of John Paul Jones, "Father of the American Navy," and speaker of those immortal words, "I have not yet begun to fight."

Last stop on the tour is the **Naval Academy Museum** in Preble Hall, a collection of over 50,000 items documenting early and modern naval history.

Paca House and Gardens

One-time residence of William Paca, a Maryland governor and signer of the Declaration of Independence, this elegant 18th-century house (it was built between 1763 and 1765) at 186 Prince George St., between Maryland Avenue and East Street (tel. 301/263-5553), has been fully restored. For many years it was a hotel called Carvel Hall, demolished in 1965 but its original structure saved from the wrecking ball by ardent preservationists. Some 80% of the original woodwork remains intact. In the wing where you enter, you'll see two guest sleeping rooms that are still in use today, accommodating distinguished visitors and conferees. In the passage hangs an engraving Congress presented to signers of the Declaration of Independence. On a 40-minute house tour you'll see the parlors (painted in Paca's favorite Prussian blue), upstairs bedrooms (wherein are some original pieces by famed furniture maker John Shaw), and the dining room. An Elizabethan porch leads to the 18th-century stone- and brick-walled garden, its intricate parterres, Chinese Chippendale bridge, terraces, and waterways restored from architectural and historical records as well as a Charles Willson Peale portrait of Paca in his garden. There's a two-story garden pavilion and cold bath house, and a visitor center/museum on the premises explains the archeology and reconstruction of the house.

The house is open Tuesday to Saturday from 10 a.m. to 4 p.m., on Sunday from noon to 4 p.m. The gardens are open year round Monday to Saturday from 10 a.m. to 4 p.m. (also on Sunday, May to October from noon to 5 p.m.; the rest of the year to 4 p.m.). Without a Ring Ticket, admission is $3 for adults, $2 for ages 6 to 18 (under 6, free), for the house tour; $4, $2.50, and free respectively for a combined house-and-garden tour.

The Victualling Warehouse Maritime Museum

An 1810 building, on the site of an earlier building confiscated from its British Loyalist owner and used to store military supplies and provisions during the Revolution, the Victualling Warehouse, 77 Main St., at Compromise (tel. 301/268-5576), today serves as a maritime museum. In Annapolis's early days the waterline of the dock came right up to it. A 1718 copy of the 1694 town plan, like Williamsburg laid out by colonial Gov. Francis Nicholson, is on display here, much of it still intact. And in the center of the museum is an incredibly detailed model of Annapolis in its premier seaport days (1751–1781). You can see block makers (wood blocks were needed to raise and lower sails, buckets, etc.), a blacksmith working in his shop, the ferry in the harbor, suckling pigs in the field, and even the Victualling Warehouse itself. Many of the buildings in this model are still extant. "We think if George Washington sailed into Annapolis harbor, he'd recognize it," a curator told us. Other exhibits include advertisements for 18th-century craftsmen, blacksmithing and shipmaking tools, navigational instruments, displays on rope- and sailmaking, advertisements for taverns (as an important seaport, early Annapolis had over 30 licensed taverns), imports (china, fabrics, spices, fruits, paint, etc.), exports (tobacco, sassafras, cedar shingles, barrel staves), and soldier's equipment. There's a basket of hands-on items for kids to examine.

Open daily from 11 a.m. to 4:30 p.m. Admission without the Ring Ticket is 50¢ for adults, 25¢ for ages 6 to 18; under 6, free.

The Tobacco Prise House

A surviving example of the small warehouses that dotted the Annapolis waterfront in the 18th and 19th centuries, the Tobacco Prise House, 4 Pinkney St. (no phone), is a reminder of the crucial role played by the tobacco industry in Maryland's early history. The soil and climate were ideal for the cultivation of this valuable crop, and the topography of the Chesapeake Bay area, with numerous rivers and waterways, make shipping it abroad feasible. Annapolis was a center where tobacco was stored before export and where leaf quality underwent official inspection. Only the best was shipped. At the Tobacco Prise House you'll see an actual prise, an 18th-century lever-operated machine that was used to compress tobacco in order to fit the largest amount possible into a hogshead (a large barrel capable of accommodating 750 to 1,400 pounds) for shipping.

There's no tour, but informative signs explain the prise procedure. No admission is charged.

The Barracks

Restored quarters of Revolutionary soldiers, the Barracks, 43 Pinkney St. (no phone), was a building in which troops were billeted while waiting to be sent to battle. Annapolis was a focal point for Maryland's war effort, and at times there were more soldiers in town than actual residents. The two-story gambrel-roofed structure, a typical mid-18th-century artisan's home (it was appropriated for wartime use), the Barracks was no Hilton. Soldiers slept on crude straw-filled mattresses on the floor, and though the lieutenant had a bed, it wasn't much of one. A card table is set up, indicative of time spent in long hours of waiting. In summer, there are "living history" programs here.

Open weekdays only, mid-April to mid-October, from 11 a.m. to 4:30 p.m. Admission is 25¢.

The Maryland State House

Built in 1772, first occupied in 1779, and completed (to its present appearance) in 1905, the Maryland State House, State Circle (tel. 301/974-3400), is the oldest state capitol building in continuous use in the country. Its dome, constructed of cypress beams held together by wooden pegs, is the largest wooden dome in the United States. Thomas Dance executed the beautiful plasterwork in the central hall, a job that cost him his life; in 1793, as the work neared completion, he fell 90 feet from the scaffolding to his death. A black line in the marble floor separates the Old State House from the annex built in the early 1900s. The facility served for ten months as the nation's first peacetime capitol. Here George Washington resigned his commission as commander-in-chief of the Continental Army in 1783; the Treaty of Paris, the document that officially ended the Revolution, was signed in 1784; and Thomas Jefferson was appointed the first United States ambassador to France. The governor's office is in the building, and his residence, the Governor's Mansion, is right across the street.

On your tour, you'll visit the **Old Senate Chamber,** which is restored to its appearance in the late 1790s. The furnishings are a mix of John Shaw pieces made in the late 18th century and replicas thereof. A bronze plaque marks the spot where Washington stood to deliver his farewell address. A Charles Willson Peale painting, *Washington, Lafayette, and Tilghman at Yorktown,* commissioned by the Maryland legislature in 1781, has hung over the fireplace for more than two centuries. And there are also Peale portraits in this room of five early governors. Note the Ladies Gallery above the room. You'll also see the rust-and-gold marble-walled **House of Delegates,** and the red-and-white **New Senate Chamber,** the colors of the rooms together being those of the Maryland state flag. Both rooms have Tiffany skylights, and the latter is hung with portraits of Maryland's four signers of the Declaration of Independence.

The State House is open daily except Christmas (it's open but no tours are given Thanksgiving and New Year's Day), and free tours are offered from 9 a.m. to 5 p.m. Before or after the tour you can view a ten-minute video show about the history of Maryland that focuses on the role of Annapolis and the State House.

The Hammond-Harwood House

Just off State Circle at 19 Maryland Ave., the Hammond-Harwood House (tel. 301/269-1714) was built by Matthias Hammond in 1774. It was designed by William Buckland, one of the most noted architects of the day. Hammond was a lawyer and planter, a patriot, and a colleague of Declaration of Independence signers William Paca and Charles Carroll. He published his opinions in the *Maryland Gazette* and served as a quartermaster of the county militia. However, in 1776, at the age of 28, for some reason (some accounts claim it was a romantic disappointment) Hammond resigned his elected office and retired to the country, leaving his "elegant and commodious dwelling" unoccupied for eight years. He died in 1786. The house passed through a series of owners and renters over the years, and just before the Civil War it was occupied by William Harwood, great-grandson of Buckland. The last occupant was Harwood's daughter, Hester Ann, a spinster who became a recluse in this Colonial masterpiece and seldom left it. She died in 1924, leaving no will. Since 1940 it has been a landmark property under the auspices of a nonprofit organization which has kept it open to the public.

The house is cited by architects as one of the most exquisite examples of the English Palladian movement (based on the theories of 16th-century Italian architect Andrea Palladio). Two 18th-century visitors, Charles Willson Peale and Thomas Jefferson, were so inspired by the mansion's elegance and pure proportions that they made sketches of it in their diaries. It has a central section with two flanking wings connected by enclosed passages known as "hyphens." The elaborately carved front door, typical of the attention to detail and richness of ornament within, is framed by columns and topped with an impressive band-leafed frieze and pediment.

The rooms are today arranged and furnished to represent a museum collection of 18th- and early-19th-century decorative arts. The reception hall furnishings include one of the oldest objects in the house, a birdcage clock (still working) dating to about 1660. Six signed pieces in the house are by famed cabinetmaker John Shaw. On a 45-minute tour, you'll also see the gentleman's library, housing about 30 books, a typical number for this era. Portraits by Charles Willson Peale and Rembrandt Peale adorn the library walls, the latter of George Washington on horseback. Across from the library is the ladies parlor, delicately furnished in Hepplewhite and Federal pieces; it is set up for tea with a fragile china porcelain service on the table. Griffin heads and leafy arabesques adorn the doors, windows, and fireplace of the dining room, wherein you'll also see a copy of a Charles Willson Peale portrait of Buckland, and three original Peale paintings of Buckland's family. Off the dining room is the withdrawing room whence the women retreated after dinner while the gentlemen remained to partake of pipes and port. An unusual feature is the kitchen, here a part of the house rather than an outbuilding as was more usual for the period. You'll also see the game room, bedrooms, boudoir, and drawing room.

The house is open for tours Tuesday to Saturday from 10 a.m. to 5 p.m., on Sunday from 2 to 5 p.m. April 1 through the end of October. The rest of the year hours are 10 a.m. to 4 p.m. Tuesday to Saturday, 1 to 4 p.m. on Sunday. Adults pay $3 admission, students 6 to 18 pay $2, and children under 6 are admitted free.

The Chase-Lloyd House

Just across the street from the above at 22 Maryland Ave. (tel. 301/263-2723) is the Chase-Lloyd House, named for its two distinguished early owners, Samuel Chase and Edward Lloyd IV. Chase was a Supreme Court Justice and a signer of the Declaration of Independence, Lloyd a planter so wealthy he was known as "Edward the Magnificent." Chase began the project in 1769 but overreached himself economically, and Lloyd took over the building in 1771, engaging William Buckland to finish the job. His family lived here through 1846, after which Hester Ann Chase, a direct descendent of Samuel, bought the mansion. Her niece inherited it, and upon her death in 1886 bequeathed the property as a home for "destitute, aged and infirm women where they may find a retreat from the vicissitudes of life." And a luxurious retreat it remains, inhabited by eight very fortunate women to this day. It's open to the public in a limited way.

Guided 20-minute tours of a few of the downstairs rooms are given between 2 and 4 p.m. Tuesday to Saturday. Admission is $1 for adults, 25¢ for children under 12.

The Banneker-Douglass Museum

Housed in the Victorian-Gothic Mount Moriah African Methodist Episcopal Church, home of a free black congregation that gained its charter in 1803, the Banneker-Douglass Museum, 84 Franklin St., between Church Circle and Cathedral Street (tel. 301/974-2894), presents cultural exhibits and programs on the history and contributions of Afro-Americans to Maryland and the nation. The facility is named for two preeminent black Marylanders. Benjamin Banneker (1731–1806) was among the team of surveyors who laid out the city of Washington, D.C. Frederick Douglass (1818–1895) was a famed abolitionist, orator, foreign minister to Haiti, and editor of his own newspaper, *The North Star.* He recruited some 186,000 blacks to serve in the Civil War, and Abraham Lincoln called him "the most meritorious person I have ever met."

Exhibits focus on Afro-American arts and crafts, black history, and black achievements. For example, a recent show called "Black Voices, Black Votes" focused on black members of the Maryland General Assembly. Other exhibits here have included "Echoes of Apartheid: Art by Black South Africans" and "In Search of Benjamin Banneker" featuring archeological discoveries from his home site in Oella, Maryland. A gift shop on the premises features Afro-American art, posters, and crafts; African art objects; and books on Afro-American and African themes.

Open Tuesday to Friday from 10 a.m. to 3 p.m., Saturday noon to 4 p.m. Admission is free.

Harbor and Bay Cruises

Annapolis's restored historic waterfront area is the starting point for Chesapeake Bay cruises offered by **Chesapeake Marine Tours,** Slip 20 (tel. 301/268-7600). A 1½-hour narrated scenic cruise aboard the 150-passenger *Providence* is offered Wednesday through Sunday at 2:30 p.m., April through December. You'll see the Eastern Shore country described by James Michener in his novel, *Chesapeake,* including the U.S. Naval Academy, beautiful residences at Horn's Point, and the Spa Creek marinas. Snacks and beverages are served on board. Adults pay $8, and children 2 to 12 pay $6; under 2, free.

The *Providence* also goes out on lunch and dinner cruises, the former Wednesday to Saturday, the latter Tuesday to Saturday. Call for details. And do inquire about other tours ranging from a 40-minute harbor cruise to a seven-hour "Day on the Bay" that includes a three-hour visit to the quaint town of St. Michaels. You can reserve in D.C. by calling 261-2719.

Guided Tours

If your time in Annapolis is limited, the best way to see the sights is via a **Historic Annapolis, Inc., walking tour** departing from the Old Treasury Building, State Circle and from the Victualling Warehouse (tel. 301/267-8149). This nonprofit preservation organization was founded in 1952 to protect the town's historic landmarks from demolition and incompatible redevelopment. Their guides are especially knowledgeable. A 1½-hour tour visiting the State House, St. John's College Campus, William Paca Gardens, and the Naval Academy costs $5 for adults, $3 for ages 6 to 18; under 6, free. Call for days and hours, and inquire about other tour possibilities; there are many options, including children's tours.

Tours are also offered by **Three Centuries Tours of Annapolis** (tel. 301/263-5401 or 263-5357). Guides in colonial attire lead two-hour Early Bird walking tours departing from the Hilton Inn lobby daily at 9:30 a.m. April 1 through October 31; the same route is followed on the Summer Stroll (departing from the Visitor Information Booth at City Dock) at 1:30 p.m. daily May 1 to September 30. Price is $5 for adults, $2.75 for students; under 6, free.

WHERE TO EAT: Annapolis's premier restaurant is the **Hampton House,** 200 Main St. (tel. 301/268-7898), serving exceptionally fine classic French fare with an Eastern European accent (owner/chef Tom Fazekas is Hungarian). Fazekas's credentials are impressive: he started out as a chef at the Plaza Hotel in New York, went on to open Charlie's Georgetown in Washington, D.C. (a top jazz club in its day), and is nowadays called upon to cater the most upscale of Maryland's state functions, including a recent party for the Lord Mayor of London. For his restaurant, he chose an elegant 1820s town house with a front porch bordered by boxwoods and planters of seasonal flowers. Afternoon tea and cocktails are served here—and on a brick terrace—daily, along with a light menu and wines by the glass. However, the pleasures of al fresco dining are more than equaled within the Hampton's cozy interior, wherein the walls are covered with 19th-century mural wallpaper by French artist Jean Zuber, here depicting Boston Harbor in 1830 (you'll see the same paper in the Diplomatic Reception Room of the White House, or at least you would if you were invited to a function there). The other walls, Wedgwood blue with cream trim, are hung with Hogarth prints. A 24-carat gold-trimmed Austrian crystal chandelier is suspended from the pressed-tin ceiling. There are stained- and leaded-glass windows, and a front window is draped in white swagged silk. A fireplace is ablaze in winter. And white-linened tables are beautifully appointed with Villeroy & Boch china, stunning flower arrangements in silver vases, and hurricane lamp candles. Classical music plays softly in the background.

We began with appetizers of the pâté du chef (it changes nightly, but on this occasion it was rich and creamy, flavored with juniper berries) and a paprika-spiced stuffed Hungarian cabbage with ground veal and pork filling. For entrees we chose Australian lobster tail topped with lump crabmeat in butter sauce and a pork loin, pocketed and filled with sautéed apples and sauerkraut, grilled, roasted, and topped with demi-glaze. Like all entrees, these were served with an array of exquisitely sauced, perfectly al dente vegetables—broiled tomato with cheeses, snowpea pods, sautéed rice pilaf, red cabbage, cauliflower, broccoli, and thinly sliced carrots. Not only were they delicious, they made for a delightfully colorful arrangement on the plate. Also artfully arranged was the salad (it, too, is included with your entree)—a refreshing affair of endive, Bibb lettuce, tomato, and fresh sliced mushrooms in a slightly sweet tarragon-flavored vinaigrette. And for dessert, we shared a Grand Marnier mousse in a chocolate cup with seasonal fruits and a chocolate hazelnut cake with rich chocolate icing. For the two of us, this feast totaled about $55, not including wine, tax, or tip. There is a well-chosen and reasonably priced wine list (mostly French, German, and Californian, though you could order a hearty Hungarian wine called "Bull's Blood"), and three premium wines are offered by the glass each night. The luncheon menu is considerably less expensive (entrees are $6 to $8).

The Hampton House is open for lunch Tuesday to Saturday from 11:30 a.m. to 2:30 p.m., for dinner nightly from 6 to 10 p.m. Reservations suggested.

Another charming choice is the **Reynolds Tavern,** 7 Church Circle (tel. 301/263-6599), opened in 1985 but housed in a 1737 residence. It was the home of William Reynolds, a hatmaker who, in 1747, decided to open his premises to the public. His tavern was a center of 18th-century Annapolis social and commercial activities until 1812 when the Farmers National Bank purchased it as a home for its president. It belonged to the bank through the 1930s, when it went up for sale. Happily, local preservationists were able to stop an oil company from buying it in order to demolish the building and construct a service station on the site.

Today this 250-year-old tavern is a restaurant under the auspices of Historic Inns of Annapolis, restored to its appearance during Reynolds' tenancy. Its white walls are hung with antique hunting and botanical prints, floors are bare pine, moldings and doors are painted in Williamsburg hues, and there are Georgian brass chandeliers overhead. Three fireplaces grace the dining rooms, and a working fireplace also warms the downstairs Tavern (a bar/lounge). The interior is especially lovely at night when tables are lit by hurricane lamps. In good weather you can sit outdoors on a large brick terrace under the shade of an ancient walnut tree, enjoying light fare and drinks, including a choice of 20 different rums and many potent rum concoctions. Waiters and waitresses are in period costume (or a reasonable facsimile thereof; an 18th-century tailor might look askance).

Some of the fare is colonial, some not. At dinner, for instance, you might begin with a seafood chowder prepared from an 18th-century recipe or crab Alfredo. Many of the entrees ($12 to $18) are proper to the period, such as game "pye"—braised venison, tenderloin, and chuck in a garlic and port wine sauce topped with a pastry crust—or crab smitty—backfin crab sautéed in butter with Smithfield ham, served with rice, sautéed garden vegetables, and salad. A basket of delicious breads (including sourdough) is served with your meal. And for dessert, you can't beat the walnut "pye," made with shortbread pastry and topped with homemade vanilla ice cream ($3.50). At lunch there are sandwiches (like smoked turkey and Stilton on whole-wheat French bread with sweet mustard), salads (such as boneless chicken breast with orange sections, toasted almonds, fresh ginger, and mint on tossed greens with a crème fraîche dressing), and entrees such as a Créole oyster loaf garnished with potato wedges and coleslaw. Most selections range from about $5 to $8.

Every Sunday from 10:30 a.m. to 2:30 p.m. the tavern offers a Plantation Champagne Brunch ($12.95 for adults, $6.95 for children under 12). It includes an all-you-can-eat buffet laden with soup, salads, bacon, sausages, mussels marinara, and desserts; unlimited champagne; coffee or tea; and entree choices such as Belgian waffles topped with fresh strawberries and whipped cream, crabs Benedict, and eggs Bienville (with filet mignon on an English muffin topped with a tomato-flavored béarnaise sauce).

Open Monday to Thursday from 11:30 a.m. to 10 p.m., on Friday and Saturday to 11 p.m., and on Sunday from 10 a.m. to 9 p.m. Reservations suggested.

For good cheap eats in the heart of town, head for **Chick and Ruth's Delly,** 165 Main St., near Conduit Street (tel. 301/269-6737), a New York–style deli complete with tin bowls of pickles on every table. It's funky and cheerful with bright-yellow walls and a high pressed-tin ceiling, orange booths, and lights with pull strings anchored by bagels. There's also a long counter with alternating orange and yellow stools. At breakfast a bagel with cream cheese is 99¢; fresh-made doughnuts, 40¢ apiece; coffee, 60¢; a cheese omelet with fried potatoes, $2.50. Throughout the day you can order sandwiches ($2.50 to $4.50) like corned beef on fresh-baked rye, cream cheese and Nova on a bagel, or the "Pres. Reagan"—a six-ounce steak with cheese and onions on a hard roll. At night, from 5 to 10 p.m., a full dinner—soup, beverage, entree (perhaps roast chicken with vegetables and bread and butter), and dessert—costs $5 to $7. And if these prices aren't low enough, discount coupons are often issued on request (ask at the counter).

Open 24 hours a day. No credit cards. Wine and beer are available.

Chick and Ruth maintain the 10-room **Scot-Laur Inn** upstairs, by the way. Rooms are charmingly furnished with brass beds and floral-print wallpapers; each contains a color TV, phone, and private bath. Rates are $50 to $65 single, $5 for an additional person. The largest room sleeps up to four. Zip code is 21401 if you'd like to write for a brochure.

Another good place for inexpensive light fare is the **Dockside Boulangerie**, 18 Market Space (tel. 301/268-1115), a tiny eatery, with six bentwood chairs at ceramic tile-topped tables. Classical music does much to enhance the setting. At breakfast there are chocolate, almond, and fruit croissants; cheese and fruit danish; ham and cheese croissants; buttered baguettes; etc., in the 80¢ to $2.50 range. Sandwiches on French bread or croissant are $4.25; try the ham and Swiss, roast beef, or shrimp salad. And a bowl of crab soup is $2.25.

Open daily from 6:30 a.m. to 8 p.m.

OVERNIGHT STAYS: Though Annapolis is just an hour from the District, you might want to spend a night in order to enjoy its charm and historic attractions at a more leisurely pace.

One of our favorite places is the very central **Prince George Inn**, 232 Prince George St. (between Maryland and College Avenues), Annapolis, MD 21401 (tel. 301/263-6418). Owned by Bill and Norma Grovermann (she also founded Three Centuries Tours, detailed above, and can tell you everything about local sights), this delightful Victorian B&B offers four exquisite air-conditioned rooms, all tastefully decorated in period style. Yours might have white wicker furnishings, a Victorian trundle bed, a leaded-glass bay window, or a turn-of-the-century armoire. There's a cozy parlor with a working fireplace, where guests gather to read, chat, and watch TV at night. Plushly furnished, it has sienna walls hung with large gilt-framed mirrors and nautical-motif paintings. Breakfast, included in the rates, is served on a glassed-in sun porch or al fresco on a brick terrace. It's a buffet of fruits, a choice of five juices, dry cereal, croissants, fresh-baked muffins, jams, butter, and tea or coffee. There's a phone in the parlor, and baths (they're immaculate) are shared.

Rates are $50 to $65 single, $65 double. Children under 12 are not accepted. No credit cards.

Five restored 18th-century inns in the central historic district are represented by **Historic Inns of Annapolis**, 16 Church Circle, Annapolis, MD 21401 (tel. 301/263-2641, or toll free

800/847-8882). Via that number, you can make reservations for accommodations in any of their 137 guest rooms. These are also highly recommended. We especially like the oak-floored, high-ceilinged rooms at Governor Calvert House, 58 State Circle, furnished with gold velvet chairs, 19th-century desks, and 18th-century Italian armoires. Call or write for details on these exquisite inns.

BALTIMORE, MARYLAND

Just an hour's drive from Washington, D.C., and en route to or from home for many of you, Baltimore abounds with tourist attractions. They range from Babe Ruth's birthplace to Edgar Allan Poe's grave, and include over a dozen museums, historic homes (among them, H. L. Mencken's), a 150-acre zoo, an arboretum, parks, and a great deal more. However, all that's another book. Here we'll concentrate on the famed Inner Harbor, the city's biggest tourist draw on the Patapsco River, which was transformed into a 240-acre attraction-filled area in 1965. If you'd like to explore further, details on all Baltimore sights, events, and accommodations are available from the **Baltimore Office of Promotion and Tourism,** 34 Market Pl., Suite 310, Baltimore, MD 21202 (tel. 301/837-INFO).

In town, stop at the **Information Kiosk** at the Inner Harbor on Pier 1, where you can pick up maps and brochures, find out about events that will be on during your stay, and get information about hotels and restaurants. Take a free copy of a monthly publication called *Baltimore Scene,* a comprehensive guide to city happenings.

GETTING THERE: From the District, take I-395 to Baltimore's Pratt Street, make a right and another right at President Street, where you'll find a huge parking lot offering all-day rates of $3. Bus (via Greyhound and Trailways) and train service (Amtrak) are available if you don't have a car.

INNER HARBOR SIGHTS: There's enough to keep you busy for a full day, and all the attractions are within walking distance of one another. But if it's hot and your feet are giving out, just hop a **water taxi** ($2.75). Mid-April to mid-October, these little boats run frequently Sunday to Thursday from 11 a.m. to 11 p.m., on Friday and Saturday till midnight, stopping at all major harbor sights. The whole route takes 30 minutes and is in itself a pleasant jaunt.

The National Aquarium

Our great favorite of the Inner Harbor sights, this seven-level complex at Pier 3, 501 E. Pratt St. (tel. 301/576-3810 or 576-3800), houses over 5,000 specimens, representing about 500 species of fish, birds, reptiles, amphibians, invertebrates, plants, and marine mammals. The aquarium holds more than a million gallons

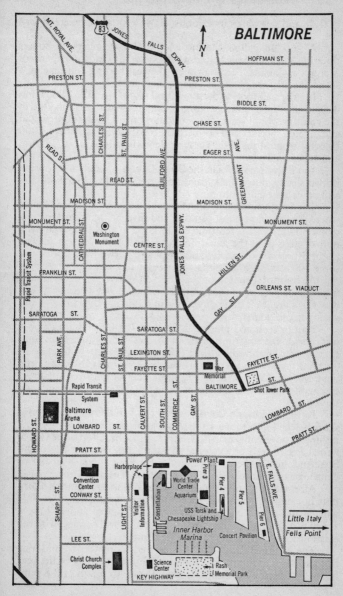

BALTIMORE

MT. ROYAL AVE.

83 JONES

FALLS EXPWY.

HOFFMAN ST.

PRESTON ST.

PRESTON ST.

BIDDLE ST.

CHARLES ST.

ST. PAUL ST.

READ S

CHASE ST.

EAGER ST.

GREENMOUNT AVE.

READ ST.

GUILFORD AVE.

MADISON ST.

MADISON ST.

MONUMENT ST.

● Washington Monument

CATHEDRAL ST.

CENTRE ST.

MONUMENT ST.

Rapid Transit System

FRANKLIN ST.

HILLEN ST.

ORLEANS ST. VIADUCT

SARATOGA ST.

GAY ST.

PARK AVE.

SARATOGA ST.

CHARLES ST.

ST. PAUL ST.

LEXINGTON ST.

JONES FALLS EXPWY.

FAYETTE ST.

FAYETTE ST.

■ War Memorial

ST.

BALTIMORE ST.

Shot Tower Park

Rapid Transit System

■ Baltimore Arena

CALVERT ST.

SOUTH ST.

COMMERCE ST.

GAY ST.

LOMBARD ST.

LOMBARD ST.

HOWARD ST.

PRATT ST.

PRATT ST.

PRATT ST.

Power Plant

E. FALLS AVE.

■ Convention Center

Harborplace

Pier 3

CONWAY ST.

World Trade Center

Pier 4

Pier 5

SHARP ST.

LIGHT ST.

Visitor Information

Aquarium

■

Constellation

USS Torsk and Chesapeake Lightship

Pier 6

→ Little Italy

LEE ST.

Inner Harbor Marina

Concert Pavilion

Fells Point

Christ Church Complex

■ Science Center

■ Rash Memorial Park

KEY HIGHWAY

of fresh and salt water; its exhibits, along a spiral route, are easy to see.

A 260,000-gallon **Marine Mammal Tray** currently houses three bluish-gray female beluga whales from the Hudson Bay area of Manitoba, Canada. Feeding times (they eat herring and capelin, a smelt-like fish) are posted at the information desk.

In the 13-foot **Atlantic Coral Reef,** a 335,000-gallon doughnut-shaped tank that is one of the largest exhibits of its kind in the country, you'll see a 100-pound tarpon, a Hawksbill turtle (an endangered species), and bonnethead sharks, along with over 3,000 colorful tropical reef fish. Feeding demonstrations are at 11 a.m. and 1:30 and 3 p.m.

You'll also see sharks in the **Open Ocean,** an oval tank housing brown sharks, nurse sharks, and sand tiger sharks, along with rays and other large gamefish.

The **South American Rain Forest** is a steamy simulated jungle where the stratification of plantlife and diversity of animal life in a tropical rain forest is reproduced. Housed in a 64-foot-high pyramid of glass atop the aquarium, it is filled with verdant foliage, about 30 species of fish (including piranha), two-toed sloths, and some 100 brightly hued birds—parrots, trumpeters, tanagers, etc.

At **Habitat Theater** (a chance to sit down), an eight-minute multimedia program called *The Chesapeake: A Bay at Risk* explains why this significant body of water is in ecological difficulties—and what you can do to help.

Harbor seals and grey seals live in a 70,000-gallon rock pool just outside the aquarium, their antics always drawing a large audience, especially at feeding times (10 a.m. and 1 and 4 p.m.).

A display of living corals provides a view of a reef habitat's striking beauty and diverse denizens; more than three dozen coral species, with evocative names like sea fans, star, and purple sea rods, are shown.

In the **Children's Cove,** visitors can handle horseshoe crabs, starfish, whelks, and sea urchins. Four local habitats—an Allegheny mountain pond, tidal marsh, Assateague Beach, and Atlantic Continental Shelf—can be explored in **Maryland: Mountains to the Sea.** And, finally, there's an electrifying exhibit of eels—capable of emitting a current of up to 800 volts, enough to stun a horse!

After we go to press, in 1990, a new **Marine Mammal Complex** housing dolphins and whales will open on adjacent Pier 4. It will be under the National Aquarium's auspices and include a 1,300-seat amphitheater and an exhibit hall. It will connect with the existing aquarium via an enclosed footbridge.

The National Aquarium is open mid-September to mid-May from 10 a.m. to 5 p.m., till 8 p.m. on Friday; the rest of the year hours are Monday to Thursday from 9 a.m. to 5 p.m., till 8 p.m.

Friday through Sunday. Admission is $7.75 for adults, $6 for senior citizens and students 12 to 18, $4.75 for children 3 to 11; under 3, free. You can purchase advance tickets to the Aquarium via Ticket Center (tel. toll free 800/448-9009). It involves a $1.75 per ticket surcharge, but in spring and summer, when tickets sometimes sell out, it's not a bad idea.

Harborplace

The hub of Inner Harbor activity is Harborplace, at the corner of Pratt and Light Streets (tel. 301/332-4191), a Rouse Enterprise Company project (like Faneuil Hall in Boston and New York's South Street Seaport) originally focusing on two glass-canopied pavilions. Together they contain over a dozen restaurants and cafés (all with waterview terraces) about 70 additional gourmet food markets and specialty eating places, and numerous shops.

In 1987, a third glass building, **The Gallery at Harborplace,** opened, adding four shopping levels (another 75 stores and eateries), a Stouffer Hotel, and an underground parking garage with 1,150 spaces (entrance at South Street or Calvert Street, between Lombard and Pratt Streets; maximum rate $9 a day). Its six-story atrium is capped by Baltimore's largest skylight. Stores in the Gallery include Brooks Brothers, The Sharper Image, Benetton Uomo, Banana Republic, Ann Taylor, and Trocadero.

More chic retail outlets are at the **Pratt Street Pavilion,** among them such well-known emporia as Laura Ashley, The Limited, Crabtree & Evelyn, Pappagallo, and Benetton. In addition there are shops purveying jewelry, cutlery, crafts, children's books, china, clothing, hats, Irish knits, dollhouse furniture, games, stuffed animals, heart-shaped items, and much more.

The **Light Street Pavilion** contains the majority of the food outlets. At the **Colonnade Market** and **Trading Hall,** you can purchase every kind of bakery item from strudel to cannoli, homemade chocolates, cotton candy, sausage sandwiches, dried fruits and nuts, wines, gourmet fare, spices, barbecued chicken, fresh fruit, salad-bar offerings, raw-bar fare, cheeses—in fact, just about every imaginable edible. Upstairs there's more to eat at **Food Hall,** where international stalls feature ethnic specialties from souvlaki to sesame noodles, along with such American staples as Häagen-Dazs and hot dogs. There are about 50 vendors. Sharing the upper level with Food Hall is the **Sam Smith Market,** where pushcart merchants and kiosks offer an ever-changing array of mostly frivolous wares—items relating to crabs, Harborplace memorabilia, a left-handed shop, and novelty timepieces like the Betty Boop clock.

All three pavilions are attractive and colorful, with chrysanthemum-bordered trees thriving under the skylights and banners suspended overhead. Shops are open Monday to Saturday from 10 a.m. to 9:30 p.m., from noon till 6 or 8 p.m. on Sunday, with extended hours in summer. Most restaurants stay open until midnight or later.

To find out about special happenings during your visit, make a stop at the **information kiosk** just outside the Light Street Pavilion or call the above-listed phone number. A typical month's activities will likely include a regatta, fireworks, concerts (everything from reggae to Rachmaninoff), an international festival, theatrical events, a parade, an outdoor art exhibit, an ice cream–eating contest, and much more. In summer there are jazz and big-band concerts at the Harborplace Amphitheater. Santa is on hand Thanksgiving through Christmas. And you can count on a big to-do every holiday—even a Mardi Gras celebration.

More on Harborplace restaurants is given later on in this section.

The Maryland Science Center

Its antecedents dating to 1797, when a Maryland academy was formed for the "promotion of science," this fascinating ultramodern science museum at 601 Light St. (tel. 301/685-2370) opened in 1976. It was conceived as a "dynamic tactile environment where visitors can interact with exhibits and participate in a variety of programs and activities." In other words, hands-on exhibits are the norm, most of them child oriented. There are intriguing live science demonstrations on special stages throughout the day, and half-hour films on subjects ranging from dinosaurs to space travel are shown two to four times a day on weekends in the Boyd Theater. You can also catch space shows in the Davis Planetarium, wherein are 350 projectors and a four-channel sound system with 12 loudspeakers.

Permanent exhibits touch on a smörgåsbord of scientific subjects—energy, ecology, perception, physics, probability, computers (numerous games here), Chesapeake Bay life, geology, etc. The viewer is always involved, be it functioning as a human battery, designing a new energy policy, or catching a falling stick to test reaction time. An IMAX theater opened in 1987. It alternately shows *Grand Canyon: The Hidden Secrets* and *The Dream Is Alive*. If you haven't yet seen a thrilling IMAX film, don't miss these. If you have, I'm sure you won't want to miss these fabulous shows. Tickets are included with your admission price; pick them up when you come in.

Additional features are a family restaurant and a terrific gift shop specializing in science-related items. For 24-hour information regarding exhibits and shows, call the above number.

The center is open early September through late June, Monday to Friday from 10 a.m. to 5 p.m., Saturday 10 a.m. to 6 p.m., and Sunday noon to 6 p.m. Summer hours are 10 a.m. to 8 p.m. daily. Admission is $6.50 for adults, $5.50 for children 12 and under or senior citizens, free for children under 3. Davis Planetarium shows are $1 extra.

The World Trade Center

I.M. Pei's 423-foot-high, 30-story pentagonal building doesn't quite vie with New York's, but it doesn't have to compete with surrounding skyscrapers either. The 27th-floor observation deck, windowed all around of course, offers a spectacular panorama of the harbor, the downtown office and hotel district, Shot Tower (a 234-foot building dating to 1828, in which 12½ million pounds of shot were once manufactured annually), and the nearby suburbs.

In addition to oohing and aahing at views, you can peruse a number of Baltimore-related exhibits up here. There's a display of artifacts from Baltimore sister cities—Luxor, Egypt; Rotterdam, The Netherlands; Genoa, Italy; Kawasaki, Japan; Gbarnga, Liberia; and Piraeus, Greece. Flags overhead represent all the countries that trade with the Port of Baltimore. An audio-visual exhibit shows what a crane operator sees while unloading goods from a cargo ship docked at a Baltimore port; still others explore Baltimore neighborhoods, industries, history, architecture, houses of worship, and monuments. And kids love the simulated ship's bridge with authentic navigational equipment they can operate—container loading, ship-to-shore communication, a ship's whistle and bell, and collision control. Of course, there's a gift shop too, specializing in international and local handcrafted articles.

Hours Memorial Day through Labor Day are weekdays from 10 a.m. to 5 p.m., on Saturday to 7 p.m., on Sunday from 11 a.m. to 6 p.m.; the rest of the year, Monday to Saturday from 10 a.m. to 5 p.m., and on Sunday from noon to 5 p.m. Admission is $2 for adults, $1 for children ages 5 to 12 and seniors, and under 5, free. For further information call 301/837-4515.

A Few Additional Notes

The **Rash Field Flower Garden,** between the Maryland Science Center and the Rusty Scupper Restaurant (tel. 301/659-7532), is a square-mile international garden of flowers from all over the world. There are wooden benches to sit on but a lamentable lack of shade trees. It's best enjoyed on cooler days.

You can board the U.S. frigate **Constellation,** the navy's first commissioned ship, launched in 1797. Called the "Yankee Racehorse," she was the first American naval ship to defeat an enemy man-of-war. She served through World War II, her final duty as a flagship of the Atlantic Fleet. The U.S. Navy's signal book and regulations, still in use, were written aboard this ship by her first captain. Today she's docked at the Inner Harbor, and a self-guided tour is $1.75 for adults, $1 for seniors, 75¢ for children ages 6 to 15; under 6, free.

From early April through the end of October, **paddleboats** can be rented in front of the Pratt Street Pavilion. The cost is $7.50 an hour, $4.25 for a half hour.

And a variety of harbor boat tours are offered, both by day and by moonlight, some of them including meals and/or musical entertainment. To find out what's available, visit the **Dockside Harbor Cruises Office** on the Light Street Promenade.

WHERE TO EAT: The Harborplace pavilions abound with restaurants and food outlets. All of the major eateries are very attractive, and it's lovely to dine in their outdoor cafés or second-story terraces, enjoying the harbor view. They all offer reasonably good, though seldom rapture-inducing, repasts, so you can just walk around and choose the kind of fare you fancy. Your options for sit-down restaurants include Chinese, Italian, Indian, Greek, American, and French cuisines, plus pub fare and seafood. And should you want to explore the fast-food outlets, you can probably find anything you've ever eaten or thought about eating.

Our real preference, though, is to leave the harbor area altogether and head over to the **Peabody Court** hotel for a really superb meal, either at the extremely posh (and pricey) **Conservatory** or the lovely (and less expensive) **Peabody's**. Not only will you enjoy food and ambience that many consider Baltimore's best at these hotel restaurants, it's also nice to get away from the harbor hustle and bustle for a while. Both restaurants are detailed in the following listing.

WHERE TO STAY: Like Annapolis, Baltimore is less than an hour's drive from the District, but it, too, has attractions sufficient to keep you overnight. Not the least of these is a hotel so elegant it would be worth driving up just to stay here.

The **Peabody Court**, 612 Cathedral St. (at Mount Vernon Place), Baltimore, MD 21201 (tel. 301/727-7107, or toll free 800/732-5301), was designed to be the "perfect European hotel" in America. The owners spent months abroad with decorator Rita St. Clair purchasing hand-cut, hand-blown crystal from Murano, Italy (12,000 pieces!), Vendôme-style customized silverplate, and thousands of yards of Axminster wool carpeting.

Guests are cosseted at every turn, from the moment they enter the walnut-paneled lobby resplendent with a six-foot Baccarat crystal chandelier and marble desks. A concierge is on hand to do your bidding, and room service operates around the clock. Your bed is turned down nightly and a gourmet chocolate left on your pillow, and each morning the *Baltimore Sun* (or other paper on request) is left at your door. Guests are welcome to gratis use of the nearby Downtown Athletic Club, whose facilities include an indoor Olympic-size pool, Jacuzzi, mile-long indoor running track, steam, sauna, massage, racquetball, and a full line of Nautilus equipment.

The 105 rooms are grand residential chambers decorated in muted color schemes (gorgeous mauves, ochres, grays, etc.) and furnished with cherrywood beds, pediment-topped Directoire armoires (also cherrywood) that conceal color satellite TVs/clock radios and mini-bars, and 18th-century mahogany brass-tipped desks with inlaid tooled-leather blotters and Louis XVI–style chairs. Framed Italian botanical prints and other fine artworks adorn the walls. About two-thirds of the exquisite verdi and cremo marble baths have Jacuzzis, and all have hair dryers, makeup mirrors, and phones. Phones here, by the way, have two lines.

The Peabody has two superb restaurants. The forest-green and sienna Peabody's, reached via a bronze-railed marble staircase, is its "everyday" restaurant, though most properties would be happy to claim it as a premier dining room. It features regional American cuisine and is open for all meals.

Even more opulent is the Conservatory, a lavish rooftop restaurant offering panoramic views from dark mahogany-trimmed curved-glass walls. It's the kind of luxury, said one reviewer, that evokes "not the excesses of robber barons, but . . . the quiet luxury of the *Orient Express.*" The room is decorated in Fabergé colors—muted jade and peach (both seen in the swirling fleur-de-lis-motif carpet), with grand verde marble pillars, lacy wrought-iron arches, and jade velvet curtains. Belle Époque gaslight-style chandeliers are suspended from peach ceilings, and gilt-framed period oil paintings adorn the inner walls. Tables covered with Italian royal white linen are handsomely appointed with hand-blown crystal, exquisite china and silver, and lovely floral arrangements. In the plush adjoining lounge, with its Aubusson-tapestried sofas and bar stools, a pianist entertains on the Steinway grand from 6 to 11:30 p.m., nightly except Sunday and Monday. You might spend an evening here enjoying the music over a bottle of wine and hors d'oeuvres. A typical Conservatory dinner might include an appetizer of quail eggs poached in champagne served with light watercress sauce and two caviars, an entree of breast of duck roasted with honey and cumin sauce, with wild rice and pine nuts, and a raspberry tarte served in a pool of white crème anglaise swirled with raspberry sauce. Entrees range from $18 to $25. Dinner only is served.

Rates at the Peabody Court are $115 to $155 single, $20 for an extra person, free for children under 16 in their parents' room. The weekend rate is just $85, single or double. A trolley that stops in front of the hotel will take you back and forth to the harbor throughout the day.

Another excellent choice is the **Shirley-Madison Inn,** 205 W. Madison St., at Park Ave., Baltimore, MD 21201 (tel. 301/728-6550), consisting of 16 rooms in a five-story Victorian brick building and another nine rooms around the corner at 716 Park Avenue, (connected via a garden courtyard). Owner Roberta Pieczenik (who also owns the highly recommended Kalorama Guest House in D.C.), has created a stunning hostelry here. Upon arrival, guests are greeted with sherry in a beautiful parlor furnished in turn-of-the-century pieces, including comfortably plush sofas; it even has a working fireplace. Continental breakfast is served daily—croissants, sweet rolls, muffins, bagels, juice, and tea or coffee. The rooms, some of them suites with living or dining rooms, and some with kitchenettes, are exquisitely appointed. Most have 15-foot ceilings, pale peach walls, mauve carpeting, muted rose silk curtains, and brass beds with white eyelet quilts. The feel is upscale residential, and all modern amenities are provided: in-room private bath, a color cable TV concealed in a mahogany armoire, clock radio, and direct-dial phone. The Shirley is just 12 blocks from the Harbor.

Rates, including morning breakfast and evening apéritif, are $55 to $80 single, $65 to $95 double, $10 for an additional person.

Index

Note: All sights and museums listed are in Washington, D.C., unless
otherwise noted.

NOW!
ARTHUR FROMMER LAUNCHES HIS SECOND TRAVEL REVOLUTION
with

The New World of Travel

The hottest news and latest trends in travel today—heretofore the closely guarded secrets of the travel trade—are revealed in this new sourcebook by the dean of American travel. Here, collected in one book that is updated every year, are the most exciting, challenging, and money-saving ideas in travel today.

You'll find out about hundreds of alternative new modes of travel—and the many organizations that sponsor them—that will lead you to vacations that cater to your mind, your spirit, and your sense of thrift.

Learn how to fly for free as an air courier; travel for free as a tour escort; live for free on a hospitality exchange; add earnings as a part-time travel agent; pay less for air tickets, cruises, and hotels; enhance your life through cooperative camping, political tours, and adventure trips; change your life at utopian communities, low-cost spas, and yoga retreats; pursue low-cost studies and language training; travel comfortably while single or over 60; sail on passenger freighters; and vacation in the cheapest places on earth.

And in every yearly edition, Arthur Frommer spotlights the 10 GREATEST TRAVEL VALUES for the coming year. 384 pages, large-format with many, many illustrations. All for $12.95!

ORDER NOW
TURN TO THE LAST PAGE OF THIS BOOK FOR ORDER FORM.

NOW, SAVE MONEY ON ALL YOUR TRAVELS!
Join Frommer's™ Dollarwise® Travel Club

Saving money while traveling is never a simple matter, which is why, over 27 years ago, the **Dollarwise Travel Club** was formed. Actually, the idea came from readers of the Frommer publications who felt that such an organization could bring financial benefits, continuing travel information, and a sense of community to economy-minded travelers all over the world.

In keeping with the money-saving concept, the annual membership fee is low—$18 (U.S. residents) or $20 U.S. (Canadian, Mexican, and foreign residents)—and is immediately exceeded by the value of your benefits which include:

1. The latest edition of any TWO of the books listed on the following pages.

2. A copy of any Frommer City Guide.

3. An annual subscription to an 8-page quarterly newspaper *The Dollarwise Traveler* which keeps you up-to-date on fastbreaking developments in good-value travel in all parts of the world—bringing you the kind of information you'd have to pay over $35 a year to obtain elsewhere. This consumer-conscious publication also includes the following columns:

> **Hospitality Exchange**—members all over the world who are willing to provide hospitality to other members as they pass through their home cities.
>
> **Share-a-Trip**—requests from members for travel companions who can share costs and help avoid the burdensome single supplement.
>
> **Readers Ask . . . Readers Reply**—travel questions from members to which other members reply with authentic firsthand information.

4. Your personal membership card which entitles you to purchase through the club all Frommer publications for a third to a half off their regular retail prices during the term of your membership.

So why not join this hardy band of international Dollarwise travelers now and participate in its exchange of information and hospitality? Simply send $18 (U.S. residents) or $20 U.S. (Canadian, Mexican, and other foreign residents) along with your name and address to: Frommer's Dollarwise Travel Club, Inc., Gulf + Western Building, One Gulf + Western Plaza, New York, NY 10023. Remember to specify which *two* of the books in section (1) and which *one* in section (2) above you wish to receive in your initial package of member's benefits. Or tear out the next page, check off your choices, and send the page to us with your membership fee.

FROMMER BOOKS
PRENTICE HALL PRESS
ONE GULF + WESTERN PLAZA
NEW YORK, NY 10023

Date_____

Friends:
Please send me the books checked below:

FROMMER'S™ $-A-DAY® GUIDES

(In-depth guides to sightseeing and low-cost tourist accommodations and facilities.)

☐ Europe on $30 a Day $14.95	☐ New Zealand on $40 a Day $12.95
☐ Australia on $30 a Day $12.95	☐ New York on $50 a Day. $12.95
☐ Eastern Europe on $25 a Day. $12.95	☐ Scandinavia on $50 a Day $12.95
☐ England on $40 a Day. $12.95	☐ Scotland and Wales on $40 a Day. . . . $12.95
☐ Greece on $30 a Day. $12.95	☐ South America on $30 a Day $12.95
☐ Hawaii on $50 a Day $13.95	☐ Spain and Morocco (plus the Canary Is.)
☐ India on $25 a Day. $12.95	on $40 a Day. $13.95
☐ Ireland on $30 a Day $12.95	☐ Turkey on $25 a Day. $12.95
☐ Israel on $30 & $35 a Day $12.95	☐ Washington, D.C., & Historic Va. on
☐ Mexico (plus Belize & Guatemala)	$40 a Day. $12.95
on $25 a Day. $13.95	

FROMMER'S™ DOLLARWISE® GUIDES

(Guides to sightseeing and tourist accommodations and facilities from budget to deluxe, with emphasis on the medium-priced.)

☐ Alaska $13.95	☐ Cruises (incl. Alask, Carib, Mex, Hawaii,
☐ Austria & Hungary $14.95	Panama, Canada, & US) $14.95
☐ Belgium, Holland, Luxembourg $13.95	☐ California & Las Vegas $14.95
☐ Brazil (avail. Nov. 1988) $14.95	☐ Florida $13.95
☐ Egypt. $13.95	☐ Mid-Atlantic States $13.95
☐ France $14.95	☐ New England $13.95
☐ England & Scotland $14.95	☐ New York State $13.95
☐ Germany $13.95	☐ Northwest $13.95
☐ Italy. $14.95	☐ Skiing in Europe. $14.95
☐ Japan & Hong Kong $13.95	☐ Skiing USA—East $13.95
☐ Portugal, Madeira, & the Azores . . . $13.95	☐ Skiing USA—West. $13.95
☐ South Pacific. $13.95	☐ Southeast & New Orleans $13.95
☐ Switzerland & Liechtenstein $13.95	☐ Southwest $14.95
☐ Bermuda & The Bahamas $13.95	☐ Texas $13.95
☐ Canada $13.95	☐ USA (avail. Feb. 1989). $15.95
☐ Caribbean $13.95	

FROMMER'S™ TOURING GUIDES

(Color illustrated guides that include walking tours, cultural & historic sites, and other vital travel information.)

☐ Australia $9.95	☐ Paris $8.95
☐ Egypt. $8.95	☐ Thailand. $9.95
☐ Florence. $8.95	☐ Venice $8.95
☐ London $8.95	

TURN PAGE FOR ADDITIONAL BOOKS AND ORDER FORM.

FROMMER'S™ CITY GUIDES
(Pocket-size guides to sightseeing and tourist accommodations and facilities in all price ranges.)

☐ Amsterdam/Holland . . . .$5.95   ☐ Montreal/Quebec City $5.95
☐ Athens. . . . .$5.95   ☐ New Orleans. $5.95
☐ Atlantic City/Cape May . . . .$5.95   ☐ New York $5.95
☐ Boston. . . . .$5.95   ☐ Orlando/Disney World/EPCOT $5.95
☐ Cancún/Cozumel/Yucatán. . . . .$5.95   ☐ Paris $5.95
☐ Dublin/Ireland . . . .$5.95   ☐ Philadelphia $5.95
☐ Hawaii . . . .$5.95   ☐ Rio (avail. Nov. 1988). $5.95
☐ Las Vegas. . . . .$5.95   ☐ Rome. $5.95
☐ Lisbon/Madrid/Costa del Sol . . . . . .$5.95   ☐ San Francisco $5.95
☐ London . . . .$5.95   ☐ Santa Fe/Taos (avail. Mar. 1989) $5.95
☐ Los Angeles . . . .$5.95   ☐ Sydney. $5.95
☐ Mexico City/Acapulco. . . . .$5.95   ☐ Washington, D.C. $5.95
☐ Minneapolis/St. Paul $5.95

SPECIAL EDITIONS

☐ A Shopper's Guide to the Caribbean. .$12.95   ☐ Motorist's Phrase Book (Fr/Ger/Sp). . .$4.95
☐ Beat the High Cost of Travel . . . .$6.95   ☐ Paris Rendez-Vous $10.95
☐ Bed & Breakfast—N. America. . . . . . .$8.95   ☐ Swap and Go (Home Exchanging). . . .$10.95
☐ Guide to Honeymoon Destinations   ☐ The Candy Apple (NY for Kids). $11.95
   (US, Canada, Mexico, & Carib). . . . . .$12.95   ☐ Travel Diary and Record Book $5.95
☐ Manhattan's Outdoor Sculpture . . . .$15.95   ☐ Where to Stay USA (Lodging from $3
                                          to $30 a night) $10.95
☐ Marilyn Wood's Wonderful Weekends (NY, Conn, Mass, RI, Vt, NH, NJ, Del, Pa) $11.95
☐ The New World of Travel (Annual sourcebook by Arthur Frommer previewing: new travel trends,
   new modes of travel, and the latest cost-cutting strategies for savvy travelers). $12.95

SERIOUS SHOPPER'S GUIDES
(Illustrated guides listing hundreds of stores, conveniently organized alphabetically by category)

☐ Italy. . . . .$15.95   ☐ Los Angeles $14.95
☐ London . . . .$15.95   ☐ Paris $15.95

GAULT MILLAU
(The only guides that distinguish the truly superlative from the merely overrated.)

☐ The Best of Chicago (avail. Feb. 1989) $15.95   ☐ The Best of New England (avail. Feb.
☐ The Best of France (avail. Feb. 1989). .$15.95   1989) $15.95
☐ The Best of Italy (avail. Feb. 1989) . . .$15.95   ☐ The Best of New York. $15.95
☐ The Best of Los Angeles . . . .$15.95   ☐ The Best of San Francisco $15.95
                                          ☐ The Best of Washington, D.C. $15.95

ORDER NOW!

In U.S. include $1.50 shipping UPS for 1st book; 50¢ ea. add'l book. Outside U.S. $2 and 50¢, respectively. Allow four to six weeks for delivery in U.S., longer outside U.S.

Enclosed is my check or money order for $_____

NAME_____

ADDRESS_____

CITY_____ STATE_____ ZIP_____